The Sex Scientists

Edited by

Gary G. Brannigan
State University of New York–Plattsburgh

Elizabeth Rice Allgeier
Bowling Green State University

Albert Richard Allgeier
Allgeier & Associates

 LONGMAN

An imprint of Addison Wesley Longman, Inc.

New York • Reading, Massachusetts • Menlo Park, California • Harlow, England
Don Mills, Ontario • Sydney • Mexico City • Madrid • Amsterdam

*To my wife, Linda, and my sons, Marc
and Michael*   GGB

*With love to our four children,
Beth, Sarah, Kate, and Don,
and to our five grandchildren*   ERA and ARA

Editor in Chief: Priscilla McGeehon
Acquisitions Editor: Rebecca Dudley
Marketing Manager: Jay O'Callaghan
Project Editor: Ann P. Kearns
Text and Cover Designer: Mary Archondes
Cover Photo: Keith Tishken
Production Manager: Alexandra Odulak
Desktop Coordinator and Electronic Page Makeup: Joanne Del Ben
Manufacturing Manager: Hilda Koparanian
Printer and Binder: The Maple-Vail Book Manufacturing Group
Cover Printer: Phoenix Color Corporation

Photo credits: p. ix (top), Robin Brown; p. 88, Joe Vericker; p. 169, Swiss Federal
Office of Public Health; p. 201, Angela N. Russo.

For permission to use copyrighted material, grateful acknowledgment is made to the
following copyright holders: p. 46, HOW CAN I KEEP FROM SINGING? additional
words by Doris Plenn, © 1957 (renewed) BY SANGA MUSIC INC. All Rights
Reserved. Used by Permission; p. 46, THIS LAND IS YOUR LAND, Words and
Music by Woody Guthrie, TRO-©-Copyright 1956 (Renewed) 1958 (Renewed) 1970
Ludlow Music, Inc., New York, New York. Used by Permission.

Library of Congress Cataloging-in-Publication Data

The sex scientists / edited by Gary G. Brannigan, Elizabeth Rice
  Allgeier, and Albert Richard Allgeier.
      p.   cm.
    ISBN 0-321-01139-2
    1. Sexology—Research—Case studies.   2. Sexologists—Case
studies.   I. Brannigan, Gary G.   II. Allgeier, Elizabeth R.
III. Allgeier, Albert Richard.
  HQ60.S494   1998
  306.7'072—dc21   97-15833
                                                                                       CIP

ISBN 0-321-01139-2

12345678910—MA—00999897

Contents

Preface

The Sex Scientists provides fifteen in-depth, first-person accounts of research in major areas of human sexuality. These interesting and informative stories will appeal to a wide audience, with issues that touch all of our lives. The book is also designed to complement textbooks in human sexuality, as well as to serve as a primary source in advanced seminars. For introductory level courses, the stories can be used to illustrate applications of principles and theories and "bring to life" the content covered in traditional texts. At more advanced levels, the stories can be used to stress the "nitty-gritty" aspects of sex research—that is, planning, design, and methodology.

The book has a multidisciplinary flavor, with contributors representing various subareas of psychology and related areas such as history, sociology, and medicine. The contributors show how they encountered interesting, unique, and/or problematic research questions that demanded some creative form of resolution or understanding. They emphasize the formal aspects of research (e.g., idea generation, development of methodology, conducting experiments, applying results), as well as the personal and situational factors that frequently influence decision making.

Human sexuality is an exciting and rapidly growing area of investigation. It is typically one of the most highly subscribed courses in the curriculum. *The Sex Scientists* covers a broad range of topics that closely parallels the major sections of human sexuality textbooks. The topics include:

- A historical perspective on sex research
- Research and theory on human sexuality
- Erotica
- Child and adolescent sexuality
- Sexual signaling and communication
- Gender and mate selection
- Sexual dysfunction
- Sexual orientation
- Sexual relationships
- Birth control
- Atypical sexual behavior
- Sexually transmitted diseases
- Sexual coercion
- Prostitution
- Sexual enhancement

In *The Sex Scientists,* we counter the notion that research is a routine, lifeless process. In addition to providing an "insider's" view of sex research, the contributors convey the challenge and excitement of the process through their lively narrative accounts. They also add the much-needed human element to research as they address many of the important questions that frequently go unanswered in textbooks and journals: Who are you? Why and how did you get involved in sex research? Can I identify with you? What keeps you excited about your work? What has your experience taught you? What personal lessons can I carry away from your story? And so on. If, as we believe, there is a lot we can learn from the experience of others, this collection of "stories" will be informative and enriching.

Acknowledgments

This book reflects the efforts of fifteen scientists who took the time to write about their personal and professional experiences so that others can understand and appreciate the process of sex research. We wish to express our appreciation to all of them.

We are grateful to the excellent staff of professionals at Longman, especially Jay O'Callaghan, whose encouragement helped to get the project off the ground, Rebecca Dudley, whose editorial expertise and ongoing support guided the project from start to finish, and Ann Kearns, project editor, and David Schecter, copyeditor, whose attention to fine detail greatly improved the finished product.

The reviewers also provided helpful suggestions to clarify and improve the book. We thank

Jeffrey Stern, University of Michigan-Dearborn
Ann Brandt-Williams, Glendale Community College
Irene Frieze, University of Pittsburgh
Katherine Bruce, University of North Carolina-Wilmington
John Long, Mt. San Antonio College
Shae Coleman, Northeastern State University
Janet Simons, University of Iowa
Thomas Langley, College of Charleston

Finally, Judy Dashnaw deserves special commendation. Her editorial and word processing skills were vital to the timely completion of the project.

Gary G. Brannigan
Elizabeth Rice Allgeier
Albert Richard Allgeier

Introduction

In *The Sex Scientists* you will hear the voices of fifteen prominent scientists as they describe their personal and professional experiences in exploring interesting and meaningful issues in human sexuality.

We asked the contributors to tell how they encountered research issues that were especially interesting, unique, and/or problematic and that demanded some form of resolution or understanding. In the process, they provided an insider's view of sex research by stressing the critical thinking and problem-solving aspects of research (e.g., generating ideas, developing methodology, conducting studies, applying results), as well as the personal and situational factors that influenced their decision making.

The use of personal narratives is not new. Phillip DeVita has used this approach in several anthropology books, and Gary Brannigan and Matt Merrens have produced several similar books in psychology and education. Reviewers of these projects have been intrigued with this approach. The following thoughts, based on input from David Myers of Hope College and Rosemary Hornack of Meredith College, are representative of their feedback. Because it's easy to be intimidated by brilliant people—who seem from a distance to come up with great ideas and execute them flawlessly—you will greatly appreciate the humanness of these personal stories. As they take you backstage to view their research careers, you will read stories of uncertain initial directions, of serendipity, of false starts, of self-doubts, of job insecurity, of the importance of supportive mentors, colleagues, and students. You will also see the passion that drives these people and the ideals that guide them, values such as lifelong learning; reading published literature; benefits of working hard; making the most of all that you know from any source of experience; turning misfortune into opportunity; observing carefully; and keeping an open mind.

We have chosen selectively among the varied topics sex researchers study to highlight those issues commonly encountered in the study of human sexuality. Also, we have avoided chapter introductions in favor of letting the stories unfold "like good mysteries." However, we want to give you a taste of what's to come and hope these samples will whet your appetite for more.

In the opening chapter, Vern Bullough provides an overview of the dominant forces that have shaped research on human sexuality. In the process, he also recounts many of his personal and professional experiences in his historical research of significant issues in human sexuality. How is a theory of sexuality developed? Donn Byrne describes the underlying basis for the Sexual Behavior Sequence and provides some insights on how it is applied. In a highly engaging account, Bill Fisher details his research on the effects of erotic material on behavior. More specifically, he recounts the impact of his work on pornography on his personal and professional life. Richard Udry takes us on an interesting journey into his research on adolescent sexual behavior. He addresses many of the sensitive issues in conducting research with children and adolescents.

How do people show interest in one another? Monica Moore weaves an entertaining account of her research on courtship and sexual signaling. Many of us wonder what we have in common with our ancient ancestors. Michael Wiederman's absorbing chapter examines the evolutionary perspective on gender differences in mate selection. Leonore Tiefer traces her research and applied experience in dealing with people with sexual dysfunctions. She also explains the contributions of the feminist approach to treatment. Michael Stevenson gives us a behind-the-scenes glimpse of our government in action as he describes his work on sexual orientation. His experience as a Congressional Fellow working on the Defense of Marriage Act is the focal point of the chapter. Bram Buunk presents a detailed discussion of his research on jealousy. His chapter highlights the effects of "having sex with others" on one's primary relationship.

What concerns need to be addressed on women's reproductive health? One issue, the use of oral contraceptives, is explored in Cynthia Graham's personal account. Gene Abel provides an interesting account of his experiences in developing and using assessment tools to identify individuals with sexual problems that violate societal and legal standards. He also provides a number of intriguing case studies to illuminate his procedures. Bill Darrow's up-close look at his research on sexually transmitted diseases is filled with personal anecdotes and observations. In the process, he traces his career from its beginning as a "Venereal Disease Investigator" to his position as Chief of the Behavioral and Prevention Research Branch of the Centers for Disease Control and Prevention. Rape is the topic of Cindy Struckman-Johnson's chapter. She provides an intriguing, touching account of her research experience in prison settings. In addition to providing a portrait of the life of a prostitute, Jacqueline Boles gives us an up-close look at her research on the streets of Atlanta. And, finally, Gina Ogden discusses her personal and professional encounters as she developed her views on sexual enhancement. She shares her research findings on women's peak sexual experiences.

We hope you enjoy these stories.

About the Editors

Gary G. Brannigan earned his B.A. (1969) from Fairfield University and his M.A. (1972) and Ph.D. (1973) from the University of Delaware. After completing his clinical psychology internship at the Devereux Foundation, he has been serving on the faculty of the State University of New York at Plattsburgh. In addition to teaching in the Psychology Department, he served five years as Director of the Psychological Services Clinic. He also maintains a small private practice and consults with local agencies. He is a Fellow in the Society for Personality Assessment and a consulting editor on two journals. In addition to coediting (with M. Merrens) *The Undaunted Psychologist: Adventures in Research; The Social Psychologists: Research Adventures; The Developmental Psychologists: Research Adventures Across the Lifespan;* and editing *The Enlightened Educator: Research Adventures in the Schools,* he has authored numerous articles, chapters, books, and tests, including (with A. Tolor) *Research and Clinical Applications for the Bender-Gestalt Test;* (with N. Brunner) *The Modified Version of the Bender-Gestalt Test for Preschool and Primary School Children* (now in its second edition); and (with M. Merrens) *Experiences in Personality: Research, Assessment, and Change.* His research is primarily on psychological and educational assessment, personality, and human sexuality (currently, sexual fantasy and daydreaming).

Elizabeth Rice Allgeier earned her B.A. from the University of Oregon in 1969, her M.S. from the State University of New York at Oswego in 1973, and her Ph.D. from Purdue University in 1976. Currently Professor of Psychology at Bowling Green State University, she has won numerous teaching awards, including the BGSU Alumni Association's Master Teacher Award in 1988, and was named the BGSU Outstanding Contributor to Graduate Education in 1992. In 1986, she was named the American Psychological Association's G. Stanley Hall Lecturer on Sexuality. She has taught human sexuality at Eastern Michigan University and at the State University of New York at Fredonia. Dr. Allgeier's interest in studying human sexual behavior began while she was living among the So, a preliterate, polygynous tribe in Uganda. Her study of this tribe resulted in a two-volume ethnography that she coauthored. Her current research interests include the societal regulation of sexual behavior, sexual coercion, and the relationship between gender-role norms and sexual interaction. On the last-named subject, she edited, with Naomi McCormick, *Changing Boundaries: Gender Roles and Sexual Behavior* (1983). Actively involved in The Society for the Scientific Study of Sex, she has served as national secretary and as president for that organization, and in 1991 was awarded its Distinguished Service Award. In 1994, she was also awarded the Alfred C. Kinsey Award for Outstanding Contributions to Sexual Science by the Midcontinent Region of The Society for the Scientific Study of Sex. She is on the editorial board of four scholarly journals that publish sex research and currently is editor of *The Journal of Sex Research*.

Albert Richard Allgeier earned his B.A. from Gannon University in 1967, his M.A. from the American University of Beirut in Lebanon in 1969, and his Ph.D. from Purdue University in 1974. He has been Clinical Director at both the Northwest Center for Human Resources in Lima, Ohio, and the Wood County Mental Health Center in Bowling Green, Ohio. He has served on the faculty of Alma College, the State University of New York at Fredonia, and Bowling Green State University. Currently, he is in private practice in Bowling Green. He has been active in The Society for the Scientific Study of Sex and is a former treasurer and member of the Board of Directors of the organization. He has conducted research on interpersonal attraction and sexual knowledge and has participated, with his wife, Elizabeth Rice Allgeier, in a series of studies on attitudes about abortion. He is also interested in the implications of evolutionary theory for the study of human sexuality.

The Allgeiers are coauthors of *Sexual Interactions,* now in its fourth edition. They have just completed a concise edition of the text.

Chapter 1

History, the Historian, and Sex

Vern L. Bullough

Vern L. Bullough (Ph.D., University of Chicago) retired from the State University of New York (SUNY) College at Buffalo in 1993 and returned to California. He currently is a Visiting Professor in the Department of Nursing at the University of Southern California. He has been researching sex for nearly a half century and he is the author, coauthor, or editor of approximately 50 books. He has contributed chapters to more than 70 books, has contributed nearly 200 articles to refereed journals, and has written numerous popular articles, book reviews, and pamphlets.

He was awarded the Distinguished Achievement Award by the Society for the Scientific Study of Sex (SSSS), of which he was earlier President. He also was corecipient (with Bonnie Bullough) of the Kinsey Award by the Midcontinent Region and the Eastern Region of the SSSS. Among other things, he is a Fellow in the American Academy of Nursing and a laureate in the Academy of Humanism. He is the father of five children (one deceased), although to maintain his credentials as an advocate of contraception, he has to state that three of his children were adopted.

Many of our traditional western assumptions about sex can be traced back to the Greeks. They picked up ideas from the Egyptians and the peoples of the Tigris-Euphrates Valley, the Indus Valley, and elsewhere. These ideas were a combination of observations, assumptions, mythology, morals, and magic. When investigators came up with modifications in traditional assumptions, these were usually incorporated into the same general fabric unless they were too radical. In that case, they were usually ignored because they countered accepted ideology. Although people asked a lot of questions about sex, which scientific investigators later answered, the science of the time was not sophisticated enough to do much more than theorize—often erroneously, at least from our point of view.

Because I have written on the development of attitudes toward sexuality and the beginnings of sex research in a number of books (frequently in collaboration with Bonnie Bullough), it might be helpful to summarize some of this here. I do so without citation, although those interested in tracing the sources can look at the suggested readings at the end of this chapter.

One of the sources of reluctance to change traditional assumptions was that sexual behavior, unlike many other aspects of human behavior, became a matter of faith and morals rather than physiology or psychology. This was particularly true in the Western world where the Judeo-Christian tradition has been dominant for the past 1500 years. The ideas about sexuality in the West, however, have not been primarily biblical, although reference might be made there to some sexual activity. Rather they are part of what might be called Christian theology, which is not so much influenced by the Jewish tradition as by Greek stoicism and Neoplatonism.

The church father who had the most influence on Western ideas of sexuality was St. Augustine (354–430). A brief sketch of his background serves to emphasize the many nonbiblical sources of Christian concepts about sex. Augustine, whose mother was a Christian, was educated in the pagan schools of the day and was heavily influenced by the teachings of Plato and the later interpreters of Plato known as the Neoplatonists. As a young man, he converted to Manichaeanism, a rival religion to Christianity based on the teachings of a messiah named Mani. Many of the same stories told about the birth of Jesus were told about Mani, who was born in the third century of the modern era into the Zoroastrian faith. He preached a new kind of dualism which led to his death, popularly said to be by crucifixion although we know he died in prison.

Mani and the religion promulgated by his disciples, Manichaeanism, taught, as did Neoplatonism, that there were two basic elements in life, the material (evil and darkness) and the spiritual (goodness and light). Life on earth was a struggle between the two because the spiritual, through birth, became imprisoned in a material body from which it strove to be free. Procreation itself was therefore evil since it continually resulted in other spirits being imprisoned in a material body. The true believer abstained from all sex or eating anything resulting from sexual union (they did not know about the birds and bees and the sex of plants). Obviously there is more to Manichaeanism, but in terms of sexuality this is the key element. The Manichaeans recognized the difficulty believers would have in achieving the abstemious life, so they adopted two classes of members: (1) the adept, the initiate who observed all the prohibitions, and (2) the believer, who intended and strove to become an initiate but had not quite done so. Augustine was a believer striving to become an adept, and one of the material factors that prevented his entrance into this final preheavenly state was sexuality.

We know a lot about Augustine's struggle with sex because he wrote about it in his autobiography, entitled *Confessions*. In it, he recounts how every day he prayed to God, the source of all light, to help him overcome his sexual weakness and follow the path of the true believer. He then reports that he always added at the end of his prayer a sort of afterthought, please God but not quite yet.

After a series of crises over his sexuality, Augustine abandoned Manichaeanism and converted to Christianity. Miraculously he found he was cured of all his sexual desires and was able to live a chaste and celibate life. Almost immediately he threw himself into interpreting Christianity for all Christians in what amounts to a small library of books and treatises. On sexual matters, Augustine, following his Manichaean and Neoplatonic heritage, held that sex in itself was a source of evil. However, he recognized that Jesus had attended a wedding feast and that the Hebrew prophets had been married and had lots of children. This led him to compromise his position on sexual activity. Although he continued to hold that the ideal Christian life was one of complete abstinence from sex, he recognized that not everyone could achieve this. Thus God had permitted marriage, but only for the purpose of procreation. All other sex was forbidden, and any attempt to prevent or inhibit procreation during sexual intercourse was a sin. Augustine also stipulated that sex was only allowed with the proper instrument, the penis, within the designated orifice, the vagina. All other sexual activities, such as fellatio, cunnilingus, or masturbation, were sins, as were premarital sex, adultery, and so on. Augustine's view came to dominate the Western Church (not the Eastern).

What the story of St. Augustine indicates (and I have greatly simplified it here), is the importance of understanding the historical and cultural background of Western assumptions about sex. Our ideas do not occur in a vacuum. Later interpreters of the Western Christian tradition, including the Protestant leaders John Calvin, Martin Luther, and others, emphasized the importance of sex within marriage (Calvin especially emphasized the satisfaction of both partners). But in general, Christian teachings about nonprocreative sex until recent decades usually have been hostile and negative. Interestingly, such attitudes have not prevented Western people from engaging in all kinds of sexual activity, but it has resulted in a widespread feeling of guilt and periodic attempts at repression. The best evidence for this is the disproportionate share of religious writings devoted to sex.

Traditional Christian assumptions about sex over the ensuing centuries were occasionally challenged by new findings but rarely modified. As dissection began to take place in the universities late in the Middle Ages, for example, physicians made new discoveries about women's reproductive systems that eventually led to new importance of women in conception. Medicine, the home of the biological sciences until the past century and a half, remained an uncertain science, and the physicians, more interested in dealing with the ills of patients than in research, had to deal with a great many unknowns that the science of the time could not answer. The easiest way to deal with the unknown was to adopt generalized theories about how the body worked and how illness came about. This allowed treatment according to theories even when the physician did not know what actually caused the illness. For much of Western medicine, Galen, the Graeco-Roman physician, served as the theoretical source, although he was supplemented by Islamic writers such as Avicenna, Averroës, and others. Gradually, as the knowledge base grew, changes occurred and, in the eighteenth and early nineteenth century, a number of new theories developed. Common to most of them (including Galen) was the assumption that good health was a matter of the proper equilibrium of the body. Although the theorists disagreed somewhat in their explanations about how the body worked, they all emphasized the importance of keeping it in balance. Much of this was based on self-evident observations. If a person has diarrhea, he or she will become progressively weaker, unless it is stopped and the balance of the body restored. Similarly, constipation is a disorder at the other extreme, and it is necessary to overcome it to bring the body back to health. Certain activities also can temporarily cause a drain on the body. Sexual activity itself was thought by many to endanger the body's balance. Two factors contributed to this assumption: one is the observable phenomenon that men's orgasm results not only in ejaculation of semen but in a brief feeling of lassitude. This led many physicians to hypothesize that undue expenditure of semen would result in growing feebleness and perhaps even insanity. The second observation was that many sexually promiscuous individuals tended to become insane or develop enfeebling diseases as they aged. We now know that many of these symptoms, believed to be due to excessive nonprocreational sexual activity, were really the result of third-stage syphilis. It was not, however, until the last part of the nineteenth century that third-stage syphilis was described and not until the end of that century that the spirochete that caused it was identified. Thus, it was not believed that a disease but sexual activity itself caused the illness.

Because physicians as a group shared the negative attitudes about sexuality common to the Christian tradition, it was also not unusual for them to see excessive sex as a source of illness. Some forms of sexual activity such as masturbation seemed to be particularly harmful. Influential in focusing medical attention on masturbation was Tissot (1728–1797), one of the more important medical writers of the eighteenth century. Tissot had observed that sexual intercourse (like any other form of physical activity) increased peripheral circulation. He concluded that this resulted in a rush of blood to the head that starved the nerves, making them more susceptible to damage. What he did, in effect, was modify what Augustine had called a sin and made it a causal factor in disease. For him, masturbation was the worst sexual activity because it could be indulged in at such a young age that excess was inevitable, and the still tender nerve ends would be more seriously damaged.

Other writers built on Tissot's ideas, claiming it was not only the actual sexual activity that caused illness but even sexual thoughts. Some diets, such as those rich in meats, were also believed to increase lascivious thinking, but so did over-seasoned dishes. By the last part of the nineteenth century, the dangers of sex had not only become part of the arsenal of all the faddists and quacks but had also entered mainstream medical teaching. But why, if sexual activity was so harmful, had not generations of individuals become insane in the past? Those concerned with chronicling the dangers of sex had an answer. It was the growing complexities of modern civilization and the higher evolutionary development of humanity that had made sexual activity so much more dangerous than it had ever been before. This theory of neurasthenia was advanced by a prominent American physician, George M. Beard (1830–1883), who believed that nervous exhaustion was particularly dangerous to the educated, brainy workers, who represented a more advanced stage of civilization than the common laborer. Thus, animallike sexual activity could be permitted in the uneducated and laboring classes but not in the educated and "better" classes. The theory, for a brief period, had widespread acceptance, perhaps because it seized upon new scientific concepts to justify class and race distinctions. For Beard, the chief cause of nervous exhaustion was sexual intercourse, and it was essential for individuals to guard against any unnecessary (nonprocreative) sexual activity.

It was in this setting that modern sex research began. Many of the pioneers were individuals who were already stigmatized by societal attitudes toward their sexual behavior and therefore had little to lose by challenging traditional attitudes. They, perhaps like the German Activist, Karl Ulrichs (1825–1895), wanted to demonstrate that same-sex love was natural.

The result was an outpouring of writings on homosexuality and other forms of stigmatized sexuality. One of the more influential investigators was Richard von Krafft-Ebing (1840–1902). His studies into medical forensics not only provided guidelines for the courts in dealing with a variety of cases but also encouraged others to do research because the growing cities of the Western world were seen by many to be "cesspools" of "perverted" sex.

Researchers in other countries also joined in. In the United States, research moved from investigating the sources of prostitution and the sequelae of sexually transmitted diseases to basic research into the physiology of sex and contraception. Much of the research in the first part of the twentieth century was sponsored by John D. Rockefeller Jr. and by what later came to be known as the Rockefeller Foundation. Interestingly, few of those who did major research were willing to call themselves sex researchers. Instead they called themselves endocrinologists, sociologists, psychologists, or physiologists because there was still a stigma attached to those who showed an undue interest in sex. Most of the researchers were very cautious in their conclusions and often were more negative in their public statements than their research findings would support. The one major exception to this appeared at midcentury: Alfred Kinsey. A major recipient of Rockefeller funds, Kinsey revolutionized research into sexuality. It was at this time that I made my first appearance on the research scene, and my own anxieties about being identified as a sexual pervert, I believe, are reflective of the attitudes of the time.

The Historian

Much of my career planning took place in the U.S. Army at the end of World War II. I had graduated from high school at age 16 and then gone on to college for four quarters before entering the army. I did so to get the GI Bill, and, although the war was over and won by the time I entered, the draft was still on. Somehow my army career was one where I continually slipped through the cracks of regular army procedure. I had been pulled out of the traditional army basic training programs because I had scored high on the army intelligence tests and because I could type. The latter was more important than the former. They needed typists; in fact, they needed them desperately because they were beginning to discharge large numbers of veterans. Someone had to type the discharges, and that was my assignment from 7 A.M., with short breaks for meals, to 9 P.M., six days a week.

I began to wonder if basic training would not have been better. One of my acquaintances in the typing pool who was a dedicated churchgoer indicated that one of the chaplains was desperately hunting for an assistant who could play the organ. I could, so I applied. On the basis of my musical skills, I found myself designated a chaplain's assistant. As part of the discharge ceremonies at the post, the soldiers were marched in groups of 150 or so into a chapel while I played appropriate music. They were then addressed by one of the chaplains, who gave a short sermon and concluded by explaining the steps the soldiers still had to go through to get discharged. I had much more free time, although I also had to play for church services on Sunday and occasionally jazz piano for midweek revival services. Fortunately, the post had a good library, and I spent my time examining my career goals. My original goal in college had been somewhat nebulous, either pre-medicine or engineering. I already had considerable journalism experience from working on major newspapers before and after school and during the summer (the wartime shortage of workers allowed students to gain tremendous job experience), but only a few universities at that time had programs in journalism. Moreover, those reporters and editors on the newspapers for which I had worked advised me to get a broad background rather than trying to major in journalism. I knew from my experience on newspapers that reporting was primarily a young person's profession, and that the older individuals usually moved up to the copy desk or became some kind of editor or entered the advertising business or wrote their long-delayed novel. I knew I did not want to be an editor but rather a writer. In my brief experience in college, I had learned that many college professors were not only scholarly writers but also wrote for more popular audiences. The problem I wrestled with in the army was how to earn a living as a writer. My answer was to seek a Ph.D. in history and become a college professor.

I think I have always tried to explain things by looking at what had happened before, and because I was more interested in culture and society at large rather than in the individual, history seemed to suit me. I shared these thoughts with my bride-to-be, Bonnie (we had become engaged when I was 18 and married shortly after I turned 19), and as we corresponded she helped me to form my thoughts and encouraged my plans. Before we were married, I transferred into the

Army Security Agency and we began our marriage in Santa Rosa, California, near Two Rock Ranch Station, the post to which I was assigned.

After my discharge, I went back to the University of Utah, majored in history, and went off to the University of Chicago to do my doctorate. I supplemented our income by working on various writing projects, including rewriting two volumes of the history of Chicago (somebody else later rewrote my version). Chicago allowed registered full-time students to sit in on as many classes as they wanted. I gorged myself on all kinds of classes in religion, philosophy, literature, sociology, anthropology, and languages. I wrote a dissertation on medieval medicine and was prepared to teach courses in the history of science, Western civilization, medieval Europe, or modern Europe, at least initially. I hoped to become more specialized when I settled in.

While at Chicago, I had an assigned desk in the basement of the main library in the HQ section, that is, the sexuality and family section in the Library of Congress classification. Needless to say, I also spent some time reading in the existing sex literature, adding to a knowledge base that had been slowly building since my high school days. Let me explain.

Bonnie and I had begun going together shortly after she graduated from high school (in 1944), and that summer I met her mother, Ruth. I knew before I met Ruth that she had deserted her children and her second husband three years earlier to move in with another woman, Barrie. For a time, Bonnie had lost contact with her mother, but in her senior year in high school, her mother had reestablished contact.

This inclusion in the affairs of a lesbian couple and their lesbian (and some gay) friends opened up a whole new world to both of us. Barrie, much better educated than any other woman I then knew, had actually done considerable research into lesbianism and had a major library on sex issues. She gave us our first copy of Richard von Krafft-Ebing's *Psychopathia Sexualis* to read and explore and explained in some detail her views of homosexuality and lesbianism. Both she and Bonnie's mother invited us to parties to meet their gay and lesbian friends. Gradually Bonnie and I became what might be called closet researchers into sexuality. After Barrie's death, we also received a box of materials that included a summary of the interviews she had compiled on some 25 members of the lesbian community in Salt Lake City in the late 1920s and 1930s, which we published in the 1970s. It proved to be a pioneering study and today it is much cited and reinterpreted by those who want to make more out of it than we believe is possible.

I occasionally and with some hesitancy wrote papers on sexual issues. I even got up enough courage to talk with some professors about doing research on sexuality-related topics, but I was discouraged by them on the grounds that it would make it difficult for me to get a college teaching job. This did not stop either Bonnie or me from continuing to read widely and from beginning to collect a library on various sexual topics. It was while I was reading in the HQ section of the University of Chicago library that I realized the tremendously rich treasure of sources that could be used to study the history of sexuality. I also realized that these sources were for the most part ignored and that what was published was usually rather sensationalist and not particularly scholarly.

I began to conceive of a role for history in the research of human sexuality, a topic I thought involved a number of different variables and disciplines: biology (including genetics and hormones), the individual (psychology), the community (sociology), and culture and history (anthropology and history, plus most of the humanities). Of these, the most untouched was really the historical area, although I was convinced that it had the richest database. The problem, however, was in re-covering this database because no indices or standard bibliographies listed such topics as sexual intercourse, homosexuality, transvestism, lesbianism, or sado-masochism. I found as I explored further that others had realized the richness of history, and that individuals such as Havelock Ellis, for example, had relied on his-tory for much of this data. I also discovered that indexers in the past had not en-tirely ignored sexual topics and had found ways of guiding readers to sexual issues by using nonsexual terms. Often references to discussions of sexuality were simply classified under the topic of women or females. I have never been able to under-stand why this was so, but wondered if the mainly male indexers simply thought of women when the discussion included some reference to sex. The one major excep-tion to this general refusal to deal with sex openly was the topic of prostitution, listed boldly in most indexes. Then again, it was a topic obviously associated with women. Other index words that sometimes proved fruitful were adultery, pornog-raphy, and venereal or sexually transmitted diseases. There were occasional refer-ences to sodomy, sapphists (a term for lesbianism), pathics (a Latin term for ho-mosexuals), pederasty, and even to the catchall category of perversion. Interestingly, there were more likely to be indexes with sexual references in classi-cal works of ancient Greece and Rome than in those dealing with American his-tory. Works in French or German were more likely to have indexes with sexual terms than those in English. Thus, part of my early research was preparing bibli-ographies on sexual topics, several of which were published.

There was also a second problem in studying the history of sexuality, namely the lack of availability in research libraries of those books that had dealt with sex in the past in any detail. The libraries well might have had more books than they ad-mitted to having; they were just not catalogued. Kinsey had collected monographs and books on the topic because he faced the same difficulty, but early in my career I could not afford a trip to the Kinsey library. Even those libraries that cataloged some of their sex books kept them under lock-and-key, supposedly for fear of theft, but I suspected other reasons. This meant that one had to ask the librarian about books or pamphlets on possible sex topics, and often go through the third degree before being allowed to see the material or in some cases being denied ac-cess. Actually it was easier to get books in foreign languages on sex in the libraries because they assumed if I could read them in that language I was a true scholar and not just a voyeur. As I grew older, I was more rarely denied access, but the as-sumption was that I must be one dirty old man. Actually I am, and my children once gave me a bumper sticker saying "we love dirty old men."

Among the better sources for books and other materials were the various medical libraries, and fortunately for a time the historical collections of the Na-tional Library of Medicine were located in Cleveland, Ohio, near where I began my college teaching career. Also, legal libraries often had books that dealt with forensic medicine, a rich source of reference materials to sexuality in the past. Still, the key to much of my research on sexual topics was building my own collection of secondary and primary sources on various sexual topics, something that I was eventually able to do with funds from the Erickson Educational Foundation. Perhaps second only to my own growing library were the sexual materials uncovered by my friends and acquaintances. For example, a woman colleague wrote me that Purdue University Library had the papers of Lillian Gilbraeth, an early industrial psychologist, who had done a survey of sanitary pads in the 1920s. My friend stated that she felt the data were important but that she would not dare publish on such a topic, and that I should. I did.

As I settled into an academic career, conscious of the fact that my professors had warned me about publishing on sexual topics, I entered the field gingerly, and carefully chose my organizations for presentation. The American Association for the History of Medicine proved to be somewhat more willing than traditional historical groups to hear papers on sexual topics. Interestingly, I found sociological journals more receptive to articles on issues of sex and gender than historical ones. All the while, however, I kept up research in traditional historical topics to certify my historical expertise to my colleagues and not to put barriers in the way of my promotion and advancement. My first tentative excursions into print on sexual topics came from my willingness to do book reviews on a variety of topics in semi-popular journals, journals probably not read by most of my colleagues. One book I reviewed in such a journal was an analysis of the Wolfenden report, a special British parliamentary group that made recommendations for public policy on prostitution and homosexuality. My review aroused the interest of a New York publisher, who said that he would be interested in a book on either homosexuality or prostitution.

This in a sense caused a professional crisis for me because I very much wanted to do the book but was worried about what its effect on my career might be. Bonnie and I talked it over and she agreed to work with me on it. But we then had the choice of writing on prostitution or homosexuality. The final choice was mine, and I must admit that I chose prostitution over homosexuality because I was fearful that I would be labeled as a homosexual. I took great care to inform my colleagues that I was doing a book on prostitution, and asked for help and references, which I received. There came to be great interest among many of my colleagues who found synonyms or slang words referring to prostitution or prostitutes. In short it became a fun project and was well received. I also eventually received a review of my study in the staid *American Historical Review,* the author of which complained that the book was rather boring. I did not know whether this was good or bad, but it indicated to me that the reviewer had looked forward salaciously to reading the book. All I wanted the study to be was scholarly.

At the first professional meeting I attended after the appearance of the book, I gave a paper in a medieval session and was introduced by the chair as the person who specialized in whores, pimps, and queers, but also occasionally was capable of doing scholarly work on other topics. Everyone laughed, and whether I wanted it or not, I was labeled.

In the meantime, I had been actively engaged in sex-law reform efforts and among other activities had chaired an American Civil Liberties Union (ACLU) committee to report a policy both on abortion and on homosexuality. I did so in 1964, urging that we legalize abortion and eliminate criminal penalties for homosexuality and transgender behavior, a policy adopted by the ACLU. If I had not been labeled before, I was now. I was invited to address a large variety of clubs and organizations in Los Angeles on sexual topics. I also appeared on a number of talk shows, mainly radio at that time, and on one I was denounced and called the most evil man in America because I advocated the removal of legal penalties against homosexuality. Most of my audiences were more receptive though, and I was increasingly identified as the sex expert in various gatherings.

From the nature of our entrance into the study of sexuality, both Bonnie and I had always insisted that we needed to know the group or groups we were researching, even when much of our research was strictly of a historical nature. We made contact with prostitute groups as well as individuals, with gay and lesbian groups, with cross-dressing groups, with free-love advocates, with those involved in alternative life styles, and many others. Some of the individuals became part of our friendship network. We also joined the Society for the Scientific Study of Sex.

Although I continued to research nonsexual topics, I also put an increasing amount of time into researching sexual topics and spreading the word about the opportunities available to those interested in sex research. In 1970, I helped organize and also presented at the first session on sexual topics ever held by the American Historical Association. I included in my presentation a discussion of homosexuality. The fact that the session was attended by more than a thousand people indicated that the barriers to the study of sex had begun to disappear in the historical profession. A couple of years later, I also organized the first session on sexual issues ever presented at a conference devoted to medieval studies. Keeping to our commitment of involvement on sexual issues, Bonnie and I helped organize caucuses and committees on gay and lesbian issues in the American Historical Association and the American Sociological Association, among other groups. We also served as sponsors and organizers of the first meeting of Parents and Friends of Gays and Lesbians.

I wrote articles and reviews for *One* magazine, the pioneering gay magazine, and *Ladder,* the magazine published by the Daughters of Bilitis (the lesbian organization). I also published in the first issue of the *Journal of Homosexuality* (and served on its board of editors), served as chair of the Institute for the Study of Human Resources, the foundation associated with One Inc., and assisted in the establishment of the first course on homosexuality in an American college or university at Long Beach State in California. I also was active in the abortion movement and in many of the sex- and gender-related groups. Finally, I ventured into teaching courses on human sexuality at California State University, Northridge, where I had been named an outstanding professor in 1969, the first one so named at my university.

My first efforts at teaching were more in the field of gender than sexuality because I had become very interested in what was then called sex roles. I had received a five-year grant from the Erickson Education Foundation in 1969 to begin a major study on sexual variance in society and history, and I had theorized that one of the keys to determining societal attitudes toward sex issues was attitudes toward women and the role that society permitted women to play. I felt this aspect of my research would cause the least academic trouble, and so I began offering a course on women's role in history, and in the process I somehow became a leader in women's studies in the United States for a brief time. Publishers heard about the course and the result was a book, entitled *The Subordinate Sex,* with Bonnie Bullough as coauthor, which appeared in 1974. As women's studies gained influence on campus, I gradually changed the focus and the title of my course to one on the history of sexuality, and this was also reflected in a number of books I published on the subject. At the same time, many of my colleagues and I organized the Center for Sex Research on the California State University, Northridge, campus, and began sponsoring conferences on a variety of sexual topics.

Interestingly, in the 1970s my opportunities for publication expanded tremendously, and much of the work I had been doing for years could finally get published. But I also found my role and status changing with some of the groups I had worked so closely with in the past. While in the 1960s I had often served as what could be called a front man for gay and lesbian groups, by the middle of the 1970s this role had begun to disappear. Gays and lesbians were speaking for themselves, and although I was welcome in the groups, especially among the older gays and lesbians, there was a feeling, with which I sympathized, that gays and lesbians should speak for themselves. My studies, although scholarly, were those of an outsider. Although they were welcome, the emphasis was not what the new insiders wanted. I should add that the whole field of homosexual and lesbian studies expanded almost geometrically, with each subspecialty of history having its own experts. The same thing was happening in women's studies, with the new generation of feminist scholars. My work and that of Bonnie was recognized and appreciated, but the field and personnel changed rapidly.

We assumed the role of supporter but I took the lesser role somewhat unwillingly because it was in this period (1976) that I returned to college to get a nursing degree. We had both written a lot on nursing as well as race and sexual activities (and other things), and it was certainly easier to become a nurse insider than to change our race, sex, or sexual orientation.

I found myself not only anxious to explore new areas and new fields of sexuality but also to meet new academic challenges. I had held various administrative tasks at Northridge, and during a year of troubles when the campus had five presidents, I had served as president of the faculty and chair of the senate and had a great deal of influence in how the school was run. I like to think it was through my efforts that major campus crises were solved. Bonnie, in particular, was interested in administration, and when she was appointed dean of nursing at SUNY Buffalo in 1979, I applied for a vacant deanship at the nearby SUNY College. Somewhat to my surprise, because I felt my studies in sexuality would eliminate me from consideration, I was chosen. It turned out that several members of the selection committee were either gay or female and had read materials that I had written. In short, instead of hurting my chances for academic administration, my research in sex and gender had helped it! Certainly the academic climate had changed and I no longer had to worry about my research into sex and gender issues.

One of the new fields we began to explore was transgender behavior, an area where we already had contact with many individuals in the club movement established by our friend Virginia Prince, who had begun publishing a magazine for transvestites in 1960. We also went deeper into the study of prostitution, and did much more research on contraception, abortion, sadomasochism, and other aspects of sexuality, as well as continuing our research in nursing.

In trying to assess my contribution to sexuality, I think I helped a new generation of historians appreciate the importance that an understanding of sexuality can bring to subjects previously ignored by professionals. I think I have also helped my colleagues in other disciplines realize the significance of historical data for some of their studies. As I indicated at the beginning, I have always been interested in the study of sexuality but had to come to terms with my own sexuality and my own self-image to commit to the studies. Such a commitment, however, is not without danger. I have been labeled a security risk by the FBI, a topic about which I have written elsewhere, and currently I am being assailed as a defender of pedophilia by some in the child-abuse industry. This last is because I have written about the changing age of consent, and because my one contact with those interested either in theory or reality in pedophilia is through my position on the editorial board of *Paidika*.

Such accusations have also been aired on the Internet. I have been accused of being a pornographer by some of the feminists against pornography. Several have accused me of being a pimp because of my association with prostitutes. Only rarely do I respond to such accusations, simply because one cannot answer them. However, when identifying me as something or other might cause harm to others, I try to respond. I was once asked by *Newsweek* about how my life as a homosexual affected my academic career. I was in a quandary because usually I keep silent when someone labels me as homosexual, but this time I felt compelled to reply that I did not know because I was not a homosexual. I am not certain that they believed me, but at least I felt I needed to respond in such a way as not to mislead. When the number of accusations or misidentifications reach the number that have been leveled against me, the very contradictions can usually allow one to ignore them. In many ways, I have been quite radical (at least in belief) in trying to bring about change in the role and status of women, gays and lesbians, racial minorities, and the other challengers of gender and sexual traditions. My own personal lifestyle, however, has always been conservative. I was married to the same woman for 49 years, did not engage in extramarital affairs, had five children, got along well with most of my colleagues, served in a variety of administrative positions, and am tolerant of those who disagree with me as long as they do so peacefully. I own my own home. I garden for a hobby, swim for exercise, and occasionally play golf. I hope that my research and teaching have helped people realize that sex is an important part of life and in the process help modify what I have elsewhere called the sex-negative attitudes of most Americans.

I should repeat that history is a tremendously valuable source of materials, and for many kinds of sexual behavior such as adult-child sexual interaction, it is now about the only source of data we can use. Historical data, however, is only valuable if it is available and interpreted. This is a problem because interpretations vary with those doing the interpreting, and the same facts can be reinterpreted or ignored by others. One of the best examples of this is my disagreement with the historian John Boswell, who perceived the medieval Christian Church to be much more friendly to homosexuality than I do. Boswell, however, was a Catholic convert and a homosexual who wanted very much to change the existing Catholic policy on homosexuality. This might well be a laudable ambition, but I do not subscribe to his interpretation and this might well be because I am a humanist and a heterosexual. The debates among historians sometimes make it difficult for nonhistorians to know what to accept, and for this I apologize. All I can argue is that the growing consensus, even among gay medievalists, tends to favor my interpretation over that of Boswell.

Recently, a friend was writing on homosexuality in Hinduism, a subject on which I had written, and he found that one author had taken me to task for my writings, denying that there was any evidence of a third sex attitude in either Hinduism or Jainism. The person, however, was extremely hostile to homosexuality, feeling that it was evil and that Hinduism could not have tolerated it. Fortunately, there are others who have written since I did on the subject, and they tend to agree with me. There are, however, fashions in history, including the current widespread belief in the social construction of homosexuality. Although I agree that each generation and each period sees homosexuality within its own perspective, I strongly believe that same-sex behavior has a long and honorable history and that many of the gays and lesbians in the past would be recognizable by their counterparts today if they could read and study their lives. In short, the history of sexuality can be fascinating, and I would urge others to study it, to challenge and correct me, or perhaps even to reaffirm what I have found.

Suggested Readings

Bullough, B., Bullough, V. L., & Elias, J. (in press). *Gender blending: Transgenderism today.* Buffalo, NY: Prometheus.

Bullough, B., Bullough, V. L., Fithian, M., Hartman, W., & Klein, R. (1997). *How I got into sex.* Buffalo, NY: Prometheus.

Bullough, V. L. (1964). *History of prostitution.* New York: University Books.

Bullough, V. L. (1976). *Sexual variance in society and history.* New York: Wiley Interscience.

Bullough, V. L. (1976). *Sex, society and history.* New York: Science History, Neale Watson.

Bullough, V. L., (1979). *Frontiers of sex research.* Buffalo, NY: Prometheus.

Bullough, V. L., (1979). *Homosexuality: A history.* New York: New American Library.

Bullough, V. L., (1993). *Science in the bedroom; A history of sex research.* New York: Basic.

Bullough, V. L., & Brundage, J. (1982). *Sexual practice and the medieval church.* Buffalo, NY: Prometheus.

Bullough, V. L., & Brundage, J. (1996). *Handbook of medieval sexuality.* New York: Basic.

Bullough, V. L., & Bullough, B. (1973). *The subordinate sex.* Urbana: University of Illinois.

Bullough, V. L., & Bullough, B. (1977). *Sin, sickness, and sanity.* New York: New American Library.

Bullough, V. L., & Bullough, B. (1978). *Prostitution: An illustrated social history.* New York: Crown.

Bullough, V. L., & Bullough, B. (1990). *Contraception today: Modern methods of birth control*. Buffalo, NY: Prometheus.

Bullough, V. L., & Bullough, B. (1993). *Cross dressing, sex and gender*. Philadelphia: University of Pennsylvania Press.

Bullough, V. L., & Bullough, B. (1994). *Human sexuality: An encyclopedia*. New York: Garland.

Bullough, V. L., & Bullough, B. (1995). *Sexual attitudes: Myths and realities*. Buffalo, NY: Prometheus.

Bullough, V. L., Elcano, B., Deacon, M., & Bullough, B. (1978). *Bibliography of prostitution*. New York: Garland.

Bullough, V. L., Legg, D., Elcano, B., & Kepner, J. (1976). *An annotated bibliography of homosexuality*. 2 vols. New York: Garland.

Bullough, V. L., & Sentz, L. (1992). *Prostitution: A guide to sources, 1960–1992*. New York: Garland.

Freeman, S., & Bullough, V. L. (1993). *A guide to fertility*. Buffalo, NY: Prometheus.

Chapter 2

Why Would Anyone Conduct Research on Sexual Behavior?

Donn Byrne

Donn Byrne (Ph.D., Stanford University) currently holds the rank of Distinguished Professor of Psychology at the University at Albany, State University of New York—summer home of the New York Giants. He is a Fellow of the American Psychological Association, the Society for Personality and Social Psychology, the Society for the Scientific Study of Sexuality, the American Association of Applied and Preventive Psychology, and a Charter Fellow of the American Psychological Society. He has been President of the Midwestern Psychological Association and of the Society for the Scientific Study of Sexuality, has been Chair of the Department of Psychology at Albany, and heads the Social-Personality Program there. He is currently on the editorial or advisory boards of *Annual Review of Sex Research, Social Behavior and Personality: An International Journal,* and *The Journal of Sex Research.* He has published a sufficient number of articles, chapters, and books to suggest a thinly disguised Type A personality. When not engaged in such academic pursuits, he devotes a considerable amount of time to reading fiction, watching movies, and interacting with his son and three daughters—ranging in age from 8 to 38.

Though the question of *why* we conduct research is rarely a central focus in our discussions of what we do and what we find, the motivation that leads a small proportion of the population to engage in empirical research is worth examining. When little boys and girls state their future occupational plans, they may mention becoming a teacher or a police officer, but none that I know have replied, "When I grow up, I want to practice behavioral science—building theories, testing hypotheses by means of empirical research, and communicating my findings and conclusions in professional publications." The reason, of course, is that children learn from books, movies, and TV about grown-ups who are princes and princesses, witches, or talking animals; they directly observe teachers and police officers. Ordinarily, however, they aren't exposed to adults who earn a living as scientists either in stories or in real life. Throughout our lives, we see depictions of the work not only of law enforcement officers and educators, but also of attorneys, criminals, physicians, firefighters, astronauts, airplane pilots, entertainers, blue-collar workers, and lifeguards watching the bay, but "Doogie Howser, Research Psychologist" has not yet made it to showbiz. Generally, scientists are depicted in fiction only if they are doing something exciting such as chasing tornadoes, cloning dinosaurs, intercepting aliens from beyond our planet, or acting out their insane plans in the basement of a fog-shrouded castle.

As a result, most of us make it all the way to college without meaningful scientific role models. How in the world, then, do some of us become scientists? Quite possibly, accidental and random events are all-important, and I will attempt to describe the major factors that influenced one such individual. Though I hope that my description may be useful, and even instructive, I am not expecting this autobiographical narrative to be the basis of a major motion picture. Despite widespread rumors to the contrary, neither Brad Pitt nor Hugh Grant has been signed to play the lead in "The Awfully Confused College Student Who Grew Up to Engage in Sex Research"!

So, Why and How Did I First Get Involved in Psychological Research?

From early childhood through college graduation, I believed that I wanted to be a physician. I had more than my share of major illnesses and operations, and doctors (real doctors) were an integral part of my life. I knew where they worked, I knew (or thought I knew) what they did, and it appeared that, in return for helping others, physicians were rewarded with high prestige and a substantial income. Such benefits were brought to my attention directly by the home and lifestyle of one of my uncles who was a surgeon. Uncle Albert, as it happens, was also the individual who circumcised me when I was about six. I toss out this little-known item of trivia for the benefit of anyone who wishes to propose deeper interpretations of my life than I am willing to offer. A second childhood tidbit is that my mother often referred to her younger son as "Professor"; maybe that nickname had a long-delayed effect on my future career.

In any event, medicine remained my occupational goal through graduation from college in 1953, and I made plans to buy a used microscope to take with me to the newly opened medical school at UCLA. While working as a substitute mail carrier during the summer, I was surprised one afternoon to be approached on my route by a fraternity brother; John's task was to inform me that my father had had a heart attack in midmorning and was in intensive care in the Fresno Veterans Administration Hospital. (Many years afterward, my daughter Lindsey fictionalized the events of that day in a dramatic sixth-grade play.) My father's prognosis was sufficiently bad that I was forced to resign my medical school slot. Strangely enough, two years earlier I had switched my premed major from biology to psychology primarily because psychology required fewer lab courses, thus providing more time for me to work on the school newspaper and yearbook. An unforeseen consequence of that seemingly irrelevant adolescent change of majors was to make it relatively easy to substitute a more affordable backup career in clinical psychology for the original goal of medicine. I simply had to reformulate my fantasies of a future self as a practicing M.D. to someone who was a practicing Ph.D. engaged in a private clinical practice that was almost like being a physician, though without a microscope.

It was too late in the year to apply to a Ph.D. program, so I decided to work on a master's degree at Fresno State during the 1953–1954 academic year. I also married just before the fall semester began, and Lois and I returned from our honeymoon to be greeted by the news that I had been classified 4-F because of my inability to see the big "E" on the eye chart. As a result, I would not be drafted to fight in Korea. As much as I desired to defend my country from the Communist menace, I reacted manfully to the news of being rejected by the military. My father's physical condition was still quite serious, so he was advised not to travel to Carmel for the wedding. He soon recovered and lived an additional full and healthy 35 years.

Continuing the life changes of that stressful year, I found myself in a graduate program and faced with a world centered on research rather than on my real goal of therapy. With a keen depth of scientific understanding approximately equal to that of the African Wild Dog, I conducted my first scientific experiment. My reason for conducting research was straightforward: I was told that I must carry out an empirical study and then write up the findings because such activity was required of all graduate students. Based on my own experiences in meeting people in various schools, I studied how friendships (or acquaintanceships) develop in a college classroom as a function of the location of the seats to which each person was assigned. I found that in a section of intro psych, students knew only 8 percent of their classmates when the semester began, but they became acquainted with 21 percent by the end of 12 weeks, a small but significant increase. Among students assigned adjacent seats, however, a mere 3 percent were acquainted at the beginning of the semester, whereas a whopping 74 percent knew one another 12 weeks later; this represented not only a large increase but one significantly greater than among those not assigned to side-by-side seats.

Subsequently I learned that this phenomenon was known as "the propinquity effect" and that the role of physical proximity had been studied by numerous investigators interested in the formation of various kinds of relationships. If I (or my advisors) had been better informed, I would probably *not* have conducted this research, because it would have been considered redundant. If that alternative scenario had played out, my first publication would not have appeared in 1955. Many years later, in looking back over what I had and had not done, the first of several insights about research burst upon me. At no extra cost, this revelation will now be shared with you: *When planning to conduct research, don't clutter your mind beforehand with the procedures and findings of others. It will only confuse and discourage you.* This does not imply that it is beneficial to remain forever ignorant; after you have conducted the research and before you embarrass yourself by writing or talking about it in public, visit the library (in person or electronically) and pursue in depth what has been said and done with respect to the phenomenon in question. The seemingly odd practice of conducting research first and then exploring the literature is very much like what is now a common practice in kindergarten and first grade when children are first learning how to write. The students "sound spell" when they create stories. That is, they spell words in whatever way they wish (e.g., "I rote mi muthr a pome"). The point is to encourage the creative flow of ideas without getting hung up on the details of spelling and punctuation until after the story has been composed. A later step, of course, is to learn how to write correctly; when students are not required to progress to such a step, the consequences are not pretty.

Similarly, the first draft of a psychological article can be written in blissful ignorance and then later improved upon by creating a historical context in which its connections with precursors and with related lines of inquiry are explicated. For example, after first writing the previous paragraph, I was made aware that Richard Nisbett had already made the same point in 1990, though in a more literate and more informed fashion. As another example, my later research on the effect of similarity on attraction was inspired by observations of my father's reaction to anyone who disagreed with him about anything. Later, I was pleased to find similar observations in the Talmud, the writings of Aristotle, and in empirical publications by Sir Francis Galton at the end of the nineteenth century and several early twentieth century psychologists and sociologists—all of which long predated my modest contribution. Anyone reading my articles on this topic may reasonably assume that I spend long hours in dusty library archives, pouring over historical documents until such times as an "Aha! experience" sends me running excitedly into the street waving an experimental design in my hand. Much more often, these events occur more sedately and in the reverse order.

Despite the fears of cautious colleagues and worried students who obsess about the possibility that a given proposal "has already been done," my seemingly backward approach has not once led me to discover that I was accidentally duplicating the work of some predecessor. It *could* happen, of course, and a room packed with monkeys pounding away on word processors *could* accidentally produce *War and Peace*. Don't hold your breath while you wait for either event.

Beyond the insight about the creative advantage provided by ignorance, the most personally crucial aspect of being required to conduct research was my surprised realization that I enjoyed engaging in this kind of work. The enterprise begins with a vague idea followed by the development of a way to test it. After the procedures are in place, data are collected from real-life human beings (called "subjects" then, but today promoted to the status of "participants"). The analysis of the data either confirms (good) or disconfirms (not so good) the idea. Then, you write a "story" describing what you did, why you did it, and what your findings mean. In my virginal research experience, I was lucky enough to obtain significant results, and the manuscript appeared in a major journal. Wow! I enjoyed seeing my name in print. As icing on the cake, the article was later mentioned in a column in *Cosmopolitan*. Honest. I don't make these things up. Friends and relatives were not overly excited about the *Journal of Abnormal and Social Psychology*, but it caught their attention when my findings were described in a real magazine.

Despite what I gained from having to do this research, one should not jump to the false conclusion that all college requirements have beneficial effects. I was also required to take Physical Education and Quantitative Chemical Analysis, neither of which resulted in the least degree of enjoyment and neither of which had a lasting influence on any aspect of my life.

Having now completed this digressive introduction, I will approach the question posed in the chapter title more closely.

Why Would Anyone Conduct Sex Research?

In the period following my propinquity study, I did what many other students seem to do. I conducted additional required research on essentially unrelated topics because that's apparently what was expected. For example, I carried out an unnecessarily painful master's project in which the original members of my committee worked diligently (if unintentionally) to convince me that conducting research and writing about it was based on an adversarial relationship in which the goal was to inflict pain and suffering on anyone sufficiently stupid and masochistic to enroll in graduate school and conduct an experiment. I finally completed the work by asking a nonobsessive and nonhostile faculty member to take over as my committee chair. The project itself, dealing with the effect of induced tension on response to humor, was equally painful because I essentially found nothing, as described in the 73 double-spaced pages of a thesis. The only reinforcement associated with this truly disagreeable experience was the M.A. degree, but the prolonged torture was the occasion of my second insight: *Research should be fun, and a negative interpersonal context culminating in nonsignificant findings isn't fun.* At that point, following two sharply contrasting research experiences, I remained pretty well convinced that my life's work should center on psychotherapy. I followed that particular star for the time being by entering the clinical program at Stanford. I remained ambivalent about research, despite being surrounded by individuals in academia and even in clinical settings (at VA installations in Palo Alto and San Francisco and at the Stanford Medical School) whose careers and interests were almost universally centered on research. I had impressive role models, but I stubbornly though discreetly resisted their influence, at least for the moment.

The turning point came because of two factors. First, much of the Stanford clinical program in the late 1950s concentrated on the inadequacy of clinical procedures. Sandy Dean convinced many students to be skeptics by exposing us to the mind-boggling evidence that clinical assessment procedures were inconsistent measuring devices that predicted behavior badly or not at all. Most of the clinical faculty also were quite convincing in detailing the inadequacy of all therapeutic procedures (this was just prior to the explosion of behavior therapy). Beyond these objective problems, clinical practice gradually became less and less personally appealing as a lifetime career once I discovered that interacting with neurotic and psychotic individuals was almost as intellectually stimulating as watching stock-car races. I was able to carry out the various inadequate clinical procedures well enough, but such activities seemed analogous to the practice of routine dentistry in a world without toothbrushes, toothpaste, dental floss, or electric drills. My disillusionment was sufficiently great that I seriously explored two alternative and quite different escape routes: reapplying to medical school versus switching to the Ph.D. program in physics. Medical school was too expensive, and physics involved too much of a shift in content; I didn't look forward to starting over again from scratch.

Second, research was looking up. My doctoral committee was composed of helpful, pleasant, and extremely competent individuals whose work I respected: Lee Winder, Al Bandura, Paul Farnsworth, and Quinn McNemar. In my dissertation research, I again turned to humor. I hypothesized that, compared to students in a nonaroused state, sexually aroused individuals would be more amused by sexual cartoons; similarly, aggression arousal was expected to increase the enjoyment of aggressive cartoons. Further, I predicted that repressing and sensitizing defense mechanisms would mediate these effects. Male students were given several measures of defense mechanisms, and then some read sexual passages taken from novels, some were insulted while carrying out a task, and some were not subjected to any kind of arousal. Afterward, each individual was shown a series of sexual, hostile, and nonsense cartoons and asked to rate the funniness of each. Though the data from this experiment yielded only a scattering of significant findings, two future lines of research were accidental by-products of this project. First, in collecting fictional passages with erotic content, I found that some of my fellow students were eager to share with me their favorite dog-eared pages indicating the "dirty parts" of various books, whereas others were disgusted that I would have anything to do with such dreck. Among the most encouraging and surprising positive feedback came from various authors (such as Norman Mailer, Erskine Caldwell, and William Breadford Huie) when they wrote to give me permission to use portions of their work. The most colorful negative response was provided by Leon Festinger, who thought that sex should be confined to the real world. His openly negative appraisal and gentle (for him) ridicule of my activities were made clear when he wondered aloud in the faculty-student lounge why I didn't just read pornographic novels rather than use research as a respectable cover for my prurient motives. His insight, as usual, was not entirely off base, as will be discussed shortly. These various prosex and antisex reactions to my research helped give birth to the concepts of erotophilia and erotophobia. Second, I discovered that the various similarly titled measures of defense mechanisms were only minimally related to one another. The need for a suitable measuring device was the impetus for the later creation of the Repression-Sensitization Scale.

With the twin realizations that research could be enjoyable and that clinical activity no longer held even minimal allure for me, I spent my last year of graduate work completing the dissertation while employed as an instructor at California State University, San Francisco. There, a new problem arose: I discovered that my born-again affection for research was not adaptive in a state-college environment. At that time, San Francisco State discouraged rather than encouraged scientific pursuits. There was no subject pool, only volunteers; no equipment except for that used in classroom teaching; no research space except for unused classrooms; and no rewards at all for engaging in such deviant activity. Nevertheless, the young members of the faculty were actively engaged in semiclandestine experimentation. I was soon involved in my own work on subliminal stimulation, my first attempt to construct a measure of defense mechanisms, a follow-up of the propinquity study, and successful efforts to salvage even the master's thesis and the doctoral dissertation with brief articles. This unacceptable flurry of activity so alarmed the department chair that he called me in to accuse me of working at a furious pace only because I was unhappy at San Francisco and wanted to leave. That certainly wasn't my conscious motive, but he was making it seem like a good idea, despite the genuine appeal of living where the little cable cars travel halfway to the stars. So, when Phil Worchel sent a reprint request from Texas asking for one of my early articles, I mailed him a copy of the paper along with a note saying that I was glad to see that something I wrote was noticed in my old home town of Austin. To my surprise, Phil soon wrote back asking if I were interested in considering a position at Texas. These were the days when the old- (or young-) boy network still functioned, and we didn't know enough to feel guilty about it. Shortly afterward, my wife, infant son, Keven, and I were off to the land of the Longhorns, complete with the world's biggest flag plus the world's biggest bass drum, not to mention cannon fire and a romp by Bevo the bull following each touchdown.

Though my doctoral degree was in clinical, and I was hired at Texas as part of the clinical program, I declared one day that I was a personality psychologist and no longer one of the clinical faculty. After a few more years, I declared that I was a social psychologist. In effect, I decided that my professional identity derived from my work rather than my training. Don't try this at home; in today's job market, such declarations might just earn you a pat on the back as you are shown the way out.

At Texas, I found myself immersed in a world in which research was highly valued; my department chair and my colleagues were strongly oriented toward and actively supportive of research. Further, bright graduate and undergraduate students were eager to assist or collaborate in conducting scientific activity. Up to that point, I was only diddling around in the laboratory, as if I was not a real behavioral scientist, but I played one at UT. Then, my genuine research career began when I conducted a little experiment dealing with the effect of attitude similarity on attraction. If this narrative really were a movie, the music would now swell and the sun break through the clouds as the third and most important insight shone through: *Meaningful scientific activity requires theory-driven investigations in which one uses consistent operations across experiments.* The sacred term describing this phenomenon is *paradigm research.*

All that I (and many of my contemporaries) had been doing was gathering data here and there and writing about our findings, activity that only looked like science. In accord with an analogy suggested by psychoanalyst Leslie Shaffer, a great many of us were spending our days collecting chamber pots in the mistaken belief that this busywork would culminate in finding the Holy Grail. Successful science involves something more than acceptable experimental designs, careful data collection, exhaustive statistical analysis, tightly written journal articles, and all the other overtly impressive trappings. Conducting research within a paradigm also leads to a conceptual framework that, at its best, encompasses more and more phenomena and provides more and more precise and accurate behavioral predictions.

My comprehension of such matters was greatly influenced by a book about scientific revolutions by philosopher Thomas Kuhn. I approached attraction research and later sex research using the broad guidelines Kuhn provided. For me, his description of paradigms constituted a coherent conceptual framework for engaging in what he labeled "normal science." Note that this third insight forces us to qualify the first insight. At the initial stages of a scientific endeavor, knowing too much about what others have done and said can be an interference that stifles creativity. To coin a phrase, one person's chamber pot can turn out to be another's Rosetta stone. In contrast to this preparadigm period, at the later stages of a scientific endeavor it is essential to know what has gone before. After the concepts and procedures and measuring devices are in place, it truly is possible to duplicate previous work, repeat unnecessary mistakes, and generally waste your time foolishly. To switch analogies with wild abandon, one can initiate a paradigm by hopping impulsively into a wading pool, but you must take the time to know what the hell you are doing before even getting your big toe wet in the Olympic-size pool of an existing paradigm. Let's throw in one more analogy. I very recently realized that my gravitation to paradigm research was guided by positive childhood experiences with one special Christmas gift: an Erector set. What *are* the lessons to be learned from these shiny metal pieces, the nuts and bolts used to join them to one another, plus the special gears and cranks and motors? I'll tell you. First, you can't build anything unless you use standard, interconnecting parts. If you assume that Tinkertoys, Lincoln Logs, and Lego parts are equivalent to one another and to the contents of an Erector Set, you are doomed to confusion, inconsistency, and failure to replicate. Children are well aware of this, but many social and personality psychologists have yet to get the word. Second, it is more constructive (literally) to build than to destroy. It is better to build a Ferris wheel or a theory than to engage in their destruction. If you don't like my Ferris wheel, go home and build whatever you want. If you don't like my theoretical model, do the same.

There's one more insight to consider, and it deals with why someone conducts research on a given topic. Why does one person invest time on interpersonal attraction and sexuality while another concentrates on interpersonal aggression or self-efficacy or whatever? The universal answer to this and many other questions was provided by Steve Allen's "man on the street" portion of his TV show. One of his interviewees always answered a why question with "Why not?" A more enlightening answer is proffered in the following section.

Why Do Individual Scientists Select Specific Research Topics?

In graduate school, studying for my doctoral qualifying exams, I became painfully aware of something that I now believe to be a universal truth. At the time, however, I perceived it as a shameful personal defect. I was totally bored by and completely disinterested in a great deal of the material published in psychological books and journals. Only slowly did it become clear that this disinterest in much of my chosen field was not unique to me. Early in my career at Texas, this same "secret" was verbalized by two of my friends and colleagues. John Capaldi on more than one occasion claimed that when certain topics or lines of research were discussed, his eyeballs involuntarily rolled back in his head, a signal that he should seek a quick escape to avoid terminal boredom. And, Lou Moran told of eagerly presenting a research paper at a convention when he was a new Ph.D. He was flattered when a very famous psychologist approached him afterward, at least until that gentleman spoke. "I'm sure that what you are doing is extremely interesting, young man, but not to me." If the truth be told, that same thing could be said by most of us about the work of many other people and by many other people about our own work. This does not imply that what we or our colleagues do is necessarily faulty, worthless, or otherwise to be condemned. Rather, we should calmly agree that there is no reason to expect everyone to be fascinated by everything. That brings us to the question of why some research topics are of great interest to Person X and quite different topics of great interest to Person Y.

Perhaps because that question is potentially quite threatening, the motivation underlying one's specific scientific interest is seldom discussed in polite company. Of course, some motivational underpinnings are cute or otherwise nonthreatening and *can* be talked about without giving rise to anxiety. More than one astronomer, for example, has ascribed that particular career choice to the influence of an early interest in science fiction that described space travel. One biologist has explained his fascination with his field in general and with the behavior of ants specifically as stemming from a lonely and disruptive childhood in which insects became his major source of companionship and intellectual stimulation.

Some psychological research interests have been similarly attributed to early experiences. One pioneering psychologist traced his interest in intelligence and individual differences to his childhood fascination with the fellow inhabitants of his small Indiana community; their diversity ranged from the village idiot to a world-famous gangster. The underlying motive for other kinds of psychological research can obviously be more embarrassing and possibly more personally and intimately revealing than the reason for one's interest in IQ. Nevertheless, tongue in cheek, some suggest that anyone who studies hostility and aggression must in fact be hostile and aggressive or that only a socially insecure investigator would be drawn to research on interpersonal anxiety. On a more factual level, it can be observed that gender issues are primarily investigated by women, gay and lesbian issues by gays and lesbians, prejudice and discrimination by members of targeted minority groups, and so on. Beyond these anecdotes and generalities, there may be basic truths to be found.

This brings us to the fourth and final insight: *An individual is intrinsically motivated to pursue a given research topic only if he or she perceives it to be intensely interesting and of great importance.* Not only do such convictions propel the research, they also prevent the scientist from giving up in response to criticism, rejection, the disinterest of others, and/or disappointing data. It is not really too much of an exaggeration to suggest that it is helpful for a successful scientist to have unreasonably high self-esteem and to be at least a little delusional about the importance of his or her research. Investigations based on intrinsic motives are quite different from investigations based on extrinsic motives.

I know what it's like to conduct extrinsically motivated research. In San Francisco, a small group of us carried out market research for an advertising firm to supplement our meager salaries. We made at least one discovery that affected events in the real world. A company developed a product that they believed would appeal to black consumers. At their request, we conducted a nationwide survey and found that Nat King Cole was more admired by black wine drinkers than any other public figure, so he was signed up to endorse a newly developed sweet wine. The winery and Mr. Cole made a lot of money while we psychologists made a little money, but that income-driven research was quickly done and quickly forgotten. Research conducted for internal, personal reasons feels quite different and has quite different consequences.

When an investigator is convinced that a given topic is of vital interest and importance, the desire to ask and answer questions can be all-consuming. This type of driven behavior suggests that the topic being investigated has some personal relevance to the investigator. It is this relevance that attracts his or her attention and commitment.

Extrapolating from work on social cognition, a person's choice of a given research focus would seem to be one more example of the self-reference effect. To take a personal example, when I had to choose a topic for that first research project described earlier, friendship formation impressed me as something well worth investigating. Why? The answer lies in my own experiences. Throughout my childhood, my parents moved multiple times, managing to live in two states and three towns (as well as multiple houses within each town). On entering the ninth grade, I was in my ninth new school. Is it not reasonable to assume that classroom friendships and, more generally, interpersonal attraction would seem interesting and important to an individual whose greatest fears and challenges as a child and then as an adolescent centered on having to confront new classmates and new neighbors and, with luck, transform some of these strangers into friends? In investigating how interpersonal evaluations are affected by propinquity, attitude similarity, affiliation need, observable characteristics, emotional states, and many other factors, I have been, in effect, reliving, making sense of, gaining perceived control over, and generally dealing intellectually with matters that were once a major concern in my life. Currently, after two long (25 years and 16 years) but nonpermanent marriages, I am not at all surprised to find myself increasingly engaged in research centered on relationship outcome as a function of adult attachment patterns. In other words, I've progressed from making sense of my youthful challenges with friendship formation to making sense of my adult challenges with establishing and maintaining relationships. If I live long enough, I may even understand what it all means. Research does not, however, necessarily provide a magic solution to life's problems. In the words of one of my graduate students who had recently experienced love, marriage, and divorce, "We know a lot about what happens and why, but it still sucks."

All right, all right, so what lurid experiences led me to the study of sexual behavior? At the risk of disappointing the curious reader, my interest in sex does not seem to be based on childhood fears, all-consuming guilt, or traumatic experiences. From my earliest years, I reacted with interest and enjoyment to everything associated with sex. In truth, sex is even more fun than research. I believe that humans innately approach sexuality at least as positively as our fellow primates and other mammals. Were it not for the societal restraints we have learned, people probably would not differ, for example, from dogs who uninhibitedly sniff one another's genitals, and then mount or are mounted whenever the appropriate cues are present. When I was about three or four years of age, an equally young female friend was at my house, and we somehow agreed to go into my parents' bedroom and play doctor, a game that primarily involved removing our clothes and examining whatever anatomical structures we found. Inquiring minds wanted to know. This game was entertaining and informative, but the reactions of my mother when she entered the room were probably all-important in determining how I encoded the events of that summer afternoon. She didn't appear surprised, shocked, disgusted, or angry. Instead, she quietly suggested that we get dressed, come downstairs for ice cream, and then play something else. She also managed to let me know that it might be wise not to repeat this particular game because the girl's mother might not approve. I had no realization at the time how totally cool this woman was being. The details of this early experience probably set the tone that led to several research questions about sexuality in my adulthood.

Is Sex Fun or Just Funny?

I don't believe that I am unique in considering sex to be a central part of my life. In childhood, sex had to compete with building model airplanes and collecting stamps, but the latter two interests have since faded away. What sparked my intellectual curiosity and (I think) later research was the fact that many people I encountered seemed to respond to sexual cues quite differently than I did. For example, I perceived sexual matters as a serious source of pleasure; Sarah and I were not giggling when we played doctor. In contrast, many of my youthful acquaintances, and my parents' friends, too, responded to sex primarily as something to snicker about. "Look at those knockers! Hee, hee, hee." Also, I never quite understood the special allure of "dirty" jokes. Though I learned that it was easy to make people laugh by making silly sex-related remarks, deep down I believe that sex is too profoundly important for giggles and snickers. Altogether, this contrast between my response to sexuality and that of others seems to have led rather directly to my relatively unsuccessful doctoral research on sex arousal, defense mechanisms, and response to sexual humor. Much later, conducting research on the effects of explicit sexual imagery, I again observed tremendous individual differences among graduate assistants and undergraduate participants who viewed explicit slides and movies. Some laughed, some were embarrassed, some became angry, some were very quiet and still, and one told me that the material was very arousing but only after he returned to his dorm and replayed the scenes in his fantasies.

The association of sex and humor still interests me, but research on this topic has not paid off in terms of meaningful results. I still don't understand exactly why simple sexual cues are amusing to some people. Repeated research failures convinced me to abandon this topic. In research, as in poker, it is important to "know when to hold 'em and know when to fold 'em."

Does Sex Evoke Approach or Avoidant Responses?

To me, in the simplest terms, consensual sexuality expressed in words, pictures, or deeds has always elicited positive rather than negative affective and evaluative responses: I like rather than dislike it, perceive it as good rather than bad, approach rather than avoid it. Such reactions constitute a second apparent difference between myself and some people. Although a great many individuals clearly share my positive judgments about sexuality, a great many others just as clearly respond negatively. Almost 30 years ago, when I was asked to conduct research on the effects of sexually explicit material on behavior by the President's Commission on Obscenity and Pornography, I agreed without hesitation. I had long wondered why people are said to "use pornography." That wording seems to imply some perverse criminal act. Wouldn't it be odd to say that some people use pizza or use museums or use classical music? Underlying the establishment of the commission was the implicit assumption that the use of pornography, like the use of drugs, has negative consequences. Many of us who began to conduct research at the request of the U.S. government did not share that assumption.

Thousands of examples of negative responses to sexual matters are readily available, but the point is easily made with just a few. Why do parents teach their young children the words for eye and nose and chin and so forth but avoid accurate labels for whatever might lie between the navel and the knees? Why don't Barbie and Ken have genitals? Why did the members of Purdue's Institutional Review Board reject proposed research in which "innocent young college freshmen and sophomores from the farms of Indiana" would be exposed to and perhaps corrupted by movies in which couples fornicate? Why does a woman indignantly state that she is amazed that the men she dates expect her to put her mouth "down there" where they urinate? Why does a departmental colleague at Albany express his dismay that undergraduates are able to major in psychology by taking nothing but sex courses? (In fact, only one sex course has ever been offered, and it cannot be repeated for credit.) Why does a graduate student invited to a party express relief at finding that people who conduct sex research do not engage in Roman orgies with clothing optional? Why, when *non*explicit sexual slides were projected on a screen as part of an undergraduate course, did a student complain about having to view "pornography displayed all over the classroom walls."

In addition to these relatively mild everyday examples, consider the public controversies about censorship, legalized prostitution, pornography, breast-feeding babies in public, nude beaches, or gays in the military. In just the past few years, it has been considered newsworthy and generally deplorable to learn that an English movie actor solicited fellatio from a prostitute, that an entertainer who hosted a children's TV show masturbated in an adult movie theater, and that members of the British royal family as well as various American presidents have committed adultery. And on, and on. For me, the curious aspect of such observations is that such nonrare sexual matters elicit feelings of disgust among a large proportion of the population. I personally may decide that interaction with a paid sex partner carries a higher health risk than smoking four packs of cigarettes a day, prefer to remain fully clothed and nonorgasmic while attending a movie, and evaluate adultery as incompatible with maintaining a loving relationship. Nevertheless, my own decisions need not imply that such activities by others offend me or that an effort should be made to force everyone to model themselves on my beliefs and actions.

The observation that emotional and evaluational responses to almost all aspects of sexuality fall along a positive-negative continuum led us to develop a test (the Sexual Opinion Survey) that assesses such differential reactions and then to conduct a tsunami of research dealing with specific behaviors that are associated with these differences. A general model (known as the Behavior Sequence) specifies that human behavior is a function of external stimulus events plus a series of internal mediating events that include affective and evaluative responses, cognitive and expective entities, and thematic fantasies that are a blend of affective and cognitive elements. In effect, what a person does is the net result of these internal and external determinants.

An example of the use of this conceptualization in sexual research is our work on contraceptive use and nonuse by teenagers (research that got under way just as my oldest offspring became a teenager. Coincidence or what?). My first step was to analyze the behavioral steps required to engage in effective contraception. Briefly, an individual must (1) possess the necessary information on conception and how to prevent it, (2) accurately anticipate the likelihood of actually engaging in intercourse with a partner, (3) obtain the necessary contraceptive products, (4) communicate with a partner about intercourse and the prevention of conception, and (5) use the contraceptive product (or make sure that the partner does) in the correct way.

At each of these steps, specific aspects of the Behavior Sequence can facilitate or inhibit the necessary actions that lead to contraception. One example is the role of affect and evaluation. Because sex-related behavior is guided by sexual emotions and attitudes, it can easily be hypothesized that each necessary step in the contraceptive process is more likely to occur among those with positive attitudes about sexuality than among those with negative attitudes about sexuality. That is, compared to erotophilic individuals, erotophobic ones are more likely to avoid obtaining sexual information, less likely to be planful about potential future sexual interactions, more likely to express anxiety about obtaining contraception, less likely to communicate about contraception with a partner, and, altogether, less likely to use contraception effectively and consistently. The result is that erotophobic individuals are more likely to behave in ways that lead to conceiving an unwanted offspring than are erotophilic individuals. In other words, our theoretical model led to research that allows us to predict with better-than-chance accuracy who will or will not engage in effective contraception and hence have differential rates of unwanted pregnancies. This research has also helped guide the development of intervention procedures (by Bill and Jeff Fisher, for example) designed to alter emotional reactions, cognitions, expectancies, and relevant role-playing images to bring about behavioral change and thus to reduce the incidence of unwanted pregnancies and also to decrease the risk of becoming HIV positive.

Is a Desired Sexual Partner an Equal Participant in a Loving Act or Simply a Target Presenting a Challenge to Be Overcome?

A third sexual difference between myself and a surprisingly large number of people involves the respective roles of two humans (whether strangers, friends, or spouses of the same or the other gender) in making a decision about interacting sexually. I believe that satisfying interpersonal sex is something that occurs when two people mutually decide that this is what they want to do. The idea that one of the individuals would try to persuade, trick, threaten, or force the other to have unwanted sex is, to me, clearly unacceptable behavior. It's difficult to imagine coercing a reluctant partner to eat Chinese food, listen to a Barbra Streisand recording, or watch the Tony Awards on TV, no matter how much I personally might enjoy sharing these experiences. Given the high incidence of stranger rape, acquaintance rape, marital rape, and other forms of sexual coercion, some people (primarily males) obviously view sexual interactions not as a mutual decision but as a challenge that can require the skills of an aggressive salesperson, a con artist, and/or a felon.

Investigations of such behavior by our research group and by many others have led to the identification of a series of characteristics that are associated with the likelihood of engaging in sexual coercion. Once again, the Behavior Sequence is useful in conceptualizing how quite different variables can operate jointly to affect the coercive individual. For example, coercive males are found to hold negative and adversarial attitudes about women, to seek out and engage in enjoyable fantasies in which force and domination play an integral part of sexual interactions, to accept a variety of stereotypical beliefs about masculinity and about rape, and to hold positive expectancies about the effectiveness of aggressive persistence in overcoming female reluctance. Recently, Matthew Hogben, Merle Hamburger, and I borrowed a sociological conceptualization outlining how a society's legitimate aggressivity can spill over into the illegitimate aggressivity of its citizens. For examples, it has been found that the per capita incidence of forcible rape in the states of the United States is associated with state differences (on a per capita basis) in such nonsexual activities as applications for hunting licenses, enrollment in the National Guard, use of the death penalty, and the popularity of aggression-oriented magazines and television programs.

In our research, we applied this theoretical approach at the level of individual college students and found that those males who are most positive about legitimate aggression (hunting, the military, the death penalty, violent media presentations, etc.) are most likely to coerce their sexual partners. Though no concerted efforts have yet been undertaken, I am willing to bet that interventions designed to alter the attitudes, fantasies, and beliefs that facilitate coercive sexual behavior will be less successful than interventions designed to increase contraceptive behavior.

In Conclusion

I believe that three aspects of my sex research can be traced to my interest in explaining differences between myself and those who respond to sex as being funny, disgusting, or an interpersonal contest. One of these lines of inquiry has produced nothing of value, but the other two have been relatively successful. In science, there is no instruction manual, and the answers can't be found at the end of the book.

Altogether, I engage in research, including research on sexual behavior, because some issues seem to me to be interesting and important. The general process is enjoyable, and I am actually paid to entertain myself in this fashion. As suggested in a 1950s Broadway song, "Brother, you can't know a nicer occupation. . . . Give it a whirl, give it a try."

Acknowledgments

I wish to thank the editors of this book as well as Julie Osland and Lisa Schulte for their very helpful comments and corrections.

Because this chapter was designed to express *my* research motivations, I saw no way to cover the major contributions of my doctoral students to the various research projects. It was never a one-person show, and the numerous collaborators were an integral part of what was done. Their work was and is deeply appreciated. Maybe I will at some point have the opportunity to write about the essential role of graduate students in conducting research. I may even name names.

Suggested Readings

Byrne, D. (1961). Interpersonal attraction and attitude similarity. *Journal of Abnormal and Social Psychology, 62,* 713–715.

Byrne, D. (1961). The Repression-Sensitization Scale: Rationale, reliability, and validity. *Journal of Personality, 29,* 334–349.

Byrne, D. (1971). *The attraction paradigm.* New York: Academic.

Byrne, D. (1982) Predicting human sexual behavior. *The G. Stanley Hall Lecture Series, 2,* 207–254.

Byrne, D. (1983). The antecedents, correlates, and consequents of erotophobia-ero-
tophilia. In C. M. Davis (Ed.), *Challenges in sexual science* (pp. 53–75). Philadelphia:
Society for the Scientific Study of Sex.

Byrne, D., & Buehler, J. A. (1955). A note on the influence of propinquity upon acquaintanceships. *Journal of Abnormal and Social Psychology, 51,* 147–148.

Byrne, D., & Byrne, L. A. (Eds.). (1977). *Exploring human sexuality.* New York: Harper &
Row.

Byrne, D., & Fisher, W. A. (Eds.). (1983). *Adolescents, sex, and contraception.* Hillsdale,
NJ: Lawrence Erlbaum.

Byrne, D., & Murnen, S. K. (1988). Maintaining loving relationships. In R. J. Sternberg
and M. L. Barnes (Eds.), *The psychology of love* (pp. 293–310). New Haven, CT: Yale
University Press.

Byrne, D., & Schulte, L. (1990). Personality dispositions as mediators of sexual responses.
Annual Review of Sex Research, 1, 93–117.

Smeaton, G., & Byrne, D. (1987). The effects of R-rated violence and erotica, individual
differences, and victim characteristics on acquaintance rape proclivity. *Journal of Research in Personality, 21,* 171–184.

Chapter 3

Sex Psych Prof Taking Heat:
Fear and Loathing on the Research Trail

William A. Fisher

William A. Fisher (Ph.D., Purdue University), shown pondering a research question early in his career, is Professor of Psychology and Professor of Obstetrics and Gynaecology at the University of Western Ontario in London, Canada. Dr. Fisher is recognized internationally for his research on the psychological determinants of reproductive health behavior. As an inevitable consequence of his risk-taking style and commitment to dispassionate scientific inquiry, unfettered by political correctness concerns, he is also widely known and frequently reviled for his critical contributions to research concerning pornography and behavior, the subject of this chapter.

Dr. Fisher is a National Health Scientist for Health Canada, has served on the editorial boards of *The Journal of Sex Research, Journal of Psychology and Human Sexuality,* and *Motivation and Emotion,* and has published more than 80 scientific papers on human sexual behavior. He is codirecting a major AIDS risk reduction education project for the U.S. National Institute of Mental Health with his brother, Dr. Jeffrey D. Fisher, with whom he has worked on AIDS prevention issues for many years.

Dr. Fisher was born in the United States and has spent the last half of his life in Israel and Canada. He and his wife Randi share a two-career, three-child family and hobbies that include travel, hiking, and collecting American folk music, Israeli art, and Scotch whiskey.

This is an allegorical tale. It is "the truth, mainly . . . with some stretchers"
(Twain, 1885). Writing straight autobiography of the events described
herein would have hurt too much, and created too many martyrs, so I de-
cided to have some fun with it instead. I hope you will too.

At dinner one night I looked proudly down the table at my charming wife and three smiling children and at the turkey that I was about to carve. Amidst the happy family chatter, I casually mentioned that I had been asked to write a chapter on my research experiences in the area of pornography and behavior, and that I was approaching this task with a measure of concern.

"Gee, Dad," said Ben, age 15. "You're an earnest young sexual scientist. Could you please tell us about the highs and lows of conducting research on pornography and behavior, and about how you have managed to offend both the political right *and* the political left, so that we may all be the better for it?"

"Please, Daddy, please," begged Danny, age 11. "Tell us what it is like to have the entire campus women's caucus, professors and students alike, shout you down as a disgusting misogynist pig, and in the same week, have conservative opponents of the sex education program you pioneered write in our newspaper that you are a slimy pimp of the drug companies."

"Yes, Daddy, yes," squealed Sarah, age 6. "These issues are of significant concern to me as a woman. I want to know how you came to be a folkie leftover from the sixties. I want to know why you believe in the dispassionate conduct of science, unfettered by political correctness concerns. I want to know why you insist on the preposterous notion that there actually is an observable truth to find and to defend, when all of my deconstructionist playmates at the sandbox know that research is simply a politically motivated act designed to manufacture so-called evidence to buttress the patriarchy that, while under ferocious attack from kids like me, still squalidly rules every aspect of our lives."

"Well, honey," said my darling wife, Randi, "your story might help the children understand why you're sometimes *so* cranky after a long day conducting scientifically rigorous research on topics of social significance, in the face of repeated and morally bankrupt attempts to sabotage or subvert the work when its findings do not fit the accepted wisdom of the day. It may also teach the children valuable lessons about anger and fear and perfidy, and about the eventual victory of those who keep the flame of independent thought alive, though I must admit, dear, that the jury is still out on that last one. So for heaven's sake, let me carve the turkey just this once, and you can tell the children all about fear and loathing on the research trail."

Overcoming my natural reticence and reserve, I rolled up the sleeves of my starched white shirt, loosened my carefully knotted tie, and began to tell a tale about some of the experiences that I've had in the course of conducting research on pornography and behavior, in terms that even a child could understand.

"Well, kids," I said, "the first thing we need to do in a discussion of this sort is to define what we mean by pornography, establish its prevalence, and review research findings on the consequences of exposure to such material."

"Gee Dad," said Ben, "that seems like an awfully sensible agenda for discussion."

"Indeed it is, lad," I smiled, "but even though the definition of pornography is a clear one, findings concerning the prevalence of pornographic material are quite literally all over the place, and research on the effects of pornography has produced exceedingly inconsistent findings.

"As I mentioned, although there is agreement that pornography can be defined as any material that depicts and endorses sexual violence, there is little or no consensus about how prevalent pornography is in society today. Off the top of my head, kids, and while we're all enjoying Mom's wonderful groat cake soup, I can think of at least five peer-reviewed publications that suggest there is a very high level of sexual violence in sex magazines, adult videos, and adult bookstore materials, but I can also come up with at least five studies that document exceptionally low levels of sexual violence in similar—and in some cases the same—sex magazines, adult videos, and adult bookstore materials. What is even more embarrassing to report, kids, is that I can also think of a number of studies showing that the level of pornography in our society is increasing steadily across time and an equal number of studies demonstrating that the level of pornography is decreasing with each passing year."

"Gee whillikers, Dad," said Danny, throwing his hands up in mock despair and inserting a bread stick into his nose, "how can any self-respecting empirical scientist accommodate these wildly varying figures and still carry his or her head high?"

"You've got a good point there, scout," I noted with pride, "but just you wait—the story gets even worse! When we look at research concerning effects of exposure to pornography on men's behavior, we see evidence that exposure to fewer than five minutes of pornography is capable of provoking men to fantasize about raping a woman and capable of provoking them to direct physical aggression against a female. At the same time, though, other studies show that exposure to hours and hours of pornography has no sustained effects on men's attitudes or behavior toward women. Just off the top of my head—and I know that this is going to get me into trouble, kids, but I just can't help myself—I can think of at least five studies that attest to the ease with which pornography can turn formerly balanced and blameless college men into sexually violent misogynist beasts, and I can think of eight studies showing that pornography has little or no effect on men's attitudes and behavior toward women."

"Once again, Dad, what's an earnest young sexual scientist to do, when the data are so conflicting?" said Sarah. "How do you deal with this chaotic state of affairs? I think I'd have a tantrum and roll around on the floor, myself."

"Well, pumpkin," I said, "the first thing a dispassionate scientist must do in a case like this is to admit that the data are very inconsistent—that's why the papers I write on this subject have titles like "Erotica, Pornography, and Behavior: More Questions than Answers." But you very quickly learn that any public discussion of inconsistent findings on the prevalence and effects of pornography will be translated by flying squads of true believers into the slanderous assumption that you think that pornography is just swell, and that you dismiss the broader social and sexual victimization of women in our culture, which I most certainly do not.

And if you insist on thinking independently, acknowledging and conceptualizing and studying these findings in all of their inconsistent glory, with the goal, heaven forbid, of finding out what is really going on with pornography and behavior, you're sure to come to the attention of the Office for the Prosecution of the Inquisition, and then, my dear children, the data will hit the fan, and you will never, ever be the same again."

"Where did it all start, Dad?" asked Ben. "When did you first begin to mess up?"

"Where did it all start?" I sighed. "Well, I suppose I'd have to trace it all back to the accident of my coming of age in the 1960s, when many of us learned—if only in self-defense—about the moral and practical necessity of scrutinizing the accepted wisdom of the day, about the need to think independently, and to find and to defend the truth as we saw it. And some of us acted on these free-thinking tendencies, and eventually came to the conclusion that it was not necessarily patriotic to Support Our Boys in Vietnam, and that it was not necessarily democratic to censor disliked opinion at the end of a national guardsman's club, and that it was not necessarily moral, nor even much fun, to adhere too closely to the conventional sexual behavior and pharmaceutical use norms of our time. And of course this kind of thinking brought us into terrible conflict with true believers and hatemongers and bigots. They tried to suppress us with bargain-basement justice (see, for example, the conspiracy trial of the Chicago Seven), they were willing to lie to prove their point (see, for example, much of the Vietnam War), they took no prisoners (see, for example, copies of my correspondence with my draft board), and they even tried to drive us from the country (see, for example, my 1960s travel itinerary, and my checkered history of countries of residence)."

Ben gave an exaggerated groan, and said in a stage whisper to Danny and Sarah, "Here comes a speech, guys. We'll *never* get to dessert." The three of them started humming "This Land is Your Land" softly in the background, but I pressed on gamely, happy at least to provide an opportunity for some solidarity among my children and secretly pleased at their taste in music.

"In the fullness of time, kids, some of us who came of age in the 1960s became social scientists, and we carried on with the conviction that there is a truth to find, and that it might best be arrived at by dispassionate analysis and independent thinking, and that it might not conform to the current view of things. And son of a gun, kids, we discovered that this kind of thinking still brings us into conflict with true believers and hatemongers and bigots. They still try to suppress us or exile us, they still take no prisoners, and they still support freedom of expression, for everyone who believes exactly as they do."

"Picture this, kids. Mom and I leave the United States at the end of the 1960s, after they've shot John Kennedy, Bobby Kennedy, Martin Luther King, and a significant number of freedom riders and Kent State undergraduates. Expatriated with that mixture of adventure and regret that has never left us, we settle and live and work and study in Israel, hunkering down during the 1973 Yom Kippur War there. We eventually arrive in West Lafayette, Indiana, of all places, to do graduate work at Purdue. It's the fall of 1974, the trees are changing color, we're amidst the amber waves of grain, kids, and in a country at peace. We set to work improving our minds, and I discover that Donn Byrne—the scientist with whom I've come to work—has shifted his focus from research on interpersonal attraction to research on sexual behavior. This appeals immediately to my sense of rebellion and strikes me as an outstanding opportunity to turn a lifelong avocation into a respectable profession. Attracted by Donn's brilliance and camaraderie and warming to our subject, I jump in with all appendages tumescent and before I know it I am analyzing a study on male and female arousal responses to sexually explicit (but not pornographic) stimuli.

"Now, kids, *everything* written on the subject of male and female arousal responses to erotica at that time stated that men are compulsively aroused by even the smallest hint of skin, whereas women are entirely uninterested in matters so tawdry. While searching the literature on this issue, I came across Dr. Alex Comfort's pronouncement that 'male sexual response . . . is triggered easily by things, like putting a quarter into a vending machine,' whereas women's most certainly is not. And I read a definitive statement in a sexuality text of the time to the effect that 'about one in three women can be as aroused as the average man' by sexually explicit stimuli. This statement sounded disconcertingly like pre–Civil War notions about how barely one in a hundred slaves was capable of learning to read, and aroused my suspicion immediately.

"So even though everyone who was anyone knew that men were aroused by erotic stimuli and that women were not, we ran an empirical study on the subject because there simply was no credible evidence for this widely accepted view of things. We wanted to examine whether men and women did in fact differ in their arousal responses to erotica, and if so, we wanted to determine if—in accord with stereotypes—men would be most aroused by purely lusty depictions of anonymous sex, whereas women would be most aroused by romantic portrayals of sexual affection.

"So we had groups of unmarried men and women come to a classroom on campus, and we told them that they were going to watch an erotic movie that had just been imported from Scandinavia. And we explained that since the film hadn't yet been dubbed into English, we were going to give them a plot summary sheet to help them understand what they were about to see. Unbeknownst to the men and women in the room, though, some got a plot summary stating that the movie they were about to see was a romantic depiction of a young man and his wife who were very much in love and eager to express their affection for one another, whereas others sitting in the same room and seeing the same movie received a plot summary indicating that the film they were about to see depicted a sexual transaction between a prostitute and a client. Everyone then saw the film, which depicted sexual intercourse between a man and a woman, and completed questionnaire items concerning the degree to which they felt sexually aroused, the extent to which they had erections, vaginal lubrication, and the like."

"What happened then, Daddy?" asked Sarah, with an interest in gender and sexuality that belied her scant six years.

"When we analyzed our data, pumpkin, we found that men and women showed virtually identical arousal responses to erotica, and we found that men's and women's arousal was *not* differentially influenced by the romantic or sexual theme of the movie. So like good little scientists everywhere, we wrote up our findings, and submitted them to a top journal. Donn Byrne believed so strongly in our chance of having these findings accepted for publication that he bet me $10 the paper would be rejected, and took the opportunity to predict that if I persisted in this research line I would end up working at a small southern university where I could combine agricultural stoop labor with undergraduate teaching.

"Donn nearly got to collect on his bet. We received reviews from the editor, who admitted that though he could find nothing wrong with our methodology, he was hard pressed to believe our findings, and just to be sure, he had checked the matter out with his wife, and she concurred with his judgment. So with regret, he would have to let another, lesser journal have the privilege of publishing our paper."

"That was it, Dad?" asked Danny. "You let them crush you like a useless yellow insect?"

"Now, kids, you know better than that!" I said, mugging my best Abe Lincoln look. "When a dispassionate sexual scientist gets mad, what should he do?"

"Tell a grown-up?" suggested Sarah.

"Play a really senseless and repulsive practical joke to retaliate against his tormentor?" put in Ben and Danny together.

"Only as a last resort, kids, you know that," I said, hoping that they did.

"A dispassionate sexual scientist's first course of action is to collect more data. And that's what we did. We had married (as opposed to unmarried) men and women take part in an additional study, in which they watched movies depicting sexual intercourse or petting to orgasm—you remember petting to orgasm, right Randi?—and we told participants that the movies' plots involved either romance, or casual sex between people who had just met, or sex between a prostitute and client. And do you know what we found, kids?"

"Kleenex on the floor when the lights went back on?" suggested Ben, Danny, and Sarah in unison.

"Enough irreverence, you little scamps," I said, "this is *science*. What we actually found in the study, kids, was that men and women again reported nearly identical levels of sexual arousal in response to each movie. The only finding of any real novelty, in fact, was the finding that married men and women alike seemed to be most aroused in response to the movie that depicted casual sex between two good-looking people who had only recently become acquainted and who would probably not see one another again." I watched carefully to see how my wife would react to this news but she betrayed nothing of her feelings beyond a wistful sigh and a half-concealed smirk.

"We quickly submitted a revised manuscript with these additional findings, and kids, I'm happy to report that at least this once, justice triumphed. In strict keeping with the tenets of empirical science—an act which has become notably rarer over the years—the editor of the journal respected the data we had collected and published the study as the lead article. There have since been literally dozens of studies that have shown male-female equality in arousal responses to erotica, and interestingly enough, this finding has been annoying to both the political right and the political left, at different points in time. Back in the 1970s when the study was published, the political right detested our findings for polluting the image of the chaste and sexually uninterested American female, whereas in those days the political left adored the results because they smacked of female equality, assertiveness, and bra burning. Twenty years later, we still get shots from the political right for popularizing the notion of the sexually responsive female—which in the right wing's view has led directly to the problem of teenage pregnancy, the breakdown of the family, the epidemic of AIDS, and the heartbreak of psoriasis—whereas those on the political left now also hate these data, because the idea that women may be sexually aroused in the same repulsive fashion and by the same repulsive images as men is absolute anathema to them."

"Let me guess, Dad," said Danny, "These negative reactions caused you to immediately rethink your research interest in human sexuality and to shift to thanatology?"

"Not exactly, son. In fact, before you could say Alfred Kinsey, I was at work on another study of reactions to sexually explicit material. The purpose of this study was to find out whether watching sexually explicit material caused people to increase their own sexual activity, and if so, what kind of people were most likely to respond to sexually explicit stimuli with increased sexual behavior.

"To explore this question, we had male and female undergraduates come to the lab and watch a sexually explicit movie like those we'd used in our previous study. After viewing the film, participants recorded their evaluations of it, in terms of how pornographic, shocking, and explicit it had seemed to them to be. Then, two days later, they returned to the lab and handed in an anonymous questionnaire assessing their sexual behavior during the time since they'd seen the erotic film.

"When we analyzed our data, we came up with an entirely unexpected pattern of results. As it turned out, kids, those men and women who rated the sexually explicit film most negatively—as being pornographic, shocking, and more explicit than expected—were the most behaviorally responsive to the erotic film and had increased their sexual activity significantly during the days since viewing the movie.

"Kids, you just can't imagine how thrilled the antipornography right was when we published findings to the effect that those most opposed to pornography typically go home and masturbate (if they're alone) or fornicate (if they have a partner) with increased frequency after contact with such hateful material.

"Why, kids, I can still remember the satisfaction and peace of mind it gave me to open my mail in those days. Much of it arrived with no return address and bearing curious contents, such as the letter that contained a page torn from the Bible with the words "I am ashamed to be a member of the same human race as you! Love, Uncle Fred" scrawled across the top. Another, arriving in a plain brown envelope, contained a copy of the latest issue of *Screw* magazine. Surprised to receive this—I thought my subscription had run out months earlier—I opened it up and found an article entitled "University Researcher Shows Fuck Films To Undergraduates," opposite a centerfold picture of a naked individual smoking a cigar out of an entirely improbable orifice. I figured that with such exposure, we were done for, but it turned out that no one who read about our research in *Screw* magazine was prepared to admit it in public, so we escaped with our lives and careers intact, at least from that one."

"What then, Dad?" asked Ben. "More smut research?"

"As it turns out, no, mister smart guy," I said, putting Ben firmly in his teenage place. "My major interest has always been the study of psychological factors that influence reproductive health behaviors, such as contraceptive behavior and STD/HIV preventive behavior, and as you know, my major work during the past decade has been in the development and evaluation of theoretically based AIDS prevention interventions. Being so identified with the pornography research that I've done over the years has always been a mystery to me. I've been a reluctant conscript who feels forced to add a small voice of dissent when science in this area has been corrupted, not one who sees it as his life's work, which lies elsewhere.

"So over the past decade, kids, I've conducted research concerning psychological factors that influence our practice of reproductive health behaviors. Oh, I admit, I've made the odd excursion into politically incorrect research, but by and large I managed to stay out of pornography research for nearly an entire decade."

"Dad," said Danny, "I don't mean to pry, but exactly what sort of 'excursions' into politically incorrect research did you undertake during your hiatus from pornography?"

"Well, Danny," I said, warming to the question, "by this point, I'd begun to realize that within psychological science, as in other fields, there is a simple and sovereign solution for nearly every complex problem, and it is almost always wrong. This is the assumption that motivated my earlier pornography research, and it served as the basis for several journeys into politically incorrect territory in the 1980s as well.

"During this time, for example, it was widely accepted that male psychologists show 'gender bias' in their professional dealings with female clients, acting on hidebound stereotypes to overdiagnose women as depressed, shunt women into traditionally female occupations, and the like. Now, kids, this sounded like an entirely reasonable hypothesis concerning psychologists' contribution to the repression of women, but I wondered why psychological scientists—who should know better—had failed to support their assumptions about the ubiquity of gender bias with convincing research evidence. So, as you might imagine, your twisted father joined forces with a like-minded friend and colleague, Azy Barak, and took the completely unjustified step of actually reading and reviewing the scientific literature on gender bias among psychologists. Today, kids," I said archly, "this kind of misogynist activity would be called *backlash* and all of us would have to hang our heads in public shame.

"At all events, kids, a thorough review of the scientific literature on gender bias in therapy and counseling revealed exceedingly little evidence for the existence of this phenomenon, and we concluded that there was a remarkable tendency in the literature on this subject to skip over embarrassing and unsupportive empirical data and to move right on to politically correct pronouncements about the widespread presence of this malignant tendency. Our review of the scientific literature was a sober one that ended with a call for stronger and more honestly interpreted work in this area, and it was published in *Professional Psychology*, the

American Psychological Association's flagship practice journal. Not content to leave well enough alone, Azy Barak and I published a companion piece, an empirical study that looked at the degree to which male versus female career counseling psychologists might influence the career choices discussed and the career paths begun by actual male and female clients, during career counseling, and at a six-month follow-up. This ambitious real-world search for gender bias in psychologists showed that there was absolutely *no* influence of the career counselor's sex on his or her client's career choices. Male counselors' female clients ended up discussing and taking steps to enter careers that were no different than female counselors' female clients. This paper was also published in a major journal of the American Psychological Association, the *Journal of Counseling Psychology.*"

"What happened then, Daddy?" asked Sarah. "Did your work finally get some respect, despite your abrasive and self-aggrandizing manner and chronic need to call attention to yourself?"

"What happened next was most instructive, you little scamp. We were taken on an extended tour of a little-known place called the gulag for politically incorrect findings, which is located in a special corner of hell reserved for people like me. When all else fails, pumpkin, and you are confronted with empirical data that disconfirms your fondest political dreams, you simply ignore the data and act as if it is not there and relegate it to intellectual exile. Despite the fact that these two papers on gender bias comment on a topic that could not be politically hotter, and despite the fact that they were published in prominent professional journals, almost no one ever cites them or refers to them. In fact, kids," I said with just the tiniest trace of anger in my voice, "the study in which we empirically disconfirmed the existence of therapist gender bias in real-world field research has only been referred to in the professional literature *four* times in its entire history, and despite the hotness of the topic and the prominence of the journals, it has only been cited *once* in the past five years in any of the many discussions of this important topic. There are papers, kids, on the psychological characteristics of people who make their living reading chicken entrails that get cited and referred to more. We wrote then, kids, that failure to improve the quality of scientific research in this area will ". . . make unbelievers of those who hope that social science may be a useful basis for needed social change," and as far as I know, the number of atheist researchers has grown exponentially during the past couple of years."

"But honey," Randi purred as the kids began to clear the table and rinse the dishes, "when did things *really* get tense? When would you say your life *really* became a living hell?"

"So nice of you to put it that way, dear.

"I guess I'd say that things really began to turn rancid sometime in the 1980s, when public, professional, and legislative opinion began to solidify around the idea that the social science case had finally been closed, and that we could comfortably and definitively conclude that the scientific evidence demonstrated that exposure to pornography does clearly cause antiwoman attitudes and antiwoman acts. Set against the scientific reality of the matter—what with evidence on the prevalence and effects of pornography so inconsistent—I found it premature to accept the proposition that exposure to pornography is a robust cause of aggression against women. So I returned to the literature in this area and began to review and analyze it and I began to conduct further research on the basis of what I found.

"In what may have been one of the most politically incorrect studies of all time, I revisited the classic research on the relationship of pornography and aggression. As you may know, in such studies, a man is brought into the lab, he's either treated equitably by a woman confederate or he is insulted and receives painful electrical shocks from her, and he is then shown a very few minutes of either neutral fare, such as a talk show, or violent pornography. During a final phase of the study, the man is told to send electrical shocks to the woman every time she makes a set of predetermined errors when performing an experimental task. Results of these studies consistently show that men who have been provoked and who have seen violent pornography send stronger electrical shocks to the woman confederate than do men who have been provoked and who have seen nonpornographic material, presumably demonstrating a clear association of exposure to pornography and antiwoman aggression."

"What's wrong with that, Daddy?" said Danny, his voice a bit nasal, as he still had a bread stick in his nose.

"I'll tell you what's wrong with that, mister smarty pants," said Sarah. "The man in this experiment is *told* by the experimenter to send electrical shock to the woman, and he does not have any nonaggressive response option to exercise. Although it is true that under these exceedingly constrained circumstances, men who have seen pornography send the strongest electrical shocks to the woman who has provoked them, I wonder what would happen if the men involved had the option of responding nonaggressively, say, by simply talking with her, or by simply walking away?"

"I couldn't have said it better myself, Sarah," I said. "That darn Montessori school we sent you to did you a world of good! And that kind of logic, sweetheart, actually became the basis for the least popular study I have ever carried out. In an effort to show that the 'classic' evidence for a pornography-aggression link might actually be due to the fact that the experimental situation forced men to aggress and that men who had seen pornography might not aggress at all if they had any choice in the matter, we ran the critical condition of the classic study once again, with one important change. Men volunteered to come to our lab, they were angered and aggressed against by a woman confederate, and they were shown violent pornography, just as in the classic research approach. Then, we gave men the chance to aggress against the woman confederate for making errors in an experimental task, by sending her electrical shocks, but we also gave the men the choice of simply talking with the woman confederate over an intercom, or of simply moving on to the experimental debriefing and terminating their participation in the study at that point. Not surprisingly, at least to me, essentially all of the men—who'd been angered and provoked and who had seen violent pornography—chose *nonaggressive* responses and either spoke with the female confederate over the intercom or simply left the study, when we gave them a choice in the matter. We were unable to find a pornography-aggression link when using procedures in which men had a choice about whether or not to aggress against a woman. In retrospect, the fact that scientists so readily accepted the proposition that five minutes of exposure to pornography could turn a college freshman into something like a rapist reflects an embarrassing belief in a grossly unsophisticated kind of monkey see–monkey do psychology. I published this study with a graduate student, Guy Grenier, who'd worked on it with me, after asking him to consider carefully whether he wanted his name associated with the study, in view of the potential professional fallout that could result. With a measure of courage, he agreed, and with a measure of courage, Elizabeth Allgeier, editor of the *Journal of Sex Research,* decided to publish it."

"Wow, Dad," said Ben, "how misguided and evil can you get? After conducting empirical research with the fundamental purpose of demonstrating that the emperor has no clothes, what twisted and heretical sphere of activity was left open to you, so that you could continue your career in a blaze of glory?"

"Well, I try my best, kids. For example, together with Azy Barak, I've taken part in a total of three studies on the effects of computer-based sexually explicit materials on attitudes and behavior toward women, and once again, we've found absolutely no effects of exposure to computer-mediated sexual stimuli on antiwoman attitudes and antiwoman acts. I've supervised a doctoral dissertation by Anthony Bogaert, which used the simple and elegant approach of permitting men to choose whether or not they want to see sexually explicit materials, and if so, what sort of materials. After men had completed their participation in an experiment, Bogaert asked them to indicate if they wanted to sign up for a later experimental session in which they could see one of a large number of types of sexually explicit videos. Most men—51 percent to be exact—chose *not* to sign up to see *any* sexually explicit videos, either because they didn't have the time or because they had completed their experimental participation for the year. Among those who did chose to see a sexually explicit video, the *least* common choices were to see sexually violent material (4 percent) or child pornography (3 percent). I've also written an invited introduction to a special issue of a major sexuality journal that was devoted to the subject of sexual coercion in dating relationships. The introduction I wrote was sufficiently searching in its discussion of the research in this area that the special issue's editors rescinded the invitation and declined to publish the introduction I'd been invited to write. In addition, together with a panel of experts and interested parties, I've coedited national guidelines for sexual health education, which were commissioned and endorsed by the Canadian government. This resulted in a variety of interesting reactions, including the publication of a "William A. Fisher Fact Sheet" concerning my infamous deeds and suspect history, which was widely circulated and which a number of friends of ours, and even some of your playmates, kids, were kind enough to pass on to me. Most recently, I've published a critique of the ethics of the practice of administering testosterone replacement therapy to HIV-positive men to boost their sex drive and by so doing to improve their quality of life. Given the fact that these men carry a sexually borne lethal pathogen, this seemed like an idea whose time, ethically speaking, had not yet come.

"On and on I go, kids, with the general theme of my work being that it is permissible, and even desirable, to take an independent look at things. If it appears that a simple, sovereign, and politically expedient explanation for a complex phenomenon is being invoked, or if it appears just plain glib, or if it rings one's ethical bullshit detector, why, heck, there may be something to it after all, and a closer, independent look might just prove worthwhile. As you know, kids, your mother has sewn a needlepoint outlining some of my more iconoclastic work, and since it's hanging in the den, I would direct your attention to it, after you finish dessert."

"Daddy, before we go upstairs to read classic children's literature, brush our teeth, and say our prayers to the God of our choice, could you please tell us the story about 'Black Friday'?" said Danny, knowing that I was a sucker for this tale, and that it would effectively delay bedtime by at least a few minutes.

"Well kids, not long ago, I was asked to give a talk to the University Women's Caucus on the subject of pornography and violence against women. Now I knew that my take on scientific research in this area would win me no friends, but I felt we would all be in basic agreement about the existence of tragic and unacceptable levels of violence against women in society, and that I would be able to frame the issue of whether pornography was a major cause of such violence in the context of careful efforts to seek out and to eliminate important causes of violence against women in society, and in the context of ceasing to bark up what might be the wrong tree. Moreover, I reasoned, I was discussing this issue with a

Table 3.1 Fear and Loathing on the Research Trail

Reasons for Loathing	Locus of Loathing	Magnitude of Loathing (1:mild censure, 7:attempted lynching)
Publication of a series of studies which failed to detect male–female differences in arousal responses to sexually explicit movies.	Political right Political left	3
Publication of results which indicate that those who are most critical of pornography are also most likely to increase their sexual behavior after viewing such material.	Political right	5
Publication of government-endorsed national guidelines for sexual health promotion education.	Political right	7
Publication of review article concerning inconsistent evidence regarding prevalence and effects of pornography, and of a series of empirical studies that failed to find such effects.	Political left	7

community of scholars and students who were eager to think through this topic with me and to work together to comprehend what it all might mean. So I went and I spoke about the problems of pornography prevalence research, about the problems of pornography effects research, about the fact that from a scientific perspective the case was not yet closed, and that in fact, based on available evidence, pornography could not yet be said to play a major role in provoking the entirely unacceptable levels of sexual violence that we all agree characterize our society.

"There was silence for a moment. Then one of the members of the all-female audience shouted 'sexist pig.' Then ten other women shouted 'sexist pig.' Then much of the audience—including female professors with whom I had worked for years, and a number of former students—stood on their feet shouting 'sexist pig' at me, while the others sat there silently.

"The president of the women's caucus, who was supposed to moderate my talk, did nothing, and I realized that it would be up to me to try to return this discussion to a substantive level. I asked for specific questions and welcomed discussion and dissent, but the chant of 'sexist pig' continued, and got even louder, and if memory serves, someone threw a paper cup at me as well.

"Now at this moment, kids, I was thinking about a story that is told about how the great and dignified African American actor and singer Paul Robeson faced the House Un-American Activities Committee during the McCarthy-era 1950s, looked his accusers straight in the eye, and bellowed, '*You* are the un-Americans!' I thought that under the circumstances, I could do no less than honor Robeson's memory, so gathering up my notes, and sizing up the route to the nearest exit, I turned to the professors and students I'd worked with as colleague and teacher for years, and I looked them in the eye, and I said, '*You* are the sexist pigs.' And I got the hell out of the room.

"Now as it turned out, kids, that wasn't the worst of it. The following week, I had planned to give the same lecture on pornography research to my Human Sexuality course. As you know, this course was the largest and most popular class on campus, and I've won nearly every university teaching award that is offered in this country in connection with teaching it. Refusing to be silenced by my recent experience with the women's caucus, I talked with my class about the shortcomings in pornography research that, for my money, leave many issues in this area still quite open. As always, my students responded with a fair amount of interest and respect, a number of them asked critical questions, and the class discussed the issue from several points of view. After class was over, however, a single student approached to complain that I had been sending the message that pornography was not a bad thing. I took the opportunity to point out that from a scientific perspective, we have to have systematic evidence that pornography has antisocial effects before we can claim that this is the case, and that my conclusion was that the jury is still out in this area. I also reminded her that the scientific discussion had focused only on identifying potential causes of what we all agree is an unacceptable level of violence against women in our society and that we were all working toward the same end. Finally, I reminded her that my last transparency was a call—if for philosophical as opposed to empirical reasons—for nonviolent and equalitarian images of people, instead of the sexual and nonsexual denigration of women often seen across all of the media. Obviously unconvinced, and probably saddened that there are now laws against publicly burning nonbelievers, she did what she probably saw as the next best thing. She went directly to our campus newspaper, asked that 'her name be withheld for fear of academic punishment,' and exposed me for the politically incorrect beast that I was. Sure enough, I became the headline story in the next edition of the paper."

"What did you do then, Dad?" asked Danny, with the genuine concern of an 11-year-old who perceives that the source of his weekly allowance may be under threat.

"Well, Danny," I said, "you've got to remember that I come from the 1960s, and that in those days, we preferred not to get mad but to get even, if possible with the greatest sense of theater and in the most twisted and irreverent manner possible. To make a long story short, scout, a number of pretty strange things began to happen, not all of which I was responsible for."

"Like about what happened at the campus newspaper office? Like what happened with the Chinese food?" the kids all asked at once.

"Now, kids, you know I had nothing to do with either of these outrages.

"It *is* true that someone sent a memo to the Panhellenic Association, announcing the First Annual Interfraternity Stairwell Vomiting Competition, to be held on Homecoming Weekend. And it is also true that judging took place in relation to color and spread, and that the target was placed on the landing in front of the campus newspaper's office door. But other than that, kids, I have no further knowledge of this tasteless and sordid affair."

"And they say you can't win a battle with a newspaper!" said Sarah, with real admiration.

"What about the Chinese food, Dad? Weren't you involved with that one?" asked Ben.

"Someone did have $115 worth of Chinese food delivered to the Women's Center's Bulimia Support Group meeting, Ben, but once again, I really know nothing about it."

"What about what you did to that woman and her poor sick husband, honey?" asked Randi. "Surely you won't try to weasel out of *that* one."

"You've got me dead to rights in this one case, dear," I said, with a mildly psychotic gleam of pleasure in my eye. "Now, honey, you could have knocked me over with a feather when one of the women who had shouted that I was a sexist pig called up and asked for advice about her husband's medical condition. She was a long-time colleague of mine, and began with what passed for an apology, noting that I just had to understand the collective rage and chronic frustration of the well-dressed and advantaged professional women who were present. She went on to ask me—because I work in the medical school as well as the psychology department and she thought that I might know about such things—about her husband's upcoming cystoscopy procedure. What would it involve? I responded with great sympathy, explaining that a thin fiber-optic shaft would be introduced into her husband's urethra and threaded upward to examine the far reaches of his urinary system. She asked whether it would hurt him, and—I was only trying to be reassuring, honest—I explained that unless her husband had an exceptionally small penis—

Sex Psych prof taking heat
Instructor says porn has no effect on viewers

By Kleri Venizelos
The Gazette

The debate over academic freedom has resurfaced in Western's psychology department—but this time the study in question has nothing to do with race.

A third-year English major—who asked that her name be withheld for fear of academic punishment—says she is upset about comments human sexuality professor William Fisher made last Wednesday in his Psychology 153 class.

The student said yesterday that Fisher told the 350-student class pornography does not have a harmful effect on its viewers.

She said Fisher taught "that aggressive pornography is not a negative thing and that it does not really cause men to act violently against women."

The student said Fisher presented to the class his own study, in which 120 men showed little tendency toward violence after being exposed to aggressive pornography.

"I don't believe his data personally and I'm concerned he is leaving these students with the notion that pornography isn't harmful to women," she said.

"Even our textbook says, 'Pornography has harmful effect on men's attitudes towards women, at least according to laboratory experiments,' but he told me what he teaches in the class is more important than the text."

But Fisher said his research is not the first

to come up with similar results. In fact, he added, his data was based on the 1985 findings of the Fraser Commission, the Royal Commission on Pornography and Prostitution.

The commission found there was no proven link between pornography and violence directed toward women.

Fisher said that in spite of his findings he made a plea at the end of his lecture for the "non-violent, equalitarian images of human beings.

"The student may just be looking for a misogynist beast, which I'm not," he said.

Psychology chair William Roberts said his professors are allowed to present their research in classroom lectures.

"Professors have a right to present their interpretations of the data. A student is welcome to challenge this by researching the data for themselves.

"I don't think (the research reflects) Fisher's personal views at all. I think the student may wish the scientific evidence would support her point of view."

But the student said the professor's presentation of the facts was one-sided.

"He kept saying there were flaws in the laboratory data against pornography but never laboratory flaws in data which stated the opposite.

"I did talk to him (after class) but he's obviously very adamant about his decision."

Source: The Gazette, University of Western Ontario, April 17, 1993. Reprinted by Permission.

---

the kind of humiliating inadequacy that you generally see only in medical textbooks—the chances are that he wouldn't even be aware that the cystoscopy was taking place, and that he'd have to ask the doctor to tell him when the procedure was over. I don't know if this helped at all, because I haven't heard from her in a while."

"Dad," said Sarah. "What about the rumor that you faked your death and left the country right after the newspaper article came out. All my friends still talk about that one!"

"That was our last sabbatical, Sarah. You're just too young to remember."

I finished reading the boys their bedtime story, a chapter-by-chapter recitation of *Huckleberry Finn* selected so that Ben and Danny would learn about the journey down the river, about the moral anxiety of bucking convention and failing to turn in a runaway slave, and about the history of America, which in their earshot I always refer to as the "Old Country." Now it was time to sing Sarah a bedtime song, which I have done for all of our children every night when they are young. So I entered Sarah's room, and stood by her upper bunk, and I decided to sing a favorite hymn.

My life flows on in endless song,

Above earth's lamentations,

I hear the real though far-off hymn,

That hails a new creation.

Through all the tumult and the strife,

I hear that music ringing,

It sounds an echo in my soul,

How can I keep from singing?

When tyrants tremble sick with fear,

And hear their death knells ringing,

When friends rejoice both far and near,

How can I keep from singing?

And just before she went to sleep, I sang her our favorite song, "This Land Is Your Land," to remind her that it is. But tonight, and just tonight, I ended the song with two verses that I'd never sung her before.

As I went walking, I saw a sign there,

And on the sign, it said "No Trespassing,"

But on the other side, it didn't say nothing,

That side was made for you and me.

Nobody living can ever stop me,

As I go walking that freedom highway,

Nobody living ever can make me turn back,

This land was made for you and me.©

And I kissed her goodnight, and I hoped for the best.

Danny, Bill, Sarah, Randi, and Ben Fisher

Suggested Readings

Barak, A., & Fisher, W. A. (1989). Counselor and therapist gender bias? More questions than answers. *Professional Psychology, 20,* 377–383.

Barak, A., & Fisher, W. A. (in press). Effects of interactive computer erotica on men's attitudes and behavior toward women: An experimental study. *Computers and Human Behavior.*

Barak, A., Golan, E., & Fisher, W. A. (1988). Effects of counselor gender and gender-role orientation on client career choice traditionality. *Journal of Counseling Psychology, 35,* 287–293.

Barrett, M., Fisher, W. A., & McKay, A. (Eds.). (1994). *Canadian guidelines for sexual health education.* Ottawa: Health Canada.

Fisher, J.D., & Fisher, W. A. (1992). Changing AIDS risk behavior. *Psychological Bulletin, 111,* 455–474.

Fisher, W. A. (1997). Do no harm: On the ethics of testosterone replacement therapy for HIV positive persons. *The Journal of Sex Research, 34,* 35–36.

Fisher, W. A., & Barak, A. (1989). Sex education as a corrective: Immunizing against possible effects of pornography. In D. Zillmann & J. Bryant (Eds.), *Pornography: Recent research, interpretations, and policy considerations.* Hillsdale, NJ: Erlbaum.

Fisher, W. A., & Barak, A. (1991). Pornography, erotica, and behavior: More questions than answers. *International Journal of Law and Psychiatry, 14,* 65–83.

Fisher, W. A., & Byrne, D. (1978). Sex differences in response to erotica? Love versus lust. *Journal of Personality and Social Psychology, 36,* 117–125.

Fisher, W. A., & Byrne, D. (1978). Individual differences in affective, evaluative, and behavioral responses to an erotic film. *Journal of Applied Social Psychology, 8,* 355–365.

Fisher, W. A., & Grenier, G. (1994). Violent pornography, antiwoman thoughts, and antiwoman acts: In search of reliable effects. *The Journal of Sex Research, 31,* 23–38.

Twain, M. (1885). *The Adventures of Huckleberry Finn.* New York: Webster.

Chapter **4**

Doing Sex Research on Adolescents

J. Richard Udry

J. Richard Udry (Ph.D., University of Southern California)
is Kenan Professor of Maternal and Child Health and Kenan Professor of Sociology.
From 1977 to 1992 he was the Director of the Carolina Population Center at the University of North Carolina at Chapel Hill. He holds a Merit Award from the National Institute of Child Health and Human Development, and is a recent past president of the Population Association of America. He has more than 200 publications in the areas of demography and sexual behavior. He is the principal investigator for the National Longitudinal Study of Adolescent Health. His principal theoretical interest is the integration of biological and sociological models of behavior.

Sex research on adolescents has been stimulated by policy concerns about adolescent pregnancy, sexually transmitted diseases, and more recently the risk of AIDS. I have been doing research on adolescent sexual behavior for 20 years, funded primarily by the National Institute for Child Health and Human Development. Over the years I have stopped thinking of adolescent sex primarily as a policy problem and have gradually begun to study it as a way of understanding the sexual behavior of humans in general.

How I Got into Sex Research

People often wonder why and how a researcher decides to do sex research. Many people imagine that the explanation lies in the sexual biography of the researcher. But no one has done a comparison of the sexual biographies of sex researchers with those who do research on nonsexual topics.

I grew up in Covington, Kentucky, with two younger sisters in a professional family during the Great Depression. We were so poor we couldn't pay the rent and had to keep moving from house to house to keep ahead of creditors (an uncle was in the moving business). My mother barred the door with her body to keep the electric company from turning off service for nonpayment. But we had a live-in maid who was so desperately poor she worked for us for nothing.

At graduation from high school I was luckily diverted from my misguided plan to become a professional symphonic musician. After finishing my baccalaureate in sociology at Northwestern University, I married and was drafted for a two-year stint in the Marine Corps during the Korean war. Under the GI Bill I got a master's degree and a teaching certificate at Long Beach State. I taught for six years (math, speech and drama, English, history, civics) in junior and senior high school in Anaheim, California, most of the time simultaneously with part-time graduate work at the University of Southern California. I liked teaching adolescents, but after six years it was getting too easy. I did my dissertation on adolescent friendship groups. Upon receiving my Ph.D. I did a few years of purgatory at a southern California junior college and an obscure cow college. Then I went to heaven and joined the faculty of the University of North Carolina at Chapel Hill, with a joint appointment in the Department of Maternal and Child Health and the Department of Sociology. I have been there ever since. I have two grown (and surprisingly complex) daughters. My wisest decision in life was marrying the woman I married. My most satisfying avocation in recent years is leading Sierra Club outings into the backcountry of North Carolina and Virginia.

I got into sex research the first time in the mid-1960s through a fortuitous research finding. I was working on a research design to explore prenatal environmental factors in pregnancy outcome. I needed an unbiased sample of early pregnancies. Immunological pregnancy tests were only just coming onto the market, replacing the "rabbit test." We thought we could get a sample of women in early pregnancy by screening a large population with pregnancy tests.

Skeptics told us the plan was impractical, that women wouldn't give us the necessary urine samples, or that they would substitute samples from their children or their dogs. (I have often wondered how our advisers thought women could get dogs to urinate in a cup on command.)

But some advisers told us that the pregnancy test would not only show positive for the pregnancy hormone (human chorionic gonadotropin) but also for luteinizing hormone, which precipitates ovulation and was then thought by some to be stimulated by coitus, at least in other animals. This provoked a pilot study of 50 women whom we studied for three months, collecting daily urine samples for hormone testing and daily reports of coitus. The pilot study showed that our advisers were wrong. But in the course of the study we made the first observation of an early pregnancy and its loss, unknown to the woman, solely by laboratory pregnancy tests. My colleague Naomi Morris said to me, "I wonder whether there is a pattern of coitus within the menstrual cycle." There was. We found there was a peak frequency of coitus at midcycle and a trough in the luteal (postovulatory) phase. Morris and I spent more than a decade confirming and explaining this finding. This began my career as a sex researcher. (We never got the grant that allowed us to do the study of prenatal factors in pregnancy outcome.)

Although I am a sociologist by training, this beginning also established a paradigm in my research of combining biological and social processes in my explanations. For of course, we had to figure out how the hormonal patterning of sex in the menstrual cycle was mediated by a social process.

The answer to that question is a long story. We found that primatologists were on the trail of a sexual pheromone from the female that encouraged successful advances from males. This pheromone caused a distribution of copulations by female monkeys that looked nearly identical to the one we obtained on humans. The pheromonal substance produced by monkeys was identical to substances produced by human females. We synthesized it, diluted it, bottled it, and performed an experiment on 50 human couples for 100 days. Each woman had a strip of capsules containing, in a random order, water, alcohol, a dime-store perfume, and the "pheromone." Each evening before retiring she opened the top capsule and spread the contents on her chest. Each day she and her husband mailed us a report of their sexual behavior the prior day. Results were disappointing in their ambiguity—no clear pheromone effect.

We also did an experiment, the details of which I will leave to the reader's imagination, in which we determined whether males and females could distinguish the sexes by smell alone. They couldn't.

In another study we experimentally manipulated the female hormone cycle by giving contraceptive pills to some women and placebo pills to others (all were practicing some method of nonhormonal contraception). We showed that if we experimentally altered the hormone cycle, we changed the distribution of coitus in the cycle. For example, the contraceptive pills that we used abolished the progesterone rise in the latter half of the cycle and also the lessening of coitus that accompanied it. This suggested that the woman's high progesterone level discouraged coitus. But did it do this by reducing her interest or by a message, pheromonal or otherwise, that reduced her partner's interest? We were able to demonstrate that the experimental manipulation, and therefore the cyclicity of the hormones, had more effect on the male partner's behavior than on the woman's. The end of this story is not yet written because both Morris and I have been diverted into other lines of research.

All of my subsequent sex research has been based on biosocial theories. A biosocial theory says that two people will respond differently to the same social environment if the two have different biology. It also says that many social patterns of behavior are underwritten by human biology.

How I Got into Adolescent Sex Research

Studying the beginnings of sexual behavior in adolescence is a natural place to combine biological and social explanations. Puberty is a biological development, and most people (with the exception of social scientists) agree that there is something biological about puberty that provokes sexual interest in the pubescent. In my first adolescent research, I reasoned as a good social psychologist. Adolescents learned from their society that the person with mature secondary sexual characteristics was more interested in sex, and also a more attractive sex partner. We didn't begin to explore a direct hormonal cause of adolescent sex interest until we were satisfied that pubertal development affected sexual behavior in ways that were unrelated to its value as a social signal.

Special Problems in Studying Adolescent Sexual Behavior

Most methodological problems in studying adolescent sex are not unique to adolescents. Certain problems are more difficult with adolescents than with adults, and certain problems are more difficult when the research topic is sexual behavior than when it is food consumption patterns.

The distinctive problems of adolescent sex research, compared to adult sex research, are created by three conditions: (1) for legal and ethical reasons, adolescents cannot participate in sex research without gatekeeper permission; (2) adolescent sexual histories are sporadic; and (3) adolescents lack experience and knowledge.

Gatekeepers Protect Adolescents from Sex Researchers

If you want to do sex research on free-ranging adult humans, the primary ethical considerations are "do no harm," informed consent, voluntary participation, and maintaining the privacy of participants. Especially if you are merely collecting information, few people believe that participating in sex research will damage individual adults. This is certainly not the case with children and adolescents. Adolescents are considered to be in a delicate formative stage. Adults do not want them prematurely exposed to either involvement in or information about sexual behavior. Such exposure is considered to be potentially psychologically traumatic, provocative of precocious sexual interest, or both. Because adolescents are not legally or socially considered mature enough to make informed decisions about voluntary research participation, a series of guardians has been set up to protect the well-being of the adolescents and to represent the interests of the guardians themselves. We will consider here the role of institutional review boards for the protection of human subjects (IRBs), parents, school administrators, and politicians.

Institutional Review Boards

Institutional Review Boards for the protection of human subjects are integral to the system of protection of research participants for all researchers in institutional settings since the early 1970s. IRB regulations, promulgated by the Office for the Protection from Research Risks at the National Institutes of Health (NIH), provide special protections for children and adolescents not extended to adults. Primary among these is that parents/guardians must give permission for adolescents to become research volunteers. IRBs usually consider adolescents to be more psychologically fragile than adults. Since my first NIH-funded project on adolescent sex research, IRBs have required me to retain a psychological counselor for adolescent survey respondents who we might have reason to believe have been emotionally disturbed by answering our questionnaires about sexual behavior. Our interviewers are alert to the possibility, and we routinely offer the name and phone number of a source of information and counseling at the end of interviews. In more than 20 years we have not discovered a respondent we thought was emotionally disturbed by our research protocols. Of course we do not know how many call hot-line numbers that we also offer. None has ever called our designated counselor.

IRBs are uncomfortable with the possibility that by asking questions about sex we may serve to educate respondents about behaviors of which they were still unaware. In response to IRB discomfort, we always work to screen questions about more intimate behavior by prior questions about less intimate acts. For example, if respondents indicate they have never kissed or held hands with a member of the other sex, we don't ask questions about more intimate behaviors. We are often required not to ask certain questions of anyone under age 15. When I first asked an IRB to allow us to ask questions about oral sex, IRB members hired two expert consultants to advise them, and finally decided that we could ask those who were at least 15 years old. Although oral-sex items were considered highly sensitive by the IRB, the behavior was commonly reported by our 15- to 17-year-old respondents. Half had experienced oral sex, and 69 percent of those who had had intercourse had both given and received oral sex.

IRB members have on rare occasions allowed their emotional hostility to sex research to lead them into unethical behaviors. During the review process for my research proposal, an IRB lawyer-member gave his wife our confidential question-naires that were under review. She gave them to a newspaper reporter. The re-porter wrote a scurrilous front-page article in the local paper that accused me of prurient interest in adolescent girls. (I had a teen daughter in the local schools at that time.) The publicity wrecked our survey plans and caused us to move the sur-vey to a different community. The dean removed the member from the IRB (a ter-rible punishment for him), but that didn't repair the damage to our research.

On balance, though, the IRBs have served sex researchers well. We benefit from their caution, their examination of our ethics, and their thoughtful concerns about adolescents. They also provide us legal protection.

Parents as Gatekeepers

Before we approach an adolescent, we exercise a cardinal rule of our practice: to obtain written parental permission for the adolescent to participate in our research if any sensitive questions are to be asked in the interviews. Our re-search shows that parents make poor estimates of the sexual behavior of their chil-dren and nearly always err on the low side. This causes them to underestimate the appropriateness and relevance of our sex questions for their adolescents. Conse-quently up to 10 percent of our potential adolescent respondents are eliminated by parental refusals. Nearly all of these refusals are courteous. But some aren't.

A few years ago an irate father pointed a pistol at my interviewer as he or-dered her to leave the house. Another interviewer drove up to a farm address look-ing for an adolescent and found herself looking down the barrel of a shotgun. The parent with the gun turned out to be a marijuana farmer, according to neighbors. We didn't get the interview. On another occasion, a politically prominent father, who refused permission for his child to participate in my project, wrote a letter of protest to the president of my university. This letter prompted university officials to direct me to close down my fieldwork while they checked to see that we were abiding by the rules and regulations of the IRB. (We were back at work in 24 hours.) I give my university high marks in both giving me free rein and in protect-ing my research when it needed protecting.

On another occasion a parent wrote a letter criticizing my project to my U.S. senator. This prompted a letter from the senator to the federal funding agency suggesting that they should close down the project. The letter released a flurry of activity on several bureaucratic levels. (The funding agency stood its ground.)

Parents sometimes try to make deals with interviewers. One father offered permission for his child to participate in my study if the interviewer would get him an autograph from a (then) famous Carolina basketball player. We got the inter-view without the autograph. But these incidents are rare, and 99 percent of parent encounters are pleasant and reasonable.

Parental refusal introduces a source of bias not encountered in adult surveys. On the other hand, the fact that only 10 percent of parents refuse to allow their adolescents to participate indicates that sex research on adolescents is not as sensitive to parents as one might have thought. Parents are sometimes surprisingly sensible people.

I am often told by parents that asking adolescents about their sexual behavior implies to the children that we expect them to be doing something, and therefore encourages their sexual activity. Parents are especially concerned that the teens will learn about new sexual behaviors they then want to try. There are certain conventional practices in asking sensitive survey questions that might justify this concern. I learned in graduate school that if you want people to admit to sensitive, illegal, or embarrassing behaviors, ask the question in a way that makes the behavior sound routine and socially acceptable, so it is easy to answer yes. Don't ask, "Since you married, have you ever had sex with someone other than your wife?" Instead, ask, "Since you married, how many other people have you had sex with?" Those doing research with adolescents should ponder carefully how to frame their questions to walk the narrow line of neutrality. Questions of the sort that say, "Many young people your age are having sexual intercourse these days with their friends. Are you?" are not neutral questions, and provoke reasonable parental doubts about sex research.

It is impossible to show that adolescents who are surveyed about their sexual behavior are (or aren't) subsequently more sexually active than those who are not surveyed. But we have shown that 13-year-old adolescent boys who were interviewed about their sexual behavior every week for two years reported no more increase in sexual activity than those who were interviewed only once at the beginning and once at the end of the same time period. Parental worries about interviews stimulating the sexual behavior of adolescents are probably unfounded.

School Administrators

School administrators have enough public relations problems without having to deal with sex researchers. Rarely does anything good happen to the principal who allows a sex researcher to collect questionnaire data in school. Yet the convenience and economy of collecting data in secondary schools makes them a magnet for research on adolescents. The Youth Risk Behavior Survey, containing sex questions, is administered in a nationwide sample of secondary schools each year by the Centers for Disease Control and Prevention. It is true that some schools decline to participate, and some whole states have opted out, but the survey has been possible. Principals, superintendents, and school board members quite often take political risks with low payoffs for themselves when they think useful information will be gathered. Superintendents are political officials. Five well-placed citizens can unseat a superintendent. One superintendent, accused of giving me a student directory to use in locating respondents for a home-based sex survey, resigned under school board pressure. But the accusation was only a pretext to nail him for more serious problems in the school.

Over the past several years, a procedure informally called "passive parental consent" has become the usual method for obtaining parental consent for surveys to be administered by researchers in the classroom. This has been recognized by IRBs and school districts as appropriate in low-risk situations. A letter is sent to a parent of each child to be surveyed, explaining the survey to be done in school. (To increase the likelihood the letters reach parents, we send one home with the child, and mail another.) The parents are asked to sign and return the letters only if they do not want their children to participate. This usually results in 1 or 2 percent of parents opting their children out, which most researchers consider acceptable.

Many schools and some IRBs do not find passive consent acceptable and instead require "explicit consent," in which the adolescent is not allowed to participate unless the parent signs and returns the permission letter. Many years of experience with explicit consent has demonstrated that unacceptably low return rates (25 to 40 percent) result, no matter what Herculean efforts are devoted to encouraging parents to return consent letters. (We tried paying the schools a dollar per returned letter, but it didn't help much, even though it could have meant up to $3,000 for a successful school campaign.) Researchers have shown that the nonreturn does not indicate parental disapproval but simply parental inaction. I advise researchers to abandon school research when explicit parental consent is required, because of risk of severe sample bias.

High Politics and Adolescent Sex Research

Developments on the national legislative scene may make adolescent research in schools a thing of the past. Legislation (the Family Privacy Protection Act) has been proposed that would require prior signed parental consent for any federally funded research to be done in a public school on a wide range of topics, including anything about sex. While this legislation has not been enacted, some school administrators are already responding to impending legislation by requiring explicit consent of parents for school-based research participation. The initial sponsor of this legislation said he was provoked to action by a constituent parental complaint about a "passive consent" school survey (which it turned out was not federally funded).

Gatekeepers protecting access to adolescents operate at high political levels. I was the codirector of the American Teenage Study, a large, proposed national study of adolescent sexual behavior, which got more than its share of political attention during the late 1980s and early 1990s. After years of bureaucratic delay at several levels, it was finally funded by the National Institutes of Health in May 1991. Two months later its funding was canceled by Louis Sullivan, secretary of Health and Human Services. His stated reason for cancellation was that the survey contradicted the abstinence message that the Bush administration was trying to convey to adolescents. Sensitive questions from our questionnaires were published in a prominent box on the front page of the *Washington Times.* (I have a long-standing maxim: Don't put items in your questionnaires you are not ready to see published on the front page of newspapers.) We have a newspaper clipping file four inches thick from newspapers across the country. Hundreds of scientific organizations and advocacy groups wrote letters protesting the cancellation to Sullivan and other administration officials, but to no avail.

Originally we thought that this was the first NIH grant ever canceled for political reasons. We later discovered that in the 1950s, during the McCarthy era, another study (of the nervous system of monkeys) was canceled because the principal investigator was accused of being a Communist. After our debacle, an NIH-funded conference on crime and genetics was canceled after pressure from the Congressional Black Caucus, though it was subsequently re-funded.

Later our project's merits were debated in the U.S. Congress. Inflammatory questionnaires from the study were waved about by senators on the floor of the Senate. The project was buried permanently by an act of (a Democratic-controlled) Congress that explicitly prohibited its federal funding, signed into law by President Clinton in June 1993.

Collecting Biological Measures

In my recent research on adolescent sexual behavior, we have always tried to integrate biological with social and psychological concepts into our theories. This means collecting physical and biological measurements. In preparation for our first foray into collecting blood specimens during home interviews, we asked colleagues at our research center to ask the adolescents if they would be willing to give blood samples as a part of a research project. The almost universal response was "no way." Then we asked for the question to be repeated, but proposing $25 as payment for the sample. This turned almost all the noes to yeses. Some kids asked if they could give two samples for $50. This was encouraging. In actual fieldwork, our cooperation is about 10 percentage points lower if blood is collected, even at $25 a pop. On a more general level, we find that financial incentives to adolescents are very effective in encouraging participation in surveys, and actually reduce the cost of fieldwork.

In a recent survey our interviewers found that some adolescents were actually tracking the interviewer down to arrange for an interview (for a $20 incentive—no blood requested) rather than the other way around.

When we collect blood specimens, we use a registered nurse in the field. Our respondents immediately dubbed her "the blood lady." Our usual procedure is to use a needle in the forearm taped in place for 30 minutes, with three draws of 6 ml each (to get an average level). The very first week, a boy fainted and fell off his chair, breaking his glasses as he hit the table. Since that day we collect blood with donors lying on a couch, where they stay during the entire procedure and for 15 minutes after we are through. We usually continue with the interview during this period. Even with this precaution, we have a rare, delayed faint.

Is it worth the trouble to collect these biological specimens from adolescents? You bet. In a series of studies over the past 15 years, we have been able to demonstrate that male sex hormone levels and their changes during adolescence have important effects on sexual behavior in both boys and girls. We make no argument that the sex hormones are the only cause or even the most important cause of the development of adolescent sexual behavior. In fact, a favorite among my recent papers is "Why Smart Girls Don't Have Sex, or Kiss Much Either." The answer is: we haven't figured out why, but they don't. As every girl knows, being fat is definitely a detriment to her love life. And as every parent ought to know, religious upbringing is the most reliable contribution parents can make to delaying the sexual debut of their children.

Our interviewers often carry bathroom scales to weigh respondents. This is a big deal for the girls, but not for the boys. Girls ask "the weight lady" whether they are gaining or losing weight. But they never refuse to be weighed.

Young Adolescents Lack Sexual Knowledge

It is a rather broadly established practice not to use obscene or street language in questionnaire interviews. We therefore sometimes precede a survey by pilot cognitive interviews in which we ask adolescents what they think words or questions mean, which words they don't understand, and how they arrived at answers to the questions. In our questionnaires, we find the word that most commonly stumps adolescent respondents is "Protestant." One bright 13-year-old boy told us that he thought "oral sex" was talking to your partner while having sex. Young adolescents are frequently incredulous when we explain in cognitive interviews the meaning of anal sex. They often do not believe that people do this. They commonly do not know the meaning of anus or rectum. It is often tempting to draw diagrams for clarification. The only diagrams I have used are stylized drawings to help adolescents grade their level of breast and pubic hair development to help us measure stages of puberty.

Sexually inexperienced adolescents are sometimes not really sure exactly what takes place in vaginal intercourse, so whatever word we use, we tell them what it means. But some do not know what a vagina is. In one panel study (a panel study interviews the same respondents more than once), we introduced an honesty question on the last round, using a self-administered questionnaire. We said, "When we interviewed you a year ago, we asked you whether you had ever had sexual intercourse. What did you tell us? Was that true?" One respondent helpfully wrote, "Last year I told you I had had intercourse, because I thought I had. But now I know that I hadn't at that time because since then I *have* had intercourse."

Panel studies often reveal things that the researcher would rather not know. Between rounds of interviews, up to 15 percent of adolescents will return to virgin from nonvirgin. Some rescind previous reports of ever having masturbated or had other sexual experiences. Even on what one would think is the memorable experience of first intercourse, adolescents have a lot of difficulty giving consistent answers of their age at the event. And their attitudes toward that first event change dramatically between interviews, with boys becoming more positive and girls more negative over time. In the honesty sequence described above, from 5 to 20 percent of respondents (depending on sex and race) admit to lying on previous interviews. The problem is even more complicated. Many respondents incorrectly re-member how they answered in a previous interview. The following sequence fre-quently occurs. Respondent answers "yes" (have had intercourse) at Time 1. At Time 2 he tells us that at Time 1 he answered "no" (hadn't had intercourse), but that his answer at Time 1 was not true. Do we count this as an example of an un-truthful answer? Then there are the jokesters who on self-administered interviews tell us they are both male and female, use a crutch, or have a twin when it is not true, just to give us trouble. Our research designs often give us an opportunity to catch the jokesters. Fortunately they are less than 1 percent among adolescents.

During our panel studies of adolescents in which individual respondents in different studies may be reinterviewed anywhere from twice to more than 50 times, a major source of research problems is inconsistencies. Most of these are not deliberate. In two cases respondents changed their sex from male to female over the course of the study. Upon inquiry by our field staff, both were males who had undergone or were planning sex-change operations. Because we analyze all our data by sex of respondent, what do we do with these cases?

In the research designs I use, we frequently interview respondents from the same schools and who therefore often know one another. Especially in panel stud-ies, this creates fruitful conditions for the growth of rumors among participants. In one school where during home interviews we were weighing, measuring height and skin folds, and collecting blood and saliva, we heard from our interviewers that the girls were spreading the rumor (did they actually believe this?) that as a part of our study we were collecting specimens of pubic hair and posting them on a public bulletin board at our research center. (It wasn't true.)

We always take great pains to reassure our respondents that everything they tell us is strictly confidential, and then go to sometimes extreme lengths to make sure to keep our promise to them. But sometimes respondents write things in their questionnaires that create ethical dilemmas for us. In one panel study, the otherwise closed-ended self-administered questionnaire contained an open-ended question: "Did anything else happen to you this week that we should know about?" This question elicited repeated notes from one respondent that her mother's boyfriend was beating her. In another case, an adolescent wrote on sev-eral repeated questionnaires that she had tried to commit suicide that week. In an open-ended section of a self-administered schoolroom questionnaire administered simultaneously to all students in the school, several students in one school inde-pendently wrote that their school needed our help because the principal was hav-ing sex with teachers in his office. In each case, rather than my revealing our course of action, I ask the reader to meditate on what our ethical course of action should have been.

Other scholars will ultimately decide what work I have done is most impor-tant. In my own not-so-humble view, my most important work is the develop-ment of integrated biological and social models of the determinants of sexuality and gendered behavior. I take credit for documenting for the first time each of the following three general findings: (1) In adolescent sexuality I have demonstrated that the hormones of puberty interact with social processes to determine the tim-ing and level of sexuality of both boys and girls. (2) In adult sexuality, I have shown that the patterns of the sexual behavior of couples is shaped by the rhythms of the woman's hormone cycle. (3) In gendered behavior, I have shown that the degree to which normal adult women are more or less typically feminine in their behavior is jointly determined not only by their family socialization experience during childhood, but also by hormone processes during their fetal period and hormone processes that continue during their adulthood.

Conclusion

Adolescents are cooperative and interested research participants. Most of the problems in studying them are ethical problems and access problems. They have a formidable array of protectors. Most of their protectors have the interests of the adolescent at heart.

Adolescents make sex research interesting. The longer I have studied adolescents, the less problem oriented and the more basic my research becomes. This is not because adolescents cannot get into a lot of trouble with sex. Anybody can get into a lot of trouble with sex.

Suggested Readings

Morris, N. M., & Udry, J. R. (1971). Sexual frequency and contraceptive pills. *Social Biology, 18*(1), 40–45.

Morris, N. M., & Udry, J. R. (1978). Pheromonal influences on human sexual behavior: An experimental search. *Journal of Biosocial Science, 10,* 147–157.

Udry, J. R. (1988). Biological predispositions and social control in adolescent sexual behavior. *American Sociological Review, 53,* 709–722.

Udry, J. R. (1993). The politics of sex research. *The Journal of Sex Research, 30*(2), 103–110.

Udry, J. R. (1994). The nature of gender. *Demography, 31*(4), 561–573.

Udry, J. R., & Billy, J. O. G. (1987). Initiation of coitus in early adolescence. *American Sociological Review, 52,* 841–855.

Udry, J. R., Billy, J. O. G., Morris, N. M., Groff, T. R., & Raj, M. H. (1985). Serum androgenic hormones motivate sexual behavior in adolescent boys. *Fertility and Sterility, 43*(1), 90–94.

Udry, J. R., & Cliquet, R. L. (1982). A cross-cultural examination of the relationship between ages at menarche, marriage, and first birth. *Demography, 19*(1), 53–63.

Udry, J. R., & Morris, N. M. (1967). A method for validation of reported sexual data. *Journal of Marriage and the Family, 29*(3), 442–446.

Udry, J. R., & Morris, N. M. (1968). Distribution of coitus in the menstrual cycle. *Nature, 220*(9), 593–596.

Udry, J. R., Morris, N. M., & Kovenock, J. (1995). Androgen effects on women's gendered behaviour. *Journal of Biosocial Science, 27,* 359–368.

Udry, J. R., Morris, N. M., & Waller, L. (1973). Effect of contraceptive pills on sexual activity in the luteal phase of the human menstrual cycle. *Archives of Sexual Behavior, 2*(3), 205–214.

Udry, J. R., Talbert, L. M., & Morris, N. M. (1986). Biosocial foundations for adolescent female sexuality. *Demography, 23*(2), 217–230.

Chapter **5**

The Science of Sexual Signaling

Monica M. Moore

          Monica M. Moore (Ph.D., Experimental Psychology, University of Missouri, Columbia; respecialization, Clinical Psychology, University of Missouri, St. Louis) is currently Associate Professor of Psychology in the Department of Behavioral and Social Sciences at Webster University in St. Louis, where she received the Kemper Award for Excellence in Teaching in 1996. She has done fieldwork on courtship behavior for 20 years and written about this research in several articles. Dr. Moore enjoys traveling, gardening, needlework, and mystery novels.

As the dark-haired man named Brad approached Jill, her behavior changed dramatically from what I had seen only moments before when she was engaged in conversation with her women friends. It was almost as though a switch had been flipped. Jill sat up straighter so that her shoulders were thrown back and her chest was pushed forward. Her face became extremely animated; her facial expressions changing rapidly and often. Jill punctuated her conversational responses to Brad with smiles and laughter and illustrated what she was saying with frequent movements of her hands and arms. When Jill got up to dance with Brad, she smoothed her palms down her jeans and tucked in her blouse. While dancing, Jill smiled and sometimes glanced at Brad from under her lashes. She frequently tossed her head and ran her fingers through her hair, pushing back her bangs. When the dance ended, Jill waited for Brad to accompany her back to her chair. Once seated, Jill raised a cigarette for Brad to light, holding his hand steady while he did so, and then drew her chair close to him so that her leg grazed his briefly.

When Brad left after a few minutes of conversation, it was as though the light had gone out. All that I had seen moments earlier, primping, smiling and gesturing, dropped to a low level, only to return when Brad approached Jill's table later that evening and again asked her to dance.

I have witnessed this scene, or scenes like it, hundreds of times over the past 20 years. As a scientist interested in describing and understanding flirting and the role it plays in human courtship, I have spent hundreds of hours in singles' bars and other places people go to meet others. I have observed the many nonverbal methods women employ to get the attention of men. My findings point to the rich variety of flirting techniques used by interested women and also call into question some fundamental assumptions about the roles of men and women in courtship.

People often ask me how I came to study flirting (although I prefer the term *nonverbal courtship signaling*). The answer lies in my history and in events that took place while I was in graduate school in the 1970s. As a child, although I never said I wanted to study sex, I did know I wanted an academic career. My father is a professor at a math and science institute and I can remember thinking to myself as a youngster, "I want to do what Dad does for a living." My reaction to my father's profession resulted from how interesting I found him to be and how much he enjoyed his vocation. It was as though he didn't work for a living, although certainly he was very dedicated and put in long hours. Of course, you have to imagine that even grading blue-book exams seems glamorous to a 7-year-old. He also was a fountain of information, much better than other dads (or moms) in the neighborhood at explaining astronomy, weather, the behavior of animals, or other curious and mysterious workings of nature.

So I embarked on a path leading to an academic career in psychology. I had always loved school, so it seemed a good way to keep being a student. Like my dad, I could get paid for doing things I liked—reading, talking, asking questions, and trying to answer them. I entered graduate school in experimental psychology at the University of Missouri, Columbia. I selected experimental psychology because, much to my surprise, the research methodology class that I took as an undergraduate turned out to be my favorite course. I liked experimental psychology for a couple of reasons. The professor who taught the course was excellent, and the senior project that I completed with a classmate was accepted for presentation at the Midwest Psychological Association Convention in Chicago. Hearing about the many intriguing topics that psychologists studied fueled my interest in an academic career.

I spent the next three years completing course work and a thesis on sand digging in rats. In my master's project I investigated whether domesticated laboratory rats still had the ability to dig burrows as well as wild rats. I found working in the laboratory with a variety of animals interesting, but I hoped to expand my horizons for my dissertation research and do fieldwork with humans. Being an academic brat, I was not surprised when my dissertation supervisor, Esther Thelen, pointed out that the choice of a topic for my final research project was crucial for me as a future academician, given that I would invest heavily in researching whatever topic I chose in the early years of my career. However, like many other graduate students, I was thoroughly convinced that I would never be able to come up with a topic for my dissertation and so would be stuck in graduate school forever. Being told I needed to be particularly careful in my selection of a problem to study only added to my stress. My adviser didn't mean to torture me, but I was her first doctoral student and she was trying to be as helpful a mentor as possible.

The first thing that popped into my mind when Esther asked me what I hoped to study was, "Well, I can think of two things I could happily study for quite some time. On the one hand there's food and on the other there's sex." Sex won. But I might now be writing about eating disorders if it hadn't been for my luck in running across some very intriguing research on women and their selection of sexual partners.

In 1978 Esther brought from a conference a paper by an anthropologist, Heather Fowler Remoff. Remoff was investigating the role that women play in choosing men as sexual partners. She thought that we had perhaps overlooked the importance of women's role in the selection of partners in a culture that portrayed men as the initiators in decisions related to sex. After all, we hand over responsibility for asking for dances or dates more often to men than to women. And, our cultural norms deem men more responsible for making the marriage proposal. But that's not the way it is in most other species, as Charles Darwin pointed out more than a century ago. In most other species the choice of a mate weighs more heavily on the female. Some biologists explain the female's prerogative in the choice of a mating partner as stemming from the heavier cost that females pay by pregnancy and bearing offspring. This is so common that some biologists refer to female choice as the driving factor in such diverse male mating behaviors as the mating songs of birds and the horn-knocking fights of bighorn sheep. Male peacocks have that large, showy tail simply to attract peahens.

Given the central role females play in courtship in other species, Remoff wondered if we had minimized women's input in our own. She decided to ask women about the criteria they found relevant for picking men. Rather than bluntly asking, "Why'd you pick the guy you're with?" Remoff questioned her participants about what they found sexy about the men they were currently seeing. She released a virtual flood of responses in many of the women she interviewed. They talked for hours or days, giving her their complete relationship histories. Her analysis revealed that most women from vastly different walks of life wanted a man who could and would support them and any children they might have. For example, in one touching story, Remoff told of a woman who decided to keep dating a man who showed particular sensitivity to her needs. When Valentine's Day arrived he presented her with a gift of two bags of groceries that she and her children desperately needed, foregoing the traditional flowers and candy that would have been silly luxuries. Remoff found over and over in her interviews that a man's ability and willingness to provide resources were major factors prompting the woman to view him as a viable partner. These criteria, Remoff believes, mirror those in other species in which females need assistance in rearing immature offspring. Her findings were reported in a book entitled *Sexual Choice: A Woman's Decision* (1984).

I found Heather Remoff's work fascinating. But I wondered whether it would be possible to investigate women's choice of partners in another way. Frankly, I was a little hesitant to rely solely on what women said they were looking for in men. After all, sometimes it is hard for us to understand what motivates us, particularly when we are asked by a researcher about situations in our past. It's not so much that I thought the women in Remoff's studies had lied but that they might not be totally aware of the personal issues underlying their own behavior. I had been trained to do observational research, so interviewing people was, for me, an unusual way of finding an answer to a problem. It occurred to me that I could use the observational approach to see and then analyze women's partner choices.

Unlike many psychologists who work in laboratories with animals or who give questionnaires to people, I had been trained to watch people in natural settings for clues to the underlying causes of their behavior. This approach to research, called human ethology, also relies on evolutionary theory as a theoretical framework. Like field biologists who hope to learn more about the hunting behaviors of lions, for example, human ethologists work in natural settings. The field for me is often places like singles' bars or shopping malls. I observe people, without their knowledge, keeping careful notes about their behavior. When more convenient, I sometimes use hidden microcassette recorders to keep track of my data until the findings can be transcribed. I suppose this aspect of my style of data collection appeals to the part of me that likes reading mystery novels. I get to experience a bit of what it is like to be a private investigator, albeit in the name of science. With this background and training it seemed natural to me to pay more attention to what women do than what they say.

But if I was to observe the process of partner selection, I had to have a way of determining that a selection was being made. Some early observations turned up the surprising finding that before a man approached a woman in a bar or at a party, she often indicated that she found him attractive by displaying specific nonverbal behaviors, facial expressions, and gestures—what we commonly call body language. After I noticed these behaviors I realized I had the solution to my problem of how to observe partner selection. When I obtained a list of these flirtatious behaviors, I could determine who women found attractive. Being a naive graduate student I assumed a library search of the literature on nonverbal courtship behavior in humans would yield the list I needed. Much to my dismay I found only a few references to human courtship behaviors scattered across the literature on nonverbal communication. Of course, there were voluminous references to animal courtship rituals. The literature on human courtship was more limited, especially that involving observational research. For example, in one study some courtship behaviors had been observed as part of greeting rituals. In another, Albert Scheflen, a psychiatrist, described several nonverbal behaviors he saw during psychotherapy sessions that, he believed, were being used to "court" the therapist. But the descriptions were brief and the listings incomplete. I had no recourse but to compile a catalog of courtship behaviors myself if I wanted to answer the questions I found so intriguing. So that's how I came to be an expert on flirting. I must say that I can't believe that researching eating behavior would have been nearly as exciting.

In fact, I have had so much fun that it is hard for me to believe that now for 20 years I have investigated the nonverbal behaviors associated with dating and mating in women and girls. I have not only compiled the catalog mentioned previously but have discovered some very interesting things about those flirtatious behaviors. These findings are what I will tell you about. But I will also try to continue to portray why I wanted, like my dad, to do research. I'll discuss the way science works, the paths of discovery and the blind alleys involved in uncovering the mysteries of human nature. If you, like me, can't resist opening Pandora's box, I think you'll enjoy my story.

Because I chose to study human female courtship behavior in actual courtship situations, I was confronted with some problems that are unique to doing research in the field. First, because the field for me involved singles' bars, I needed the cooperation of bar owners. After I had obtained permission to proceed with my research from the sponsoring university, I tackled bar owners in town. With a description of how I planned to study flirting in their establishments and assurances that their businesses would not be harmed, I found most owners receptive to my plan. In fact, not only did most proprietors grant permission for the use of their facilities, but many bar owners were quite interested and wanted to talk about the research. Some often gave me and my team of observers valuable assistance by providing us with drinks disguised like alcoholic beverages so we would blend in with the crowd or by reserving a dark corner of the bar for us to sit.

Second, I wanted to protect the identities of the people I would watch. To invade their privacy as little as possible, I neither talked with the people I watched nor gathered any personal information about them. The men and women we watched (I worked with teams of trained undergraduate and graduate student observers) were unaware that they were taking part in an investigation of female courtship behavior because we made our observations secretly. This not only protected their privacy but allowed us to record flirting as it naturally occurred, without worrying that people were changing their behavior because they knew they were being watched by researchers.

To keep track of what we saw we recorded our observations into microcassette audio recorders concealed in our pockets, purses, or laps. We made our observations while sitting in mixed-gender groups after we discovered that singles pay little attention to couples. We also sat in dark corners of the bar, and we blended in with the crowd by adopting whatever attire was worn at that bar or party. This sometimes entailed calls to bars to determine if a theme night was planned so that we could be prepared with the proper country-western gear or other costumes. By taking such precautions we were never caught in the act of doing our research or bothered by people approaching members of the research team.

In our attempt to catalog nonverbal courtship behaviors in women, we used several procedures that have evolved through observational studies of animals by scientists. The use of these methods minimized bias, making the kind of systematic observation we practiced different from the casual people watching done by many in bars. After we numbered the women sitting in the vicinity of our table, we used a random number generator to select the women we watched so as not to be influenced by personal appearance or level of flirting. And we watched only those women who came to the bar without a male companion and with at least one other woman. We made our observations on the weekends and on occasions such as "Ladies Night," when women could buy drinks at reduced prices, because at those times the bar was full. Over the years we have observed hundreds of women and men in this fashion. Some people were watched briefly and a few were observed for several hours.

Our data on flirting was compiled through description of all the nonverbal behaviors, such as gestures and facial expressions, exhibited by women selected for observation at the time. We also kept track of all of the nonverbal behaviors of the men with whom the women interacted. In this method, providing consequential evidence, it is assumed that if the behavior being studied is followed by a relevant behavior, the function of the behavior in question has been isolated. In other words we defined flirting as nonverbal behavior that attracted male attention. So we later combed the transcripts of our taped data for those nonverbal behaviors that occurred just prior to some form of male attention. Male responses included approaching a women, talking to her, touching her, leaning toward her or moving closer, asking her to dance, or kissing her. Applying this method, we gathered 52 different kinds of courtship behavior for our flirting catalog.

It has been great fun to learn what works and what doesn't in courtship. So now I would like to introduce you to the science of sexual signaling. I think you'll be intrigued by the work of those sexual scientists like me who study this aspect of body language.

For me, the most striking finding to come out of the research so far is that although both men and women engage in flirting, it is women who initiate the first stage of courtship. They flirt often, using a great many nonverbal behaviors to signal their interest, and show great ingenuity in their quest for sexual attention.

Initially, a woman will usually indicate her interest through glances at the man she finds attractive. These glances may be brief and darting or direct and sustained, or a woman may look up at a man from under lowered lashes. Often she smiles at the man at the same time. Laughing, giggling, and smiling are common to a flirting woman. The courting woman is extremely animated, moving a great deal to attract attention to herself. She gestures with her hands, often with an open or extended palm, while speaking. She runs her hands through her hair and tosses her head. A flirting woman primps; she adjusts her clothing and pats her hair. She makes herself look noticeably more attractive by standing and sitting straight, with her stomach held in, her breasts pushed out, and her shoulders squared. When there is music, she rocks her body to the beat, as though asking for someone to dance with her. If these signals are not effective in getting the man to approach her, the woman may get up and walk by him. Occasionally, we have seen a woman stumble and introduce herself while making amends. Of course, some women approach a man and ask him to dance. But this occurs rarely, at least in the Midwest.

After contact of some sort has been made and the couple is seated at a table (usually hers) or dancing together, the woman uses other behaviors to express continued interest in the man. She orients her body toward him and leans close, perhaps whispering in his ear. We found that courting women often whisper into a man's ear in a noisy bar rather than shout across the table. When in conversation, a woman interested in a man frequently nods and smiles in response to his comments. Sometimes she tilts her head to the side to expose her neck. On a few occasions we have seen the man react by kissing the woman's neck. An interested woman may seek help from a man in lighting her cigarette, refilling her drink, or putting on her jacket. Or she may tease him, perhaps by stealing his hat or tickling him. Most significant, the courting woman touches the man or allows herself to be touched. A hand on his knee or her foot next to his is a powerful indication of her interest. Women in the process of rejecting a suitor pull away and rebuff any attempts to make physical contact. In fact, women are often very careful about regulating who touches them and how. As the evening and courtship progress, it is not unusual to see hugs and kisses being given and accepted by women in singles' bars.

Although the description provided above is a summary of the first complete catalog of women's nonverbal courtship behaviors, other observers labeled some of the same gestures and facial expressions as flirtatious behavior. This is important because in science you hope to have confirming evidence provided by a variety of researchers. In this regard, both Ray Birdwhistell and Desmond Morris have drawn comparisons between the courting behavior of humans and other species. Morris and Birdwhistell agree that it is the woman who most often regulates the movement from step to step. Similarly, Mark Cary, working both in the laboratory and in singles' bars, found that an initial glance on the part of the woman was interpreted by men as permission to start a conversation.

Adam Kendon and Andrew Ferber have seen some of these courtship behaviors during American greeting rituals, for instance, when hosts greet guests at a party. Still other researchers, such as Joan Lockard and Robert Adams, have made note of the variety of flirting behaviors found in couples of various ages observed in shopping malls and along paths in public parks. Both Timothy Perper and David Givens have done fieldwork in singles' bars to detail the stages of the courtship dance in humans. Ethologist Irenaus Eibl-Eibesfeldt has compared the flirting behavior of people from diverse cultural backgrounds. He found flirting to be very much the same the world over. Again, there is a striking amount of agreement between his work and what I have observed in American women.

More recently, Karl Grammer brought unacquainted couples into his video laboratory. While they were ostensibly waiting for their turn to participate in an experiment, he was documenting their interaction on a hidden camera. He, too, found that women used a variety of nonverbal behaviors such as smiling, laughing, touching their hair or clothing, and leaning closer to signal interest in a man.

After the catalog had been completed, I wanted more assurance that we truly had described human flirting. I assumed that if these behaviors functioned as courtship signals, they would be used in settings where courtship is expected but not in other, inappropriate situations. In this approach, consequential evidence is used to determine the function of behavior. Therefore to test the catalog we watched 40 women in four contexts: a singles' bar, the snack bar on a university campus, a library, and meetings at which only women were present. Again we randomly selected women to observe from those who were without a male companion. We found that the women in the singles' bar averaged 70 flirting acts per hour compared with 19 in the student union, 10 in the library, and 5 in the women's center meetings. Regardless of the situation, where men were present, women who signaled often were most likely to be approached by a man. Taken together, these two studies allow me to feel confident that we have described most of the nonverbal gestures and facial expressions that women use in the early stages of courtship to attract the attention of potential dating partners. In fact, this is the way most field researchers studying animals try to determine the function of certain behaviors they see in the wild. They look at the consequences of certain actions and compare the animal's behavior across contexts.

Looking at the data from the two studies described previously, I believe that flirting is a negotiation strategy for women who are interested in attracting the attention of men. A woman, using a number of categories of flirting behaviors not directed at any particular man, may elicit approaches from several suitors. On the other hand, by selectively turning her behavior to one person, a woman may discourage others and indicate interest in a particular man. By glancing at him and smiling or by dancing in her chair, a woman can demonstrate to a man that he is likely to meet with acceptance should he approach her. Of course, there are no guarantees that she will continue to demonstrate interest, because when the man approaches the woman and initiates conversation she has more information on which to base an evaluation of his attractiveness to her.

Not only does flirting provide an opportunity to elicit approaches from men, but flirting also influences the pace of courtship. By moving closer to her partner or allowing brief physical contact, such as a knee touch, the woman may be able subtly to encourage the man. Conversely, a woman who pulls away from a man or does not smile and nod when conversing may effectively put off potential suitors. In fact, my most recent work has been directed at trying to describe the comparable nonverbal rejection signals in women.

Now that you know what to look for, I encourage you to take a field trip of your own to your nearest singles' bar to see firsthand what I've been describing.

Of course, many of you are quite aware of these signals and have used them skillfully yourselves. When I give talks about my research, it is not uncommon to look out into the audience and see many people nodding their heads. The women I'm speaking to have employed some of the signals to let a special man know they find him attractive. And the men have looked for these indicators of interest before they approached a woman and so have lessened their chance of being rejected out of hand.

For those of you who feel unsure of your flirting skills, I hope you will find, through reading this chapter, that understanding human courtship can have personal benefits. When I hoped to move the friendship of five years that I had with the man who is now my husband to a more serious relationship it helped to be an expert on flirting. In fact, the female students who have been observers in my research also report becoming skilled flirts themselves.

Indeed, at one point this expertise in flirting on the part of my student observers presented me with a bit of a problem. It became apparent to me that I needed to have some ethical guidelines about the use of these enhanced flirting skills when a student returned from spring break to report how successful she had been using nonverbal courtship signaling on her trip. To pass the time during an airport delay, she used her enhanced courtship skills to indicate interest in a young man in the seating area. She was quite excited to discover that her newly honed skills in flirting not only got his attention, but also encouraged him to approach her in record time. She assumed I would be as thrilled as she was. And although I was happy to discover that the signals were as effective when wielded in the name of science as they appeared to be when used in the context of love, I was dismayed to find that she had no real interest in the young man in question. So now I tell my students that I want them to use their enhanced flirting skills only when genuinely interested. I feel very strongly that students who learn to be better flirts through working on research projects should reserve those skills for times when they want to attract or maintain the attention of a particular man they find attractive. I don't want these findings to be used to hurt the feelings of men who are being toyed with for amusement, although that, of course, happens sometimes in courtship. I must say, however, that the opportunity to learn to flirt better at the same time they learn about research has meant that I have not lacked for student observers.

Not only have my students and I benefited personally from the results of this research, but I had a great deal of fun learning what works and what doesn't in the nonverbal language of love. And, I think a lot of the fun in my research comes from the fact that it's part of my job to watch people. Of course, research is not all fun and games. There are many times when it is boring, exhausting, and frustrating. The noise and the smoke in bars sometimes get to me and my students. The good news is that this line of inquiry contains so many as yet unanswered questions that it's possible to move on to a new research project in a different setting. So now I would like to talk about a few other projects that emerged from the basic work of pulling together the catalog of women's nonverbal courtship behaviors.

After the catalog had been completed and tested, I presented it at meetings of several professional associations. Not surprisingly, I found that some people were critical of my methodology. One man, a more traditional laboratory psychologist, suggested an experimental test of the effectiveness of the behaviors in the catalog. In other words, he wanted me to train women to give off particular courtship signals and then count how long it took to elicit approaches from unsuspecting men. I had grave concerns about using this methodology. First, I think that it is insensitive of a researcher, in the name of science, to perpetuate the notion that a woman finds a man attractive when that is not the case. I also feared for the safety of the student used to dupe men in this fashion. For these reasons, I viewed such a research protocol as highly unethical so I looked to devise another type of test of the power of these signals.

Luckily, I remembered another ethological study done by Gail Ziven in which predictive ability had been used to demonstrate understanding of particular categories of children's nonverbal behavior. I was convinced, after having watched countless women flirt, that I knew flirting as well as Ziven knew children's facial expressions. After hundreds of hours watching courtship, I could sometimes tell which of my friends was interested in a man by watching her primp, smile, and tease him. So, in the next study we tried to test our predictive power. We had a trained observer watch a woman for a certain specified amount of time. The researcher kept track of the number and type of courtship signals the woman used. Then the observer, using those pieces of information, made a prediction about whether or not the woman would be approached. If, for example, the woman was employing a number of different courtship signals, some of which were quite strong indicators of interest in a particular man, then the observer would predict that she would be approached. If, on the contrary, a woman we were watching was involved in a conversation with her female friend and was paying little or no attention to the available men, then the observer would predict that she would not be approached. After the prediction was made, another researcher looked for confirmation. We were correct in our predictions about 90 percent of the time. In fact, we were most often wrong when a woman changed her behavior after the prediction had been made. In these cases, a woman who had been signaling a particular man ceased to do so when he walked to a part of the bar where she couldn't see him, or a woman who had been patently disinterested perked up at the entrance of a new man.

But perhaps more important than the fact that these behaviors can be used to predict behavior is our finding that the more signals a woman gives off, the more likely she is to have contact with potential suitors. In several of our studies we found that signaling is strongly related to approaches. These behaviors work when the goal is to attract men. This is not to say that a woman may be successful in attracting any man she wants, because men play an active role in courtship too. But still these nonverbal behaviors can be effective if used judiciously.

In fact another study points out that the use of nonverbal courtship signals is more important than what one looks like. Women and men often assume that the most beautiful women in the world don't really have to use the signals we've been talking about, that men flock to them regardless of whether or not they show interest. This belief stems not only from the stereotype of beauty in America but also because a number of studies in psychology have pointed to the importance of physical attractiveness in partner selection, particularly in the beginning of a relationship.

What I have found is that nonverbal courtship signaling can be a powerful tool in the hands of less-than-stunning women. In one of our studies we had observers make judgments of the attractiveness of the women we were observing. It may seem like this would be a difficult task, but if broad categories are used, there is often remarkable agreement among raters. The ease in reaching consensus when rating attractiveness has been demonstrated in several studies using yearbook pictures. In fact, there are some studies that show that people in non-Western and Western cultures use similar criteria for measures of attractiveness. Particularly important are indices of health and well-being such as bright eyes, clear skin, shiny hair, and symmetrical facial features. On the other hand, it is also true that what one person finds attractive may be a real turnoff for another. Sometimes someone reminds you of someone you didn't like or an unpleasant event in your life. So it's important to take note of our idiosyncratic views on physical attractiveness.

We decided to put the issue of which was more critical—the use of flirtatious behaviors to signal interest or how beautiful the woman was—to the test. We had a team of three raters estimate the attractiveness of women we watched in singles' bars. Each rater used three categories—unattractive, attractive, and very attractive. After the women had been labeled, we sat back and simply counted the exhibition of courtship signals. We also tallied how many men approached the women we were observing. What we discovered was that a less attractive woman could be as successful as a more attractive woman when she used flirting to her advantage. It appeared that men looked for signals of a woman's interest. In this regard, we found that the more flirting behaviors a woman used, the more likely she was to be approached. If a beautiful woman and her less attractive friend both signaled their interest, then the more attractive woman was more likely to be approached. But if a gorgeous woman ignored the available men, then less attractive women found that flirting got men to pay attention to them.

I have never tested this finding by using modellike women in my research as decoys because I think it is unethical to fool a man, who has not agreed to participate in a research project, into believing a beautiful woman wants his attentions. I would hate to be the man who discovers that the woman flirting with him was doing so in the name of science. However, such a demonstration was staged recently on television. A beautiful model was hired and told to sit in a bar and show no interest whatsoever in any man. At the same time an attractive woman, although not so beautiful as the model, was told to use flirting behaviors to show interest in those men whom she found attractive and would like to meet. Although this was show business, not research, things turned out as I would have predicted. Only one man approached the model. When interviewed, he said he did so because he was concerned about her, given how sad she looked. The second woman attracted a great deal more attention, collecting the names and numbers of several men in a short period of time.

Although I have no control over the way the results of my studies turn out, I must say I was happy to find that beautiful women don't always get the guy. I believe that women have often been discouraged about their dating prospects by experts and the media touting the idea that it is necessary to be beautiful to attract a mate. It has been rewarding to broadcast the idea that maybe we've made too much of beauty. Given the enormous pressure put on women to be beautiful and the billions spent every year in this quest, it is nice to be able to point out that it is more important for women to be obvious about their interest. The burden of making an approach is more often put on men in our culture. Because men want to prevent the humiliation of a public rejection, they are often cautious about whom they approach. We have observed that many men require several indicators of interest on the part of a woman before they will go up to her and introduce themselves, start a conversation, or ask her to dance. The woman who is shy about showing her interest misses out on opportunities to meet a man with whom she may have something in common. Men who approach women who have demonstrated that they are patently uninterested are more likely to experience rejection.

But what if you are a woman and you are not particularly good at indicating to a man that you find him attractive? In other words, if you are a poor flirt? The good news is that there is no reason to despair because flirting, like a lot of other skills, can be learned. I say this with such confidence because one study that I did indicated that girls in their early teens learn a great deal about courtship from one another as they begin to interact more with boys.

Because young teenagers don't go to singles' bars, I watched them in surroundings more conducive to teenage courtship—shopping malls and recreational settings such as swimming pools or skating rinks. I must confess that this project appealed to me because I was burned out on late nights and smoky bars, yet I wanted to continue to do fieldwork. After a number of boys and girls had gathered, I began to observe their behavior, using the systematic approach we employed while researching women's flirting. What I discovered in girls was that although there were some similarities to the courtship behavior of women, there were also a number of key differences.

First of all, girls flirt. They use many of the same signals that women use, but they are less likely to use the more overt nonverbal behaviors such as skirt hikes, buttock pats, or caresses. At least I found that to be true in the venues I studied. Although this information doesn't really help the woman trying to improve her flirting skills, I suspect that it will allow parents of young teenagers to breathe a sigh of relief. Girls tend to concentrate their flirtatious expressions and gestures on those behaviors seen early in the sequence in adults, the glancing, smiling, primping signals.

In addition, they don't use as many signals as do women and so attract fewer approaches from boys. Now it certainly can be argued that one problem could be that the places I used to observe teenage courtship were not comparable to singles' bars. It is also the case that girls getting fewer approaches from boys may have as much to do with boys as it does with girls. Perhaps boys are more reluctant to approach girls given their lack of experience in dating. Maybe boys at this age just aren't as interested in the opposite gender as are girls.

In any case, there was less flirting activity in the kids I studied when I compared their behavior to that of adults. In fact, girls paid a great deal more attention to one another than they did to the boys. I found this particularly interesting, given that on the rare occasions I could overhear conversations, girls tended to talk about boys a lot. But by paying attention to one another, girls had the opportunity not only to cement their relationships, but also to make use of the behaviors of other girls in the group. When girls pay attention to one another, they see which behaviors are effective and which don't work. Then girls can copy one another's flirting techniques. More specifically, I found they copy the facial expressions and gestures of the dominant girl in the group, the group leader.

Mimicking the behavior of another person is virtually unheard of in women. In fact, it seems that women take pains to make sure they are not engaging in the use of similar flirting signals to those of another woman at the table. Women operate independently from one another. One woman may be signaling fast and furiously, while another is exhibiting few, if any, flirting behaviors.

Not so with the girls I watched. When one patted her hair, they all did. If one girl glanced over at a group of boys, they all did. I believe that this makes it possible for girls to have experience in the flirting arena before they begin dating seriously.

Because girls are just practicing skills they will use more frequently later on, another quality I noticed in these 13- to 16-year-olds was that their signaling didn't have the grace and subtlety of that used by women. Girls' nonverbal courtship behavior is exaggerated, similar to other behaviors. Most flirtatious expressions and gestures used by these girls are delivered in a very noticeable, even theatrical manner. When a girl primps she goes through an elaborate process of smoothing her clothing. When she tosses her head and pats her hair she throws her head back dramatically and fluffs her hair for quite some time. Now you could argue that perhaps this is because girls cultivate hairstyles requiring a lot of maintenance, but that wouldn't explain the fact that other courtship signals are similarly exaggerated.

In women these same behaviors are subtle, fluid, even elegant. They are executed smoothly and sometimes go unnoticed to all but the careful observer or the man for whom they are intended. In women, the appearance of nonverbal courtship behaviors is often quite refined in its simplicity. Some researchers have found the interaction between courting men and women to be so beautiful that they have compared it to a dance. It should come as no surprise, therefore, that something this complex takes practice. And girls appear to get this practice by observing one another and then trying the behaviors out. Because this is unfamiliar territory, the results are often signals that are awkwardly executed, lacking in refinement.

But with time and practice girls get better. And so can any woman who feels awkward flirting. Like the girls I observed, she can watch the skilled flirt and copy her technique.

Another lesson I learned from girls has to do with their reliance on flirting behaviors with which they are familiar. Girls devote a high percentage of their nonverbal courtship signaling to play behavior or teasing. When they want a boy to know they like him, they pinch, hit, push, or grab him. A teenager will steal a boy's french fries out from under him and then throw them at him. Childhood teasing is translated into the newly adult world of male-female relationships. Play behaviors are safe remnants of life as a child or preteen.

Women use play behaviors as well. In fact, you also find it in the courtship behavior of a large number of other species. In human females, playing or teasing occurs less regularly in the courtship situation than it does for girls. But when it does appear, it adds a note of fun to the interaction between a woman and the man in whom she is interested. We have seen women come up behind a man they danced with earlier and place their hands over his eyes so he has to guess their identity. One evening in a singles' bar with a Western theme, a woman "stole" a man's cowboy hat and ran away with it. Needless to say, he chased after her and she was able to capture his attention along with his hat. Because we can't hear what courting couples are saying, we miss the joke that is told or the double entendre used in conversation. But I believe that these verbal gambits reinforce the playful facial expressions and gestures we can observe from afar. These play behaviors not only inject humor into what can be a stressful situation for both parties, but I believe they also allow a woman to test the man's receptivity to humor. When a man doesn't appreciate her silliness, we have sometimes seen a woman use rejection signals to end the relationship or cool it considerably with fewer expressions of interest and attention.

After seeing women use nonverbal indicators of disinterest, I decided to turn my attention to documenting their form in the field. So rejection signaling is what I am in the process of observing now. Because little has been done in the way of naturalistic observation, we are back in the bars, after our hiatus in shopping malls studying teenagers, looking at how women signal a lack of interest. After that research is completed, there are many other questions to be answered about human nonverbal courtship behavior. There has been little work done looking at the courtship behavior of gay men and lesbians, of people of color and the elderly, and of people with disabilities. There are issues related to the effectiveness of courtship signaling and the interpretation men and women put on the use of flirting. As you can see I no longer worry about not being able to come up with an original idea to research.

Just like my father I have been lucky to find work that is so interesting that sometimes it's hard to believe that I get paid for opening Pandora's box. Luckily, too, now my daughter can brag to her friends that her mom is able to give some answers about interesting human behaviors, although she is not all that great on astronomy or geology.

Acknowledgments

I gratefully acknowledge the valuable suggestions and comments offered by John Sterling and Gloria Grenwald-Mayes. I continue to rely, as well, on the suggestions made by DeAun Blumberg when we exercise together.

Suggested Readings

Eibl-Eibesfeldt, I. (1971). *Love and hate*. New York: Holt, Rinehart and Winston.

Givens, D. (1978). The nonverbal basis of attraction: Flirtation, courtship, and seduction. *Psychiatry, 41*, 346–359.

Grammer, K. (1990). Strangers meet: Laughter and nonverbal signs of interest in opposite-sex encounters. *Journal of Nonverbal Behavior, 14*, 209–236.

Kendon, A., & Ferber, A. (1973). A description of some human greetings. In R. P. Michael & J. H. Crook (Eds.), *Comparative ecology and behavior of primates* (pp. 591—668). London: Academic.

Lockard, J. S., & Adams, R. M. (1980). Courtship behaviors in public: Different age/sex roles. *Ethology and Sociobiology, 1,* 245–253.

Moore, M. M. (1985). Nonverbal courtship patterns in women: Context and consequences. *Ethology and Sociobiology, 6,* 237–247.

Moore, M. M. (1995). Courtship signaling and adolescents: "Girls just wanna have fun"? *The Journal of Sex Research, 32,* 319–328.

Moore, M. M., & Butler, D. L. (1989). Predictive aspects of nonverbal courtship behavior in women. *Semiotica, 3,* 205–215.

Perper, T. (1985). *Sex signals: The biology of love.* Philadelphia: ISI.

Remoff, H. T. (1984). *Sexual choice: A woman's decision.* New York: Dutton/Lewis.

Scheflen, A. E. (1965). Quasi-courtship behavior in psychotherapy, *Psychiatry, 28,* 245–257.

Chapter **6**

She Should Be Young and Beautiful, He Should Be Older and Successful: Gender Differences in Mate-Selection Preferences

Michael W. Wiederman

Michael W. Wiederman (Ph.D., Bowling Green State University) is Assistant Professor of Psychological Science at Ball State University in Muncie, Indiana. He has published numerous articles on mate selection, jealousy, gender differences, and eating disorders. He is a member of the Society for the Scientific Study of Sexuality and served as Assistant Editor for *The Journal of Sex Research*.

"**W**hy would anyone want to spend their time conducting research? Such individuals must be nerds, or at least not have anything better to do." These were my thoughts as I started a doctoral program in clinical psychology. I realized that to earn a doctoral degree in psychology I needed to complete a master's thesis and a doctoral dissertation, but these were not endeavors that thrilled me. I had earned my bachelor's degree at the University of Michigan, Flint, a small branch campus where I had not been exposed to individuals who conducted research. The entire process of conducting psychological research was a mystery and I viewed it as simply an unavoidable and intimidating hurdle toward my ultimate goal of becoming a therapist.

During the initial week in graduate school, my clinical classmates and I had an orientation meeting with the coordinator of the graduate program. I still remember his words: "All of you said in your applications that you are interested in research. We know that you had to say that to have a chance of being accepted into the program. Now that you're already here, we can't kick you out, so be honest: How many people really are interested in conducting research?" Not one hand was raised. Apparently I was not alone in my perceptions.

Despite our apparent lack of interest, we were encouraged to generate topics for our master's thesis research as soon as possible. I figured I would probably do something related to cognitive forms of psychotherapy, but I wasn't sure. To introduce us to the various faculty members in the psychology department who were involved in research, the graduate coordinator arranged for a series of informal meetings wherein faculty came to our group to talk about their research interests. One of these faculty speakers was Betsy Allgeier, a social psychologist, whose white hair and warm smile led me to believe she probably studied group cohesiveness, or friendship, or even religiosity. You can imagine my surprise when she said that she conducted research on human sexuality.

I was fascinated as she described some of the projects she and her students had completed. As she spoke I began to realize that I had always been interested in such issues as why we are attracted to certain individuals and not others, how people decide whether to be sexually intimate with a particular dating partner, and why certain romantic relationships dissolve whereas others progress to greater commitment. Up to that point, however, attempts to satisfy my curiosity had been limited to occasionally reading through one of the hokey sex surveys in *Cosmopolitan* or listening with interest to a snippet on the evening news about the results of a recent poll on sexual attitudes. Now, right in front of me was a woman who investigated these inherently interesting topics for a living. It was the first time I realized that research could be interesting and "juicy." My curiosity was sparked.

What Do We Look For in a Potential Mate?

Shortly after the meeting, I approached Dr. Allgeier about the possibility of supervising my master's thesis. She explained that such a working relationship required a substantial investment from each partner and that it was best to engage in a trial working relationship before making a greater commitment.

She also thought I might be interested in a recently published article by David Buss, a psychologist at the University of Michigan, who had surveyed adults in 37 different cultures regarding their preferences for potential mates. His hypothesis was that, through thousands of generations of natural selection, men and women have evolved differing strategies in choosing a potential mate. That is, choosing a mate who could successfully provide for her and her offspring would have been important to our female prehistoric ancestors because it was the women who became pregnant and nursed the infants. Women who chose mates who could not or would not provide for them and their children were probably less likely to survive during pregnancy and nursing and, thus, less likely to have children who survived.

Rather than finding a mate who could provide material resources, for our male prehistoric ancestors it was probably more important from a reproductive standpoint to mate with females who were relatively fertile. Women can get pregnant only during a portion of their lives, while they are relatively young. Prehistoric men who preferred older mates were probably less likely to have children who survived. Certain physical characteristics (such as smooth, unblemished skin, shiny hair, good muscle tone, white teeth, and so forth) that humans have come to find attractive are reliable indicators of women's relative youth. If women who preferred resource-providing men and men who preferred women with "beautiful" characteristics had more children compared to those without such preferences, and these preferences were something that could be inherited to some degree, then each generation would have a greater proportion of individuals who exhibited the particular mate preferences. Eventually, these preferences would be universal, or a part of human nature, just as a general preference for sweet foods over bitter foods is inherent. Notice that we do not even question why sweet is a more pleasant taste than bitter, or why smooth skin is more attractive than wrinkled skin; humans as a species have these general preferences.

With regard to mate preferences, Buss hypothesized that contemporary men would place more emphasis on a potential mate's physical attractiveness, whereas women were hypothesized to pay relatively more attention to a potential mate's ability to earn financial and material resources. To test these hypotheses, Buss used a mate-selection survey that had been given to numerous samples of college students over the past 50 years. The survey consisted of a list of 18 characteristics such as "sociability," "similar religious background," "emotional stability," and "dependable character." Respondents were asked to rate how important each characteristic would be to them in selecting a potential mate. The two items that Buss hypothesized men and women would respond to differently were "good looks" and "good financial prospect." Remarkably, across cultures, men rated "good looks" as more important in a potential mate than did women, whereas women rated "good financial prospect" as more important in a potential mate than did men.

Dr. Allgeier was correct in assuming that I would find David Buss's article of interest. Just prior to starting graduate school I experienced a sudden and unexpected divorce. The experience left me pondering gender differences in what people look for in a mate and what they expect from their romantic relationships. I had noticed that when I tried setting up my guy friends with potential blind dates, typically the first question was, "Is she good looking?" I had also been struck by the observation that freshman males, who had the lowest status on campus, seemed to have the most difficult time getting a date or having a girlfriend, whereas senior males seemed to have the easiest time. Similarly, I was intrigued at hearing various male celebrities, who were considered sex symbols, describe how difficult it was to find anyone willing to go out with them before they became famous.

Dr. Allgeier and I decided to follow up on David Buss's work to see if the gender difference also existed on our campus. In this way, we would get a chance to satisfy our curiosity, and we could gauge how well we worked together. To obtain results we could compare to Buss's we decided to use the same mate-selection survey.

Some of Buss's critics noted that perhaps women place more emphasis on men's earning power not because of some inherent gender difference in the way men and women process information about potential mates but rather because women generally earn less than men and may be dependent on their spouses to secure enough money to live comfortably. In other words, some critics hypothesized that if women were financially independent, they would not need to be concerned with the earning capacity of a potential mate. Men, on the other hand, could afford the luxury of being concerned with a potential mate's physical attractiveness because they did not need to worry about relying on their spouses financially.

We decided to test this assumption by correlating women's ratings of how important a potential mate's "financial prospects" were with how much money women expected to earn themselves after graduating from college and becoming established in the workforce. To do so we included a question about the amount of money they expected to earn three to four years after graduation. We chose to measure each student's expected income a few years after graduating from college because we figured it would take that long, on average, to find the kind of job for which the students had been trained. In other words, we were afraid that if we asked how much money each student made currently, we would get low numbers for just about everyone (most traditional students do not work or only do so part-time). Similarly, if we asked how much money each student expected to earn in the first year after graduating from college, the estimate might not reflect what they would earn once they were somewhat established in their profession. Of course, there is no way to determine how accurately the students estimated their future income. However, with regard to how their income might affect mate selection preferences, it is most important to measure the students' *perceptions* of their own earning capacity (i.e., how financially independent they believe they will be).

We had a research idea and we had a methodology for addressing it. What we still needed was research participants. We figured that college students were not only a convenient sample for our study, but an ecologically valid one. Who better to survey about mate selection than young adults involved in the process of courtship?

By this time I was excited about finding out whether men and women on our campus differed in the relative importance they placed on physical attractiveness versus earning capacity in potential mates. Also, Dr. Allgeier and I appeared to have figured out a way to test the assumption held by some other researchers that the gender difference in mate-selection preferences is due to men's and women's unequal access to financial resources. If this explanation was correct, we hypothesized that women who expected to earn the most money themselves would be least concerned with the earning capacity of a potential mate and might place greater emphasis on physical attractiveness because they could afford to do so. To test this notion we needed a large sample of students representing a variety of preferences and expected incomes.

Fortunately Dr. Allgeier was well liked by her colleagues in the psychology department and she had friends who were faculty in other departments as well. We were able to coax several instructors who taught large sections of various courses to allow me to come into their classes, introduce the brief survey, and ask students to take a few minutes to complete it. Data collection then consisted of me running up and down the aisles of large classrooms carrying a box into which students could anonymously throw their completed questionnaires. I felt like an evangelist with a basket collecting contributions from the congregation at a revival meeting. Instead of money, however, I was gathering a resource that was beginning to be equally as important to me: empirical data.

In the span of one week I had questionnaires from about 1,000 college students. I beamed with pride over such a substantial haul in such a short period of time. However, one more task lay ahead: entering the ratings into a computer file so that we could analyze them statistically. I didn't look forward to the prospect of typing several thousand numbers into a computer; in fact, I have yet to meet *anyone* who enjoys data entry. Usually the job falls to the person lowest on the research totem pole, which, when you're a graduate student, usually means you. So, between my classes and homework, I began chipping away at entering data. It seemed to take longer to input the data than it did to collect it (the reverse of the old rule "time flies when you're having fun"). After I finished the tedious chore, I learned, much to my chagrin, that there was a small staff on campus whose job it was to enter data for faculty and students conducting research.

Consistent with David Buss's findings, the students on our campus displayed noticeable gender differences. Men rated "good looks" as more important in a potential mate than did women, whereas women rated "good financial prospect" as more important than did men. However, the other results surprised us. When we correlated women's expected income with their ratings of "good financial prospect," the correlation was positive rather than negative! Critics of Buss's findings hypothesized that as women's personal income increased, their ratings of the earning capacity of potential spouses would decrease. We found just the opposite: Those women who expected to earn the most after graduating from college actually gave the highest ratings to the mate characteristic "good financial prospect." Among men, expected income after graduating from college was totally unrelated to ratings of "good looks" or "good financial prospect" in a potential mate.

What About Mate Preferences Among "Real People"?

Our findings among college students were interesting; women's expected income and the emphasis they placed on the earning capacity of potential mates were positively related. However, college students are not representative of the community at large. So, whenever one uses a college-student sample, one is always left with questions regarding the generalizability of findings to people other than college students. In graduate school, when discussing such findings with classmates, we would jokingly ponder whether our findings from college student samples would hold up with samples of "real people." When it came to mate-selection preferences, perhaps college students can afford to be less concerned with the earning capacity of potential mates because they themselves expect to earn a college degree. What about women who do not have means of self-support, those who do not have an education or a job? To satisfy our intellectual curiosity, Dr. Allgeier and I decided to administer the same questionnaire to men and women in the general community who represented a wider range in age and socioeconomic status.

Accessing a community sample is always difficult. How can one locate typical community members during a time when they might be willing to take a few minutes to complete a questionnaire? After pondering the question for some time, our best answer was to catch people while they were out shopping. Accordingly, we recruited ten undergraduate and graduate students to assist us in approaching people in the local grocery stores and shopping mall and asking them to complete our brief, anonymous survey on mate-selection preferences. The only change we made in the questionnaire had to do with expected personal income. Rather than asking how much money they expected to earn after graduating from college, we asked how much they expected to earn during the next year.

Preparing to collect the data proved to be somewhat challenging. One of the many chores involved meeting with the manager of each grocery store to make my pitch for allowing us to come in and accost their customers. After checking with their regional or corporate managers, the two largest grocery stores in town granted us permission to come in one Saturday afternoon to collect data. It seemed that everything was going to work out well, until the data collection day drew closer. Then, one week before the upcoming event, I was horrified to learn that, at one particular store, the manager recently had left the corporation and the interim manager had never heard of me or our project. Thankfully, after a few frantic telephone calls to the corporate headquarters, we again secured permission to gather data on our designated Saturday.

On the day of data collection, we divided our forces among the two grocery stores and the local shopping mall. The scene in the grocery stores was a sight to behold. Several research assistants, complete with name tags and clipboards, approached customers as they milled about the produce and frozen-food sections of the stores. Although the prospect of taking a mate-selection survey in a grocery store must have seemed strange, people were generally friendly and cooperative and took a few minutes out of their shopping experience to stand among the broccoli, potatoes, or frozen desserts and share with us what they most valued in potential mates.

I led the group collecting data at the shopping mall, which seemed like an ideal place to survey adults. There was a food court in the center of the mall where people sat to have a bite to eat or something to drink. Because they were already sitting down and not doing too much, most people we approached agreed to complete a questionnaire. In my zealous pursuit of data, however, I failed to anticipate how we might be perceived by the store owners or mall management. In my mind, the food court in the shopping mall was a public place. Was I wrong! We had been collecting data for only a short time when a mall security guard singled me out as the ringleader and asked me to join him in a trip to the mall manager's office. There, I was informed that, indeed, permission is needed to approach mall customers and that this particular shopping mall did not allow solicitation of any kind. In short, we were to leave the premises as soon as possible. With some degree of embarrassment, I rounded up the troops and left the mall under escort of the security guard. (I guess he figured psychology researchers were a shifty bunch, not to be trusted—he seemed to be afraid we would set up shop in the parking lot).

Data collection in the grocery stores went well, but because of the shopping mall fiasco, we did not get to approach as many research participants as we had hoped. We decided to add one session of data collection in a different setting. In a nearby city (about 30 minutes away) there was a park downtown on the banks of a river. When the weather was pleasant, people tended to congregate there on their lunch breaks. A couple of other graduate students and I took our clipboards and surveys to the riverfront park and began approaching people with my spiel about who we were and the nature of our study. We were sure that the park was a public place and that permission was not needed to approach park goers.

However, data collection at the park posed other potential problems. To ensure that everyone present had an equal opportunity of being sampled for our study, I tried to approach every person who came into my immediate vicinity. As I approached one particular man, I realized that he was a homeless person who apparently lived in or around the park. Still I continued my speech until he interrupted me by ranting, "I'm not a registered voter! I'm not a registered voter, I tell you!" My first impulse was to explain that one did not have to be a registered voter to participate in our study, but because his ranting was causing an unpleasant scene, I simply responded, "I'm sorry to hear that," and walked away.

As a result of our concerted efforts, we collected responses from 282 community members ranging from 18 to 78 years of age. Similar to the findings with our college student sample, men placed significantly more emphasis on "good looks" in potential mates than did women, whereas women rated "good financial prospect" as significantly more important in a potential mate than did men. Also similar to the college students, men's personal income was unrelated to their ratings of either "good looks" or "good financial prospect." In contrast to the college women, for women in the community sample, personal income was totally unrelated to the importance they placed on the earning capacity of potential mates. We also found that age of the respondent was unrelated to ratings of "good looks" and "good financial prospect" in a potential mate.

The apparent gender difference in the value placed on physical attractiveness versus earning capacity in potential mates was consistent across samples of college students and community members of various ages. Also, women's greater emphasis on the earning capacity of potential mates seemed not to be the result of women perceiving that they would be unable to support themselves financially.

"Single White Male Seeking . . . "

By the time we completed our small mate-preference study with college students and community members, I was hooked on research. It was an activity that I truly found intellectually stimulating and challenging, and there was great excitement in the prospect of testing ideas and sorting out findings.

Even though I had grown to enjoy the research process thoroughly, I was trying to complete a doctoral degree in clinical psychology and I did not have a lot of time for conducting research. Plus, the reward in conducting research comes when one has data to analyze and results to ponder—actually getting research participants to complete surveys is a mundane, if necessary, part of the research process. I began trying to think of a way I could continue to investigate gender differences in mate-selection preferences without having to recruit research participants and without relying on a college student sample. The answer turned out to be as near as the personal ads printed in the Sunday issue of the newspaper.

Nearly every major newspaper prints personal advertisements, and it seems that many people read them, even if "just for fun." Although many people consider them a suspect way to meet the individual of one's dreams, a single issue of some large newspapers contains literally hundreds of personal ads. Personal ads start with the assumption that the writer wishes to meet someone for friendship, dating, or marriage. Typically such ads include a bit of information about the advertiser and a brief description of the type of person the advertiser hopes to meet. A standard, run-of-the-mill ad might run something like this: "Single white male, good-looking business professional, age 28, looking to meet attractive, single woman, 21 to 28, who is into movies, scuba diving, and quiet dinners. Am tired of blind dates and bar chit-chat. Looking for compatible life partner. I'm eagerly awaiting your reply."

Although the personal ads are typically brief and I could not question the writers of the ads, they do have a high degree of ecological validity. That is, the information conveyed in personal ads comes from real people actually engaged in the mate-selection process. Rather than college students who are completing a questionnaire to obtain course credit, or community members who may agree to complete a survey even though they are married, personal ads are written by people actually in the trenches of courtship. People write personal ads in an attempt to meet the kind of potential mate they are seeking, so one can assume that they are invested in the process of crafting their advertisement to reflect the characteristics they are seeking and the characteristics they think will be most attractive to potential mates. But, how could I use personal advertisements to investigate gender differences in mate-selection preferences?

First, I had to develop a coding scheme for making sense out of the various words advertisers might use to convey similar attributes. For example, I was interested in whether men as compared to women advertisers more often requested physically attractive potential mates. So, I had to decide what words, out of those I encountered in ads, would qualify as meaning "physically attractive." Some of the descriptors I anticipated in advance, whereas others I did not think of until I encountered them in the actual advertisements. For example, I encountered the following descriptors that I considered the equivalent of "physically attractive": attractive, above-average looks, appealing physical appearance, better-than-average looks, beautiful, cute, good looking, good looks, gorgeous, handsome, nice looks, pleasant looking, pretty, stunning, visually appealing.

Based on previous research, I was interested in investigating potential gender differences with regard to the emphasis placed on physical attractiveness, body shape, financial success (or the qualities which are associated with financial success), type of relationship sought, and the age of desired mates. In addition to exploring whether men and women differed in what they sought in potential mates, personal ads allowed the opportunity to test whether men and women differed in the qualities they offered or highlighted in their self-descriptions. For example, are men more likely than women to emphasize their financial success when trying to attract a mate? Are women more likely than men to highlight their physical attractiveness and body shape when trying to attract the attention of male readers?

After securing several issues of three different papers published in Ohio, I ended up with a total of 1,111 different personal ads placed by 630 men and 481 women. The actual coding of the ads took place in my apartment, often while eating my meals or during commercial breaks from my favorite television programs. In many ways the results were remarkably similar to those we had found with the mate-preference questionnaires. Many more men advertisers (24.8%) than women advertisers (6.7%) explicitly requested a physically attractive mate, and more men (25.6%) than women (2.7%) asked for a potential mate who possessed an attractive body shape. Similar to this gender difference, more men (21.3%) than women (8.5%) requested that individuals responding to their ad include a photograph. What about financial resources? Women (12.1%) were much more likely than men (1.1%) to request that potential mates possess financial security, and women (17.3%) were more likely than men (8.4%) to seek mate characteristics related to earning capacity, such as education, intelligence, and ambition.

These findings were very consistent with previous research using surveys. The personal ads, however, offered the advantage of allowing for investigation of the types of characteristics men and women offer to attract potential mates. I was curious whether men and women more often offered the types of characteristics the other gender sought. Interestingly, I found that women advertisers were only slightly more likely than men advertisers to cite physical attractiveness (38.5% vs. 33.2%), but that women were about twice as likely as men to mention their own attractive body shape when trying to attract a potential mate (19.1% vs. 10.5%). When it came to financial resources, men (18.7%) were much more likely than women (5.0%) to describe themselves as financially stable; however, men were only somewhat more likely than women to describe themselves as possessing qualities related to earning capacity (29.4% vs. 23.1%). In general, it appeared that, when trying to attract a potential mate through personal advertisements, men and women emphasized the qualities more valued by the other gender.

The personal ads also allowed for exploration of other variables such as the type of relationship sought and the desired age of potential mates. Interestingly, the proportions of men and women advertisers who sought either dating, a long-term relationship, or marriage did not differ. However, women advertisers were more cautious than men, with women more likely to specify that they were seeking a friend or companion, or a friendship with the possibility of developing a more committed relationship. In contrast, nearly one out of every five men advertisers (19.1%) was seeking an erotic or sexual relationship (compared to only 2 out of 481 women advertisers who were looking for such a relationship). Although most men and women who advertised in the personals clearly were seeking long-term romantic relationships, among those who were not there were marked gender differences in the type of relationship sought (sexual vs. platonic).

Because men placed relatively more emphasis on physical attractiveness and women placed relatively greater value on financial resources and earning capacity, I expected to find gender differences in the desired age of potential mates. Women's physical attractiveness is associated with youthful features, whereas relatively older men are more likely to be financially secure. Accordingly, I expected to find that men would typically desire mates younger than themselves, whereas women would desire relatively older mates. Even though the men advertisers ranged in age from 19 to 79 years and the women advertisers ranged in age from 18 to 75 years, the men advertisers were generally younger than the women advertisers. This finding made sense in that relatively younger men (without financial resources?) and relatively older women (less physically attractive?) seemed to be the most likely to use personal advertisements to begin with.

What about the desired age of potential mates? In personal ads, the advertiser typically states his or her age as well as an age range for the type of mate he or she is hoping to meet (e.g., "seeking woman age 20 to 30"). So, I calculated the upper and lower acceptable age limit relative to the advertiser's own age. In other words, if a 35-year-old male advertiser requested a potential mate age 25 to 40, this advertiser was coded as accepting someone up to ten years younger or five years older than himself. I then graphed the upper and lower acceptable ages for potential mates according to gender and age of the advertiser. A difference between men and women advertisers was apparent. On average, women in their 20s sought a potential mate their own age or up to 10 years older. Women in their 30s or older sought a mate ranging from a few years younger to about seven years older than themselves. In other words, regardless of their own age, women advertisers generally sought a potential mate their own age or older. For men, the relative age desired in mates depended much more on their own age. On average, men in their 20s sought women ranging in age from five years younger to five years older. However, as men advertisers increased in age, they sought women progressively younger than themselves. In fact, among men in their 50s or 60s, the average acceptable *upper* limit for a potential mate was about four years *younger* than the advertiser (and the acceptable lower limit was 15 or more years younger than the advertiser). Regardless of their own age, nearly all of the men advertisers were trying to attract relatively young women.

The analysis of the personal ads confirmed earlier findings based on questionnaires completed by college students and offered an opportunity to investigate other variables not explored in surveys. It was clear that, despite many similarities, men and women prefer some distinctly different characteristics in potential mates. Also, the entire project was a lot of fun. In what other field could someone read through more than 1,000 personal ads all in the name of science?

In Conclusion

For me, conducting research on sexuality-related topics is a primary source of intellectual and professional satisfaction. This is not to say that everyone has been happy with my career choice. My first recollection of such a case involved an undergraduate I was dating during my first year of graduate school. She seemed to find my work interesting but made me swear not to tell her parents that I participated in sex research (apparently to have a research interest in sex would be interpreted as having a sexual interest in their daughter). I also remember attending my first sexuality-related research conference. As other hotel guests boarded the elevator with me, they seemed friendly enough, that is until they noticed the name tag I was wearing that identified me as attending an annual meeting of The Society for the Scientific Study of Sex. At that point all eye contact was broken and the pleasant small talk ceased. I can only imagine the images that might have crossed these innocent hotel guests' minds.

As I have grown accustomed to viewing relationship and sexuality issues through scientific eyes, I sometimes forget that others outside the field may not appreciate my fascination. Recently I was made aware of such a discrepant view when visiting my in-laws. As typical for me, I brought along several research articles I had been looking forward to reading, as well as some statistical results over which I needed to ponder. As I spread out my materials on the floor one quiet evening, my father-in-law remarked, "It sure is a shame they make you work even during the holidays." Up to that point I had forgotten that my involvement in sex research may appear as work to others. To me, however, involvement in research is more akin to a hobby or recreational activity than a chore. Any time the line between work and play becomes blurred, one can become more confident that the correct career path has been chosen. My arrival at this place in my professional life is even more remarkable to me given that I started the process asking, "Why would anyone want to spend their time conducting research?"

Suggested Readings

Allgeier, E. R., & Wiederman, M. W. (1994). How useful is evolutionary psychology for understanding gender differences in human sexuality? *Annual Review of Sex Research, 5,* 218–256.

Buss, D. M. (1994). *The evolution of desire: Strategies of human mating.* New York: Basic.

Ellis, B. (1992). The evolution of sexual attraction: Evaluative mechanisms in women. In J. H. Barkow, L. Cosmides, & J. Tooby (Eds.), *The adapted mind: Evolutionary psychology and the generation of culture* (pp. 267–288). New York: Oxford University Press.

Symons, D. (1979). *Evolution of human sexuality.* New York: Oxford University Press.

Symons, D. (1995). Beauty is in the adaptations of the beholder: The evolutionary psychology of human female sexual attractiveness. In P. R. Abramson & S. D. Pinkerton (Eds.), *Sexual nature, sexual culture* (pp. 80–118). Chicago: University of Chicago Press.

Wiederman, M. W. (1993). Evolved gender differences in mate preferences: Evidence from personal advertisements. *Ethology and Sociobiology, 14,* 331–352.

Wiederman, M. W., & Allgeier, E. R. (1992). Gender differences in mate selection criteria: Sociobiological or socioeconomic explanation? *Ethology and Sociobiology, 13,* 115–124.

Chapter **7**

A Feminist Activist in Sexology

Leonore Tiefer

Leonore Tiefer (Ph.D., University of California, Berkeley) is an independent scholar and clinical psychologist–sexologist in private practice in New York City. Until recently, she was Associate Professor of Urology and Psychiatry at the Albert Einstein College of Medicine, Montefiore Medical Center, in The Bronx, New York. The vicissitudes of life as a sexologist, together with emerging dislocations promoted by the revolution in managed care, however, have catapulted her into a new career phase. She has served as National Coordinator of the Implementation Collective for the Association for Women in Psychology, President of the International Academy of Sex Research, Secretary of the Society for Sex Therapy and Research, and cofounder (in 1991) of the World Research Network on the Sexuality of Women and Girls. She is or has been on the editorial board of every sexological journal, including the new British journal *Sexualities*. She also serves on the Board of Directors of the National Coalition Against Censorship and on the Board of Trustees of the Community Church of New York (Unitarian Universalist).

The Big Picture

The whole thing began with a struggle over shaving my legs. Growing up as a New York girl teenager in the fifties and early sixties, I learned to shave my legs as part of the adolescent rites of passage and thought nothing of it until—*shazaaam*—the women's liberation movement struck me in the early 1970s. Then, whether to shave my legs, like so much else, became part of the struggle to reconcile my personal and working life with my growing understanding of gender politics and my commitment to change.

Shaving my legs helped me understand how "the personal is political." Should I continue to shave my legs because I was used to it and found it hard to get over the self-consciousness associated with unshaven legs? Or should I take feminist theory to heart, "realize" that leg shaving had multiple misogynist meanings, decide that this was an important political issue, and quit shaving?

I quit shaving. The cognitive dissonance over not shaving was too unpleasant, so I stopped shaving my legs somewhere in the mid-1970s. I never really got used to the look or the feel of my furry legs, but I figured feminists were all struggling with one form of change or another and that feeling awkward was part of being in the vanguard of a revolution. I deeply believed that American women's leg shaving was part of the whole scheme of valuing women for their looks and keeping them in thrall to an endless parade of beautification products and services, and I felt that drawing the line was part of being a feminist.

In 1984 a watershed event for American feminists occurred (or, at least so it seemed at the time). Geraldine Ferraro, a member of Congress from New York City, was nominated by the Democratic Party as its candidate for vice president. When (I didn't think too much about "if") she won, she would be a heartbeat away from the presidency. Given the vicissitudes of American life, she could well become president.

I took Ferraro's nomination as a sign that I could resume shaving my legs! Something important had been accomplished by that nomination, and I could celebrate this big feminist triumph by ending my decade-long battle with feminine socialization and social pressure. Shaving my legs didn't seem to be an important statement anymore.

Learning to recognize and resist gender socialization is the story of my life in sex research, too. It sounds easy, it sounds straightforward, but as with leg shaving, it is neither. Higher education and professional and academic careers are largely about doing well within certain prescribed boundaries, and talking too much about politics is not well tolerated. How does one live acceptably within those boundaries while continuing to insist that scientific, educational, and clinical work is political and our professional decisions can make a political difference? Because sexuality is so obviously a contemporary political football, it may be easier for the sexologist to recognize her place in larger political schemes than it may be for the poetry professor or the physicist.

A Feminist in Sexology

The simple way to describe most of my work is to say that I do feminist sexology. For over a quarter century as sexology author, theoretician, researcher, educator, public speaker, sex therapist, and active member of numerous professional organizations, I have been a feminist—a person with political priorities to make the world more fair and more fun for women.

Pursuing this agenda has not been simple and straightforward, although it may sound that way on paper. There is first of all the whole problem of developing a perspective to uncover the subtle and complicated ways in which professional and scientific issues are political. What is it about sexology that needs to be liberated by feminism? That took me years and years to figure out, and maybe the honest thing to say is that now I realize that developing a political perspective is a lifelong and evolving process.

And, once you have the theoretical grasp, there is the question of when and where and how to act. I never got concrete advice on this, and so I have had to figure it out by myself, step by step. Stopping shaving my legs at one point seemed like a big feminist statement. Later I used professional opportunities within sexology to educate and advocate about feminism. Each year is different, and there are new challenges. Should I spend my time writing about this topic or that? What audiences should I speak to? What should I say to each group? What kind of research would be best? How much is too much explicit advocacy?

I've yet to develop a definitive game plan, but one principle I have learned is that the motivation to make feminism a priority must come from elsewhere than the professional career itself. Routine or career-focused tasks can easily fill up one's time unless there are equivalent or stronger obligations from nonsexological feminist sources. So, I have learned to stay connected to as many feminist as sexological organizations, to subscribe to as many feminist as sexology publications, to attend feminist meetings that have nothing to do with sexology, and so on, to help keep my priorities in mind.

Getting into Sex Research

People often ask, "How did you get into sex research?" as if it were a matter of obvious choices. Actually, it wasn't that way at all. First of all, when I was an undergraduate and then a graduate student in psychology there was no clear-cut field of sex research. There was no "career path" to become a sexologist then, and that still remains true to this day.

I got involved in sex research before the feminist movement, and so I was an "insider" in sexology before I ever got political. This is an important insight into my career. I had already established a position and reputation in sexology before the women's movement and women's studies came along. Had I been born just a little later and gotten into feminism before college or graduate school, I doubt if I would have gone into psychology and sexuality. But, I was already a sexologist, and it seemed best to persist and use the position I had.

I attended graduate school in psychology at the University of California, Berkeley, in the 1960s. One of the best known members of the faculty was a comparative psychologist (does that term even exist now?), Dr. Frank A. Beach, with an international reputation based on decades of experiments on mating behaviors in rats, mice, hamsters, and dogs. His goal was to develop concepts and theories that would describe and explain "mammalian sexuality" (rather a large jump from rat copulation, but the farther back you go in psychology the bigger the jumps). I had worked with several other psychology professors without getting very excited by their areas of research, but in the middle 1960s Dr. Beach's laboratory was full of activity, and students and visitors were continually discussing sexual behavior and physiology. Some of his students worked in the psychology building basement laboratory with mice and rats, and a sizable number studied beagles at an outdoor station in the hills above campus. Most everyone conducted experiments on various prenatal and postnatal influences of gonadal hormones on different aspects of animals' sexuality, hoping to contribute to the overall theory.

Dr. Beach, unfortunately, was not at all supportive (at that time) of women conducting the experiments he himself designed, and he would not permit women to work at all with the dogs, but he was perfectly willing to supervise a woman doing her own experiments with rodents in the lab. So, although I had to earn my living throughout graduate school by being a psychology teaching assistant while the men students in Beach's lab got paid directly for working on sex-behavior research, Dr. Beach did pay for animals, test materials, and the like for any experiments I wanted to do that seemed worthwhile.

This misogyny or prejudice of Dr. Beach's is and was no secret, but he was a terrific teacher and brilliant editor, and with the exception of his gender prejudice, he was an excellent role model and mentor. He changed as the times changed, and by the end of his career in the late 1980s, Beach fully supported women students. Thinking back to the 1960s reminds me how much gender prejudice and career obstacles were part of the territory. I didn't really think of Dr. Beach as prejudiced—*that was just how things were.* My experiences in graduate school certainly didn't make me into a feminist. They were just how things were until a new way of understanding came along that reframed these experiences as unjust, as part of a political system, and as something I could do something about.

The first rat sexuality study I completed didn't relate to hormones, and it was, in retrospect, perhaps the least feminist rat sex study ever done! It was a study of the difference in male rats' behavior between a group sex situation (wherein a male was paired in a test arena with five females) as compared with the same male rat's behavior when he was paired with only one partner. Each test continued until "exhaustion," that is, until one hour had passed without the male rat ejaculating. As I recalled, I was more exhausted than the rats most of the time because I had to pay close attention while they could snooze for long intervals! The research focus was entirely on how the situation would affect the male, and my published article doesn't tabulate anything that the female rats did in the test situation. This was typical of animal sex research at the time; the focus was always on the male's behavior and the female's reproductive capacity.

My dissertation was about hormones and mating behavior in hamsters, and its contribution was to attempt to replicate, in another rodent species, some of the rat and mouse findings. Even after I graduated, I continued for several years to study hamsters, playing with different surgical and endocrinological manipulations and always making interpretations of the findings in relation to the larger theory about mammals.

By the time I finished studying at Berkeley I saw myself as a sexologist, in the sense that I read and published in sex-research journals and attended sex-research conferences, although now I would say that almost everything I knew at that point had to do with animals. I had adopted Beach's panmammalian attitude. It wasn't until about ten years later that I decided animal sexology and human sexology were actually only linked for political and rhetorical reasons to provide the study of sexuality with academic credibility through the legitimacy of science. Feminism ultimately persuaded me that the many articles Beach (and I) had written about mammalian patterns didn't really have theoretical or empirical relevance to the things I was interested in about human sexuality. But I am getting ahead of the story.

Feminism Arrives

After getting my Ph.D. degree in experimental psychology in 1969, I became an assistant professor at Colorado State University (CSU) in Fort Collins, Colorado. This was a less prestigious job than I had expected, but women didn't easily get jobs at top schools before 1970, even Phi Beta Kappa women from Berkeley. In Fort Collins I was the only woman in a 27-person department for three years, which wasn't exactly a piece of cake. I was lonely and had more than a little trouble finding a comfortable social role in my department. So, when the first writings and notices about the women's liberation movement came to my attention in Fort Collins in 1972, in part via the hiring of another woman in the psychology department, it wasn't difficult to persuade me to take a look.

What I read made immediate and profound sense, and I rapidly became swept up in the new movement. It provided a persuasive analysis of my situation and experiences, it gave me appealing goals to work toward, and perhaps above all it gave me excited and enthusiastic comrades and teammates all over the world. Although I was still conducting sex research on rodents and teaching experimental and comparative psychology classes, I began eagerly to clip articles about women and feminism from newspapers and magazines and to write letters to their editors. I developed public speaking and organizing skills. I suddenly had dozens of meetings to attend every week to work on short- and long-term projects. I made friends with women professors all over my campus, suddenly seeing linkages where I had seen none before. I read like a madwoman.

In the university and the town, in my psychology classes and social life, with students and colleagues, I began to view the world through the lens of gender. For years, and even to this day, not an hour passes without some feminist issue crossing my mind and my lips. Of course, this is how it was and has been for millions of American women of my generation. I became part of a revolution, and it suited me.

From Animal to Human Sexuality

A crucial moment in my development as a feminist sexologist came in 1973 when I was invited to help plan CSU's first course in human sexuality. It would be team taught, with participants from different departments each giving their discipline's perspective. But something odd happened at the initial organizational meeting. Always on the *qui vive* for sexism in those days, I was offended by the locker-room humor of the faculty member who convened the meeting. I smelled a sexist skunk and decided that this person was going to give a sexuality course over my dead body.

I went to the chairperson of my psychology department and asked permission to give a course in human sexuality the very next semester. This course, limited to 30 students, preempted the team-taught project, and became the talk of the campus. The course was so in demand that the chairperson suggested I offer it every semester forever. Unfortunately, I knew next to nothing about human sexuality!

I asked my old friend Dr. Beach to suggest someone with whom I could study human sexuality during my upcoming sabbatical in 1975–1976. He recommended me to a colleague in the Psychiatry Department of Bellevue Hospital in New York City (my hometown, which I was very glad to be back in), and overnight I was plunged into "human" sexuality, which seemed to mean sexual disorders and dysfunctions. For a year I talked with transsexuals and with couples complaining of sexual problems. I observed interviews of psychiatric patients and honed my own interviewing skills. Of course, I continued to gobble up the new women's liberation literature and to attend feminist events.

By the end of my sabbatical year I was through with hamsters, I was through with Colorado, and I even decided I had had enough of college teaching. I was attracted by the energy, drama, and sense of mission I'd experienced at Bellevue, and it seemed that someone with my research background would have many opportunities to study the sexuality of people in a medical center setting. At the end of the year, I gave my first feminist sexology presentation, and there was no turning back. Along with all his other students, I was invited to a day of sex-research talks in honor of Frank Beach's sixty-fifth birthday celebration in April 1976.[1] Full of feminist energy (read: hope and defiance), I volunteered to give a presentation on "Changing Conceptions of Sex Roles: Impact on Sex Research." I worked very hard on it and put in practically everything I had read in the new women's studies literature. I was the only woman speaker, needless to say.

---

[1]Chapter 9, "An Activist in Sexology," in my collected essays, *Sex Is Not a Natural Act* (Tiefer, 1995) tells this story in greater detail.

Rereading that talk, I am amazed by how many themes I am still working on 20 years later. For example, I observed that sex research was overly preoccupied with genital coupling, as if that constituted the universe of sexuality. I complained about the emphasis on physiology and the neglect of cultural and social variables. I commented on how limited and stereotyped the ideas about men and women were, and I noted how few research methods seemed to be acceptable within sex research. The irony is that these observations I made rather casually 20 years ago relate to themes that are deeply embedded in sexology. It has not been easy to persuade my colleagues that sexology has ideologies and assumptions.

The overt politics of the presentation made Beach angry because he felt that sexology had to steer clear of politics to survive. Now that more has been written about the history of sexology, I understand his reaction better. I am also much more sophisticated about psychology now than I was then, and I understand that my presentation was a way of working out some personal issues with Beach as well as advancing feminist politics. Nevertheless, seizing that opportunity to theorize about gender and sexology marked the beginning of what I now see as my life's work.

The Eighties: Splits in Feminism over Sexuality

I did leave Colorado and animal sex research after that sabbatical year and embarked on a career in human sexology. I learned to do sex therapy, but my background as a psychotherapist was inadequate, so eventually I completed a postdoctoral respecialization program in clinical psychology at New York University. I had little time for research for several years. I discovered that the feminist Association for Women in Psychology (AWP) offered an annual conference that was amazingly different from other academic and professional meetings in its informality, noncompetitiveness, and explicit commitment to a political agenda. AWP became a sanctuary for me, and its conference offered me an annual opportunity to present feminist sexological ideas.

In my "spare time" for a number of years I did a lot of work on issues of rape in New York. I served on a citywide committee that developed a rape evidence collection kit and made sure it was available in every hospital emergency room. From surveys and interviews we had learned that the haphazard way physical evidence (e.g., injuries, semen stains) was noted and collected contributed to the low conviction rate of rapists. A standardized evidence collection kit and instructions made procedures more useful. Even more importantly, our committee provided sensitivity training for hospital personnel and supported volunteer programs for "companions" for rape victims during their traumatic hospital encounters. This was important feminist sexology work for me although I did it by snatching time from my "real" employment.

The 1980s made being a feminist sexologist challenging in other ways. As the decade advanced, it became difficult to be unthinkingly "prosex," just promoting clitoral and whole-body pleasure while advocating that women's interests lay in overcoming the double standard. Feminist discourse turned from advancing the "pleasure" side of sexuality to revealing the "danger" side, to use Carole Vance's memorable phrase. Although rape work was not controversial within feminism, pornography certainly was. As a prosexuality sexologist I found myself at odds for the first time with many feminists and with much feminist theory.

I became active in the feminist debates over pornography through connections I made in the worlds of feminist literature and the humanities. While working as a sex therapist at one hospital and undertaking the NYU retraining, I participated (again in my "spare time" and ultimately for eleven years!) in an extraordinary monthly humanities seminar called "Sex, Gender, and Consumer Culture." Most of the participants were self-employed writers, or academics at various New York–area universities. The seminar subjects had to do with art, history, and journalism—topics completely foreign both to my graduate education and hospital employment. I was the only trained scientist who attended regularly and the only member of a health profession. I often didn't understand the vocabulary and references, but I knew that sexuality was being discussed in social, political, and historical ways I had never come across in my career as "sexologist." Attending that seminar, and reading its papers and books, opened my eyes to whole new domains of sexuality studies. If sexual identities and opportunities were so diverse, what did that mean about sexology's reliance on mammalian universals? How were sexologists themselves part of the construction of sexuality in the twentieth century? I began to think about ways I could use my knowledge of sexology to make a contribution to progressive theory.

One contribution I could make as a sexologist was to affirm that, as a sex therapist and educator, I knew that explicit sexual images could be used (in fact were necessary) to empower women to achieve greater self-respect, assertiveness, and sexual pleasure. I wrote and lectured about this viewpoint and felt that I used my professional knowledge to contribute to my political goals. Moreover, the cross-disciplinary work in the seminar helped me understand how sexological research was used in a political way by the Attorney General's Commission on Pornography (final report published in 1986) to further a repressive agenda. I realized that just as I could use sexological information for progressive ends in the public world, I could also be progressive by bringing new ideas to sexological audiences.

In 1985 I gave a presentation at the International Academy of Sex Research that attempted to tie some feminist and sexologist threads together. I described the events and politics surrounding the Contagious Diseases Acts in England in the 1880s and how a coalition of feminists and other reformers attempted to use journalism-inflamed popular outrage about the seduction of young working women to promote their progressive goals for women.[2] However, partly because of the conservative rhetoric everyone, including the reformers, endorsed, the outcome was that repressive sexual legislation was ultimately passed.

---

[2]This was all taken from Judith R Walkowitz's brilliant and influential 1980 book *Prostitution and Victorian Society: Women, Class and the State* (New York: Cambridge University Press). I had met Judith in the humanities seminar where her book and ideas were often mentioned. I felt confident that Judith knew what she was talking about; whether I could communicate it properly to a nonhistorian, nonfeminist audience was another question!

I argued that in the 1980s, groups in favor of sexual liberalization, such as sexologists, were again being swamped by a repressive political tide and were unwittingly contributing to it by some of their studies. I remember being very nervous about this presentation because history was rarely a topic at sexological meetings and I was very much a newcomer at discussing broad political trends. Nevertheless, as at Beach's party almost ten years prior, I was passionately determined to show how academic ideas about sex and about women were linked to social trends and to insist that we sexologists pay more attention to the real-world consequences of our work.

The 1990s: What's a Sexologist Doing in a Urology Department?

Since 1983 I had held a series of hospital jobs doing sex research, education, and therapy in the world of urology. Urologists, surgeons specializing in conditions of the kidney, bladder, and (mostly) male reproductive organs, were beginning to see many men complaining of sexual problems, especially difficulties with penile erection. As I began to conduct psychological interviews as part of sexual complaint evaluations, I realized that there would be numerous opportunities to conduct research with feminist aspects and to provide clinical services informed by feminism.

The very first study I undertook exemplifies this. I separately interviewed men and their partners and simply asked them to tell me the nature of their sexual problem and its duration. I found large discrepancies between the facts reported by the women and men, which did not surprise me, since feminist research and theory had long suggested that men and women often bring different priorities and goals to their shared sexual lives.

Over the years, I included the patients' wives and other sexual partners in the evaluation process, something which wasn't being routinely done. In my treatment recommendations, I included women's goals along with those of the men patients. I conducted several research studies following up patients who chose various treatments, and I always included the opinions and evaluations of the women. I repeatedly insisted in presentations and publications that it made more sense to view sexual problems from the perspective of both partners rather than focusing simply on sexual problems as malfunctions of organs. This of course makes good clinical sense, but as a feminist I felt that it was worthwhile in and of itself to raise the issues and insights of the women partners to give them more power in their sexual relationships.

Another contribution I could make as a feminist was to broaden the topics in my evaluation interview beyond intercourse function to include issues typically of interest to women: improved communication, intimacy, foreplay, tenderness, women's bodies, women's sexual entitlements, and so on. I think that the men patients and other doctors tolerated my raising such issues because they attributed my interest to my being a woman. That trivializes the politics involved in introducing such topics, but the bottom line was that I was able to promote in my follow-up research, my medical school teaching, and the clinical work itself a broader range of sexual topics.

The most lasting contributions I've been able to make as a feminist are the theoretical essays I've written and presentations I've given about "the medicalization of sexuality," based on my experiences in the urology setting.[3] A few of these have been obviously and explicitly feminist, describing how the interests of women are neglected in contemporary sex research, in the clinical management of sexual problems, and even in the official terminology of sexual problems. In recent years, however, my feminist sexology has expanded beyond the specific advocacy of women's interests to advocate a sociocultural perspective in sexology.

A Broader Feminism

Criticisms about Eurocentrism have made feminists more sensitive to the ways in which gender is only one among many important social dimensions that bear on values and behavior. Women are not *just* women, but are white or Asian women, immigrant or American-born women, lower- or middle-class women, and so on. That is, women have particular social locations and interests, as well as being members of a single class. In the hospital setting where I have worked, for example, I have been able to help women by thinking not just about interests related to their gender that have been neglected but also about issues relating to race, ethnicity, class, immigrant status, language, education, and religious values.

As with so many other kinds of political awareness in my life, this broader awareness of how sexuality is related to sociocultural realities results in large part from continuing to read intensively in new areas of scholarship, such as gay and lesbian studies, cultural studies, and science and technology studies. Years ago I realized that by being book review editor of an academic journal, I could receive publishers' catalogs and many new books, so I have managed to stay book review editor of one journal after another for more than a decade! In addition, I spend hours browsing bookstores and book exhibition sectors of professional conferences with notebook in hand, making lists of interesting new publications, authors, and ideas. Sometimes I think I do this because working in medical centers has kept me out of the academic loop of seminars, conferences, and informal chat, but actually I think I would browse bookstores and scan journals in libraries wherever I worked.

I have tried to bring ideas from broader feminism to sexology. For example, I was recently invited by SIECUS (the Sex Information and Education Council of the United States) to describe my ideas about sexuality and social constructionism to their board of directors and staff. I particularly wanted them to reconsider

---

[3]Most of these are reprinted in *Sex Is Not a Natural Act* (1995), but a lengthy new presentation is forthcoming in the 1997 *Annual Review of Sex Research* titled "The Medicalization of Sexuality: Conceptual, Normative, and Professional Issues."

SIECUS's mission statement, which begins, "SIECUS affirms that sexuality is a natural and healthy part of living. . . ." My politics and scholarship over the past decade have led me to believe that terms such as "natural" and "healthy" serve to locate sexuality within a biological and universalizing discourse that underestimates the influence of race, ethnicity, age, and all the other sociocultural variables. Thinking about sex mostly in psychobiological terms has led, I suggested, to less-effective educational strategies in AIDS prevention and less-effective educational strategies in teen pregnancy than might have resulted from thinking of sex as socially constructed and thus deeply influenced by cultural and regional considerations. "Sex is natural and healthy" had served as a positive image decades ago when SIECUS was founded by a crusading physician-reformer, but I argued that our times called for rhetoric more sensitive to contemporary political realities. I saw this social constructionist, sociocultural point of view as deeply feminist, but it had evolved beyond the usual rhetoric of "women's" interests.

SIECUS had also invited a sociobiologist to present her ideas, largely about the influences of hormones and evolutionary strategies. I think she probably sees herself as a feminist, too, but it was clear that her view of feminism had led her in quite a different direction. By inviting two "experts" with different views on the nature of human sexuality, SIECUS implicitly acknowledged that views about sexuality are political, which in its own way validated my beliefs over the past two decades. Both the sociobiologist and I were academic "experts" on sexuality, but we chose widely different types of information to support our claims.

Finding Myself

When my sexological career began, I adopted without question Frank Beach's perspective that studying rodent sexual patterns was a valid way to make a contribution to understanding mammalian sexuality, which would eventually contribute to making the world a better place. I could probably still defend aspects of this point of view, but it hasn't really worked for me. As I look back, I realize that I have *always* been interested in contemporary politics. My sojourn in animal sexology was the deviant phase!

The women's movement offered me a platform of action and solidarity with others, and this resonated deeply within me. Yes, I had a career that was important to me, and yes, I was intellectually challenged and stimulated by conventional sex research and the life of a professor. But I was probably too much of an iconoclast to have settled into that life permanently. I also think that my return to New York City was inevitable, and that whatever path seemed to lead here most directly would have been the most attractive. Had I started out as a college professor in New York I probably would not have been as ready to throw over the traces when feminism struck.

I am actually turned off by the contemporary psychobabble that stresses "getting in touch" with your "inner self" or some such route to choosing a career or life path because it seems to deny how much of the self is created in social interaction. Thus I am somewhat surprised to find myself writing that my career as a feminist activist in sexology taps into deep personal rivers. In fact, happenstances and accidents have played much of a role in this particular career.

Publishing a book of my collected essays in December 1994 has had a lot to do with seeing themes in my life and work. It seemed an act of considerable hubris to think the world needed such a book, but once the plan was set into motion, I had an opportunity to look for themes in my previous work. This led to seeing more consistency than probably actually existed! Since the book was published I have sought out opportunities in lectures and interviews to promote my central ideas about women and sexuality, further streamlining and distilling a specific message. Now I can say in a way I certainly couldn't several years ago what my work is all about. Maybe eventually I can even get it boiled down to a 30-second soundbite. Just kidding.

An Insider-Outsider

In this treacherously clear light of retrospect, it seems that the struggle over shaving my legs was about learning to make choices and live with the consequences. It was about taking action at one point in time that might later be abandoned. It was about learning how to take a political stand and resist social pressure. It was about trying to deal with the social construction of woman-ness. It was a training opportunity for much that has followed. However it has happened, I am now a designated iconoclast among my sexologist friends, an insider-outsider. They expect me to use political ideas in my research and writing and my evaluation of theirs, and so I will. I still find it a daunting challenge, though, both politically and personally.

Suggested Readings

Ellis, K., Jaker, B., Hunter, N. D., O'Dair, B., & Tallmer, A. (1986). *Caught looking: Feminism, pornography and censorship*. Seattle: Real Comet.

Irvine, J. (1990). *Disorders of desire: Sex and gender in modern America*. Philadelphia: Temple University Press.

Jackson, S., & Scott, S. (Eds.). (1996). *Feminism and sexuality: A reader*. New York: Columbia University Press.

Snitow, A., Stansell, C., Thompson, S. (Eds.). (1983). *Powers of desire: The politics of sexuality*. New York: Monthly Review.

Tiefer, L. (1978). The context and consequences of contemporary sex research: A feminist perspective. In W. McGill, D. Dewsbury, & B. Sachs (Eds.), *Sex and behavior: Status and prospectus*. New York: Plenum.

Tiefer, L. (1995). *Sex is not a natural act, and other essays*. Boulder, CO: Westview.

Vance, C. S. (1984). *Pleasure and danger: Exploring female sexuality*. Boston: Routledge & Kegan Paul.

Chapter **8**

Reconciling Sexual Orientation

Michael R. Stevenson

Michael R. Stevenson (Ph.D., Purdue University) is Professor of Psychological Science at Ball State University, where he served as the Director of Women and Gender Studies from 1988 to 1991. He was recognized as an outstanding teacher in 1984 by the American Psychological Association. He has received a variety of grants and awards. He was named Fulbright Senior Scholar to Indonesia in 1993–1994 and spent 1995–1996 in Washington, D.C., as an American Psychological Association Senior Congressional Fellow. Actively involved in the Society for the Scientific Study of Sexuality, he served as its secretary in 1996. He has also served on the Board of Directors of the Midcontinent Region of the society for several years, becoming president in 1997. Dr. Stevenson is book review editor for *The Journal of Sex Research* and serves on the editorial boards of the *Journal of Men's Studies* and the *Journal of Psychology and Human Sexuality*.

The day after I agreed to write this chapter, the *Washington Post* (April 26, 1996) started a series of articles on Daniel Gajudsek. The front-page headline read, "A Life of Rare Purpose and Passion: Doctor's Work in Exotic Lands Led to Nobel Prize, Suspicions About Relations with Children." The cover story included a delightful 1957 photograph of Gajudsek surrounded by children. It had been taken in New Guinea where he did the work that led to his Nobel Prize for basic research on the neurology and microbiology of a new disease. This work helped to establish the idea of "slow-viruses" as a cause for human disease. His early insights later proved useful to researchers studying other diseases caused by viruses, including AIDS. Over the years, Gajudsek had unofficially adopted more than 50 children on expeditions to the Pacific Islands. He brought them to live at his Maryland home. Now, accused of sexually abusing one of the many youths who had lived with him, his work in New Guinea and his devotion to his adopted family were being questioned.

What, you may ask, does this have to do with sexual orientation or sex science—or me for that matter. Although not an anthropologist, Gajudsek, like any good scientist, was fascinated with the cultures he studied. He became particularly interested in the Anga people and their sexual practices. As is now well documented, the Anga believe that masculinity is fostered by the ingestion of semen. Sometimes referred to as "ritualized homosexuality," it is simply part of their cultural belief system.

Gajudsek's journals reveal his emotional and physical intimacy with the children of Papua New Guinea. "I slept well again, like a bitch with her half dozen pups lying and crawling over her, and I awoke to the dramatic skies of a Papuan morning." Among the Anga, it was common for adult men and young boys to sleep together. However, you can imagine how such behavior would be interpreted outside of this cultural context, particularly in the climate of America's obsession with child sexual abuse.

According to the newspaper reports, a group of people from the National Institutes of Health, where Gajudsek has worked for years, brought some of his journal entries to the attention of the U.S. Senate. The subsequent investigation led to allegations of sexual abuse.

In addition to my interest in sexual orientation, this story caught my eye because I had recently published a report based on my experiences as a Fulbright Senior Scholar in Indonesia. Although very different from Gajudsek's, the article was based on a journal that I had written as a way to document my responses to this life-changing experience and to keep others, back in the United States, informed of my daily life there. Soon after arriving in Indonesia, it became clear that systematic data gathering would be impossible. Any formal research must be cleared by the government, and that takes months. Furthermore, my knowledge of the language was limited, and interviews about sexuality would be difficult to complete through interpreters. In the end, I had to be satisfied with gathering information informally from the people I met and carefully recording their stories in my journal.

My manuscript was published under the purposefully ambiguous title, "Searching for a Gay Identity in Indonesia." On the one hand, it reflects my curiosity about how Indonesian men who have sex with men come to understand their own behavior and identity, as well as what their perceptions tell us about Western theories of gay identity development. On the other hand, the title implies something far more personal about how my own self-concept was influenced by the people I met and the friendships I developed. Keep in mind that I grew up in rural Indiana. I received my degrees from Purdue University, a prominent but conservative research-dominated institution in Indiana. By the time I left for Indonesia, I had been teaching for a decade at Ball State University, also located in the corn fields of Indiana. I had never lived in a major urban area and rarely traveled outside the United States. Need I say that moving to Indonesia was a big step?

Although I will never have the status of a Nobel Prize winner, the attention Gajudsek's work had received made me wonder if my own contributions to the literature on sexual orientation might later come back to haunt me. Although the feminist perspectives I fight so hard to promote show us how important it is to use and incorporate our own experience into our scientific endeavors, in some circumstances there are consequences. At least my journals are stored in a safe place—never to be published.

"Searching for a Gay Identity in Indonesia" begins with this anecdote:

On the plane from Tokyo to Jakarta, I was seated next to a middle-aged Indonesian man and his aunt. Initially, I had the window seat, she sat next to me, and he was on the aisle. He kept asking questions, much like I was told Indonesians would. As soon as he discovered that I am divorced, he really got friendly. After trading seats with his aunt, he told me that he was married and had several children, but that he had been to the States and "knew" what single men did to take care of their needs. He suggested that we should get together. Because I did not yet know where I was staying, he said he would give me his phone number so that I could call him. Although I told him several times that I was not interested, he kept on. At one point he even asked whether I had been circumcised. I kept telling him that his questions were too personal but he continued until I got off the plane. I wondered whether this was going to be typical of Indonesian men. As I relayed this story to others, I was told that although this was not typical, it was not unusual either. (p. 93)

Although I never repeated this particular experience, it did foreshadow a variety of conversations and relationships that taught me a great deal about sexual orientation, my own as well as that of the collective. I often wonder what I would have learned had I responded to this man's questions with some of my own. How often did he approach younger, Western men with these obvious propositions? Does his wife and/or children know about this part of his life? If so, what do they think? If not, why not, or what would happen if they found out? Does he talk about them with other men? The list is nearly endless.

Indonesia consists of a variety of cultures probably more easily distinguished than those in the United States. For example, Indonesians speak many different languages, have different traditions, and different cuisines. So it is senseless to talk about what "Indonesians" think about sexual orientation. This is nearly as true for Americans (even though we are often reluctant to admit it explicitly). Nonetheless, I think it is fair to say that there are at least two generalizations that describe important distinctions between conceptions of sexual orientation in the two countries. Unlike in the United States, in addition to women and men Indonesians recognize a group of people they refer to as *waria,* who are usually working-class males who dress as women and often do sex work for heterosexual male clients. They are visible in the community and are tolerated although not necessarily respected. Second, unlike most Western societies, a variety of traditional cultures in Indonesia accept or even encourage sex between men for at least some of their members. I hasten to add that in contemporary Indonesia, although there are no laws prohibiting homosexuality as there are in much of the United States, Islam, the religion claimed by the majority of Indonesians, clearly prohibits same-sex sexual behavior.

Asian/Western comparisons of concepts of self show that westerners learn to think of themselves as individuals with a consistent identity over time. When gay men say, after coming out, that they have always been gay, they are expressing an implicit desire to conceptualize the self as constant over time. Asian identity, on the other hand, is more relational, more private, and situation or time specific. As a result, sexual behavior can be seen as less indicative of some private immutable concept of self. Erotic interests can then be conceptualized as fluid, not unlike some Western feminist conceptualizations of women's erotic identity.

Unless they had prolonged contact with Western ideas about sexual identity, most of the Indonesians I came in contact with did not conceive of sexual orientation as an identity in the way most Western theorists suggest. They knew that two people of the same sex could engage in sexual behavior, but this did not lead them to conclude that those who engaged in such behavior were different in any other way. Several of the young men I met indicated that they liked sex with men, but when the time came they would probably marry and have children. They did not imply, as westerners might, that they thought of themselves as bisexual, only that there was a time and place for everything; now was the time to enjoy sex with men, and later they would meet their cultural obligations (and reap the rewards) of heterosexual married life.

I would relish the opportunity to return to Indonesia to locate these young men after they have passed the age when they are expected to marry. Such a trip would provide an opportunity to discern how their lives had changed. Would they follow in the footsteps of my seatmate on the plane and have a wife and children as well as boyfriends or brief encounters with other men? Under what circumstances would they develop a Western sense of being gay, perhaps even pursuing a long-term same-sex sexual relationship (as a few of those I met were attempting to do)? Would this even be possible without dramatic changes in the cultural milieu? For those who marry but continue their relations with men, how do they distinguish these behaviors? Do they define their encounters with men as play and intercourse with their wives as duty?

Although sexual theorists might like simple, parsimonious conceptualizations of sexual orientation and sexual identity or unidirectional theories of sexual-identity development, familiarity with how people from other cultures understand their own behavior clearly shows that there are many ways to understand sexual behavior. Recent studies of various groups in the United States show that simple conceptualizations of sexual orientation and sexual identity development do not accurately reflect the rich variation in behavior or self-classification. These inconsistencies also raise questions of unfathomable proportion. For example, as a researcher interested in sexual orientation, how do you define the group "homosexual men"? Do you base this classification on same-sex sexual behavior, as Kinsey advocated? If so, how many same-sex experiences does it take? One? Many? Does it matter if that person also has some history of engaging in sexual behavior with women? Alternatively, perhaps "homosexual men" should include only those who self-identify as "gay" or "queer" or "homosexual." In either scenario (and there are a variety of other possibilities), the research is focused on a different subset of the population of men who have or have had sex with men. Furthermore, the results of the research and the policy and treatment implications of the findings will be drastically altered depending on the operational definitions the researcher chooses.

Most models of gay identity development, based on observations and experiences of Western men (and to a lesser extent women), assume that to be a well-adjusted person who engages in same-sex sexual behavior, one must necessarily adopt a gay identity and experience an increased desire to make this private sense of self known to others. This certainly does not fit the behavior and experiences of the men I met in Indonesia. As I have suggested elsewhere:

> Although this belief may be politically expedient in decreasing anti-gay prejudice or advancing civil rights for sexual minorities, we must not assume that the mental health and development of men who have sex with men rests on coming out as gay. There are inevitably a variety of ways to enjoy and interpret one's own sexual behavior and those must be understood from the participant's point of view (Stevenson, 1995, p. 108).

Heading for Capitol Hill

A few months after my return from Indonesia, my department chair suggested that I apply for a congressional fellowship sponsored by the American Psychological Foundation. I had considered applying for similar fellowships in the past, but I had not been in a position, personally or professionally, to pursue such a placement. At the urging of friends, I applied.

Some time later, much to my delight and surprise, I was informed that I had made the first cut. The next step in the application procedure was to write a briefing memo. The instruction for the assignment read:

> As a Congressional Fellow . . . you have been asked to respond to one of the following requests (your choice). Your boss has a lot of material to

review, so your briefing memo must be limited to two pages (no cheating with appendices, footnotes, etc.).

Of the seven options, I knew immediately which I wanted to answer, but was not sure if it was the politically wise choice. Option 4 read:

> Your boss has been contacted by Speaker Gingrich to garner support for hearings on whether activities or programs funded by the federal government have the effect of "promoting or encouraging" homosexuality. While your boss believes that such programs, if authorized by local school boards and approved by communities that sponsor them, are not the business of the federal government to investigate, he has been receiving considerable pressure from a religious group in his district to participate in an investigation into such "questionable" programs as federally-funded school sexuality education programs. Your boss has asked you to find out if there is any evidence that discussions or presentations on homosexuality encourage children and teens to "experiment" with their sexuality. He is especially interested in scientific evidence about the causes of homosexuality, so he can make an informed decision about this political "hot potato."

Now, here was an assignment I could sink my teeth into. But was it the right choice? Perhaps it would be better to downplay my interest in sexual orientation and my experience teaching courses in human sexuality and emphasize my more general training in developmental psychology by choosing a less controversial topic like the consequences of day care. After weighing the odds, I decided if I was to be chosen for this position, I may as well let them know who they were choosing. I wrote the memo.

The only challenge left was to complete the task as I had been instructed: in "less than 15 hours" and in no more than two pages! How could I condense what I thought should be at least be a 30-page journal article, if not a full-length book, into just two pages. I can now say from experience that this assignment was realistic. During my fellowship, I wrote many brief memos on a variety of topics. Even after working in the Senate for nearly a year, I am still amazed that those making important policy decisions have little firsthand knowledge. The adviser, legislative aide, policy analyst—whatever the title—has a tremendous amount of influence on the process. This also helps explain why policy decisions are often made on the basis of ideology or public opinion rather than science or scholarship.

Much to my satisfaction, I finished the memo (which is included here in the accompanying box). After editing several times, it was two lines too long to fit on two pages. I just could not find anything else to cut, so I admit with some discomfort, I decided to change the font size and play with the margins. After all, there was nothing in the instructions prohibiting this! Not long after, I was invited to Washington, D.C., for an interview. My strategy had worked and I vowed to use the same approach for the interview. I would tell them exactly what I thought, in as diplomatic a fashion as I could muster. It had been years since the last time I

Briefing Memo/APA Congressional Fellowship Application
Michael R. Stevenson (1995)

We have no choice as to whether children are sexually educated because they acquire sex education from birth. Our choices concern the extent to which this education is systematic, comprehensive and accurate. Although children most often want their parents to be their primary source of information about sexuality, parents rarely provide it so this responsibility has been given to schools.

Formal sex education varies from a few hours of instruction on anatomy and menstruation to a semester long course. Only a few have been exposed to systematic and comprehensive programs. Those who argue that sex education is ineffective fail to realize that we have not yet tried comprehensive sex education programs.

Programs generally come in two varieties: Abstinence only programs popular during the Reagan/Bush administration and Postponement and Protection Programs. Abstinence only programs typically prohibit discussion of masturbation, homosexuality, birth control, and abortion. Evaluation data from abstinence only programs show that they may increase sexual behavior by stimulating rebellion rather than decreasing sexual behavior by inspiring responsibility.

Postponement and protection programs do not withhold information and promote the ideal that adolescents should postpone sexual behavior but should be knowledgeable about protection from disease and pregnancy so that when they decide to become sexually active they will be prepared.

These programs have been successful in decreasing the likelihood of participation in sexual activity, particularly for those who are not already sexually active. The programs also increase the likelihood of use of appropriate birth control and disease protection when youths do choose to become active. Such programs are more effective at reaching the goal of decreasing sexual behavior among adolescents than the "just say no" approach.

There are no data on pre-college students concerning same-sex sexual behavior. Data from college students suggest that discussion of homosexuality can decrease prejudice but have no effect on the incidence on homosexual behavior. In other words, discussions of homosexuality can lead students to be more accepting of homosexual behavior in others but do not lead them to experiment with same-sex behavior themselves.

had been interviewed face to face. In fact, I had not done an interview since I was hired by Ball State years earlier.

Needless to say, I was offered the fellowship and eventually came to work on the personal staff of senator Paul Simon. I spent the first several months of the fellowship working on one of the senator's bills that had nothing to do with my interest in sexuality. In many respects, this was a good experience. It gave me the opportunity to learn how quickly I could master new material. After about two weeks of study on the economics and psychology of gambling, I became the staff

Taken together these findings suggest that the "don't tell" approach or the "just say no" approach may lead to reactance among adolescents and greater experimentation whereas talking openly and honestly about the varieties of sexual behavior and identities, including homosexuality, is likely to lead to less experimentation and greater acceptance. Such discussion could also decrease prejudice, victimization, and perhaps even the suicide rate given that a considerable number of adolescent suicides are associated with confusion about sexual identity.

Sexual identity is the process through which people come to understand their sexual attractions and behaviors and incorporate them into their self concepts. Most people grow up with expectations of sexual interest in members of the other sex and most find confirmation of these expectations. Therefore, most adopt a heterosexual role rarely questioning the social expectations of heterosexual attraction, courtship, marriage, and parenthood. Others find that they are uncomfortable in these roles and perhaps that they enjoyed or desired to participate in sexual or gender behaviors that are contradictory to their role expectations. Open discussion of homosexuality and bisexuality would be particularly beneficial for these children and is likely to decrease the amount of experimentation.

Sexual orientation is the result of a complex interaction of environmental, cognitive, and biological factors. There are probably multiple causes and it could be that the causes are different for different people. However, considerable evidence suggests that sexual orientation may be genetically controlled to some degree. Gay men, lesbians and bisexuals are part of a class of people that is discriminated against, so some may have socialization experiences that contribute to the development of a homosexual identity. Many gay and lesbian people report feeling different from others. This realization leads them to try to discover why they feel different, so cognition also plays a role. People often ask whether gay and lesbian people choose their orientation. We can choose whether to engage in sexual behavior and with whom as the data on the effects of postponement and protection sex education programs illustrates. However, we cannot choose whether to be gay or lesbian because we do not have volitional control over who we dream about, who we are attracted to, or how we see the world.

"expert." Perhaps more importantly, becoming responsible for advising the senator in an unfamiliar area allowed me to learn a great deal about the legislative process while working on an issue for which I held few preconceived ideas. Then came the Defense of Marriage Act.

Defending Marriage

The Defense of Marriage Act (DOMA) has two primary provisions. The first exempts states from recognizing marriages between same-sex couples that may occur in other states. The second defines marriage for purposes of federal law. Under DOMA, "marriage" is a legal union between one man and one woman, and "spouse" refers to a person of the other sex who is a husband or a wife.

The sponsors argued that this bill was necessary and timely because of a 1988 Hawaii court case. In 1988, three same-sex couples sued the State of Hawaii, arguing that denying them the right to marry violated the state's constitutional ban on sex discrimination. The state Supreme Court sent the case back to the lower court indicating that the state must demonstrate a compelling interest in denying marriage to these couples. Keep in mind that the final decision in this case was not expected until well into the next legislative session, and the Hawaiian legislature could delay enforcement and could amend the state constitution before same-sex marriages became legal. In spite of these facts, supporters in Congress insisted that this bill must pass now, "before it is too late."

Never before had Congress enacted legislation dealing purely with domestic relations. Family law, including regulations concerning who can marry whom, has always been left to the states on constitutional grounds. Many states (34 as of this writing) were already dealing with the issue of same-sex marriage. Half of these chose not to go forward with legislation.

I jumped at the chance to assist in staffing DOMA for Senator Simon, who was a member of the committee that was responsible for the bill. Staffing an issue for a senator includes being knowledgeable about the issue, participating in meetings where staff from various Senate offices and committees gather to share information and contemplate strategy, and coping with telephone calls and correspondence from constituents and lobbyists on both sides. It can also include drafting legislation or potential amendments and preparing speeches and correspondence. It most certainly involves keeping your boss apprised so he or she always appears knowledgeable. The initial staff meetings were disheartening. Although we agreed that this bill was unfair, politically it might be difficult to vote against. Senator Simon was among the first to speak publicly, taking the position that this was an issue best handled by the states.

The staff's first task was to choose witnesses for a hearing. On Capitol Hill, hearings have two purposes. Sometimes they are intended as situations in which experts have the opportunity to provide information on which Members of Congress may make decisions. However, more often than not they are media events, and witnesses are chosen not for their expertise but for how well what they say will play in the press. In the House, attempts were made by witnesses at hearings to goad the more explosive and conservative Representatives into making statements that they might find embarrassing later. In the Senate, a more sedate and deliberative body, such tactics are less successful.

Scheduling a hearing in the Senate turned out to be complicated. It was scheduled several times and postponed. At one point, after a hearing date had been set, Senator Edward Kennedy pointed out to Senator Orrin Hatch, chair of the committee holding the hearing, that there appeared to be time for a hearing on same-sex marriage but not time to hear testimony on church burnings. At the time it seemed that another southern African American Church burned at least weekly. Hatch, apparently unaware that the hearing date had been set, protested until staff indicated that Kennedy was right. The hearing on DOMA was promptly postponed and one on church burnings scheduled.

Pressure from the Right Wing

Off the Hill, that is, outside of Congress, right-wing groups were working hard to drum up support for DOMA. The "right wing" consists largely of religiously motivated groups that attempt to bring public policy in line with their religious beliefs. Congressional offices continued to hear from constituents. Some were concerned individuals; others were the result of lobbying campaigns. I was responsible for handling the telephone calls, mail, and faxes for Senator Simon.

The Family Research Council, an influential right-wing lobbying organization, staged a lengthy briefing that was televised repeatedly. Their "experts" made a variety of claims. They argued that heredity had little to do with sexual orientation and that "homosexuals" can change if they want to, just like the "ex-gay" man on the panel. They claimed that without DOMA, primary and secondary education would change dramatically. If same-sex marriages were condoned by government, schools would be obliged to teach that homosexuality was OK. Books like "Heather Has Two Mommies" and "Daddy's Roommate" would become part of the school curriculum, and this would have devastating consequences.

These "experts" basically dismissed or at least misinterpreted much of the available research on gay identity development and gay and lesbian mental health. This was the first time I had seen social science research applied in the debate on DOMA. I wondered if these issues would be raised in the context of debate on the Hill or if they would remain in the domain of the media. I watched carefully for the opportunity to correct these misrepresentations and misconceptions.

One Last Chance

I was scheduled to leave the Simon office when the Senate went into recess for the 1996 conventions. Just before they adjourned, Senate Majority Leader Trent Lott announced which bills he intended to take up as soon as the Senate reconvened. DOMA was among them. If the bill could not be kept from coming to the floor altogether, taking it up in early September was to our advantage. The Hawaii court case was expected to begin on September 10, and it would be best to get this over with prior to the trial.

Among my last contributions to the Simon office were two briefing memos that were attempts to clarify two important issues raised during the Senate hearings. My hope was that these memos would be useful to the Senator and my colleagues on the staff when the bill came to the floor for debate. One dealt with same-sex marriages in other countries. The other involved the distinction between sexual orientation and sexual behavior.

At the Senate hearing, witnesses gave the impression that no other culture legally recognized same-sex couples. This is simply false. In 1996, Iceland and Hungary joined Denmark (1989), Norway (1993), and Sweden (1995) by enacting laws that allow civil recognition for gay and lesbian couples. Each has marriage or domestic-partner laws that allow gay or lesbian couples at least some of the same benefits enjoyed by heterosexual married couples.

"Same-sex marriage" and "domestic-partner" laws have different implications. When marriage laws apply regardless of the sex of the partners, everyone is given equal status. Domestic-partner laws, on the other hand, typically provide fewer benefits. Calling the unions of gay and lesbian couples something besides "marriage" may quell some of the fears of those who oppose government recognition of same-sex marriages. This may be a practical approach to gaining at least some benefits or protections for gay and lesbian couples. However, such laws imply second-class status, particularly if they are specific to gays and lesbians.

It was also clear from the Senate hearings that proponents of DOMA confuse "sexual orientation" with "sexual behavior" and that this distinction has implications for the role of volition. Adults of any sexual orientation are capable of making choices about sexual behavior. The same person can make different decisions at different points in life. For example, we encourage young people to postpone certain sexual behaviors until they are older. Some religions expect clergy to abstain from sexual behavior for life. Conventional marriage vows convey a conscious choice to engage in sexual behavior only with one's marriage partner. Although each of these examples implies control over behavior, none suggests that attractions or desires have changed. Heterosexual men don't stop noticing attractive women when they say "I do." Those whose religious commitments require celibacy often struggle to maintain their vows. In other words, we continue to have sexual feelings regardless of whether we choose to act on them.

In contrast, humans do not have volitional control over their sexual orientation. We do not wake up in the morning and decide whether to be sexually attracted to Bob or Brenda. In fact, young people become aware of their sexual desires long before they choose to act on them. Furthermore, claims that sexual orientation can be changed are not supported by research. We can help people inhibit behavior, but attempts to change sexual orientation are generally unsuccessful. If they are motivated to do so, we can, for example, help heterosexual people stop engaging in particular sexual behaviors, but we cannot change their sexual orientation such that they become attracted to people of their own sex.

There is considerable evidence that sexual orientation has a genetic component. The Hawaii court case relies, in part, on this conclusion. Many criticize the behavioral genetics research on this issue and some criticism of individual studies is deserved. However, these same criticisms are appropriately waged against genetic arguments for other characteristics. For disorders like depression or schizophrenia, genetic explanations are welcome, so supportive studies are less likely to be criticized. Research supporting a genetic component to sexual orientation is more harshly criticized because it is politically expedient for those who support discriminatory legislation. Data show that those who believe that genes play a role in sexual orientation are more tolerant in their attitudes toward gays and lesbians in comparison to those who claim that sexual orientation is a choice.

Most importantly, regardless of the extent to which sexual orientation is influenced by genes, gay and lesbian people deserve to be treated like their heterosexual counterparts. Responsible choices concerning sexual behavior should be encouraged. Everyone should be held to the same standard.

No one questions government interest in regulating coercive sexual behavior. Whether it occurs between adults as in rape or with minors as in child sexual abuse, it can have severe consequences for victims. In spite of the fact that most perpetrators of such behavior are heterosexual men, the sex of perpetrators and victims should be irrelevant under the law.

If government has a compelling interest in regulating private, consensual, sexual behavior (and I do not believe that it does!), then laws should apply regardless of the sex of the participants. For example, if the military prohibits consensual extramarital sexual behavior among the enlisted, then this policy should apply regardless of sexual orientation.

More to the point, if government has a compelling interest in promoting lasting relationships (and I believe that it does!), then, again, laws that promote such relationships, like those regulating marriage, should apply regardless of the sex (or the sexual orientation) of those involved.

Epilogue

My return to the university was frustrating. It is very difficult to track legislation from outside the beltway. Outside of Washington I did not have direct access to internal documents and lobbyists. My former colleagues helped when they could by sending E-mail messages and copies of the Congressional Record, but my desire to contribute to the process remained unsatisfied. After considerable political maneuvering, the Senate passed DOMA on September 10, the same day the Hawaii court case was to begin. President Clinton signed it soon thereafter. The new law will undoubtedly be challenged in court and opponents of this policy will continue to work toward introducing some form of domestic-partnership legislation.

My purpose in life is to help people expand their understanding of the world, to change the way they think, and to help them identify the assumptions they make about themselves and about others. The way people think about sexual orientation has implications for their evaluation and understanding of their own behavior and that of others. It also has implications for public policy, for what behaviors the law ignores, promotes, or punishes. Conceptualizing sexual orientation as they do in Indonesia has very different implications for understanding the self and for public policy than the conceptualizations that are currently advocated by gay civil rights groups and sexual scientists in the United States. Perhaps, as Stephanie Riger (1992) has noted, there is some truth to the argument that science helps to create reality, rather than simply discover truth. As my Indonesian friends learn more about Western sexual science, the way they make sense of their own behavior and the way they construct their sexual identity may change. Similarly, if sexual scientists are successful in helping members of Congress, as well as the general public, think more clearly about sexuality, reality will change. Fewer gay, lesbian, and bisexual youth will grow up misunderstood; fewer hate crimes will be perpetuated against members of the lesbian, gay, and bisexual community; and perhaps, just perhaps, government policies will foster healthy relationships regardless of sex or sexual orientation.

Acknowledgements

This chapter was written primarily while I was an American Psychological Association Senior Congressional Fellow working as an adviser to Senator Paul Simon. I am deeply indebted to the Fulbright Scholars Program and to the American Psychological Association Congressional Fellowship Program for the experiences on which this chapter is based.

References

Stevenson, M. R. (1995). Searching for a gay identity in Indonesia. *Journal of Men's Studies, 4*(2), 93–108.

Riger, S. (1992). Epistemological debates, feminist voices: Science, social values, and the study of women. *American Psychologist, 47*(6), 730–740.

Chapter 9

Social Psychology, Jealousy, and Extradyadic Sex

Bram P. Buunk

Abraham P. Buunk (Ph.D., Utrecht University) is Professor and Chair of Social Psychology at the University of Groningen, the Netherlands. Previously he held positions as Lecturer and Senior Lecturer at the University of Nijmegen, the Netherlands. He was a Visiting Professor at Hebrew University, Jerusalem (1986), and Arizona State University (1995). He also was a Fulbright Scholar at the University of California, Los Angeles (1983–1984). He has written and edited 15 books and has published more than 200 scientific articles in the areas of social comparison, social exchange, jealousy, extradyadic sex, occupational stress and burnout, absenteeism, social support, and AIDS prevention. He is a member of the editorial boards of the *European Journal of Social Psychology*, the *Journal of Social and Personal Relationships*, and *Personal Relationships*. He is a nature lover who enjoys jogging, ice skating, hiking, bicycling, and canoeing.

I have to admit that I feel a little out of place among the sex researchers contributing to this book. Most of my work in the past decades has *not* been on sexual behavior but on such issues as social comparison, social exchange, occupational stress and burnout, and social support. Why then, have I accepted the invitation to be a contributor to this book when I consider myself primarily a social psychologist? Well, because jealousy and extradyadic sex (sex with someone other than one's primary partner) are the only topics that I have continued to study from the beginning of my academic career. I may have been "unfaithful" by studying other issues, but I always returned to my first academic love (although the relationship is not as strong as it once was).

Why Sexual Jealousy?

Questions about why I became interested in jealousy and extradyadic sex have been asked at least 143 times. Frankly, there is something exciting about studying a topic that everyone finds fascinating. Even after 25 years of work in this area, I still find that jealousy and extradyadic sex evoke many interesting research questions.

So how *did* I really get into this area? It began toward the end of the 1960s when I was studying at the University of Groningen for my master's degree in psychology. I was hired by Geert Sanders as an assistant on a research project on homosexuality. This project was funded by the Dutch Ministry of Health at a time when homosexuality was becoming a public issue and interest in preventing discrimination against gay and lesbian individuals was growing. The project focused on ways in which individuals became aware of having a homosexual orientation, how they developed an acceptance of their homosexual identity, and how this was related to their family background and social environment. This project was my first direct experience with social psychological research, and it made me realize what a creative experience the process of doing research could be.

Although the project was not concerned with sexual behavior per se, it brought me into contact with the fascinating study of human sexual behavior for the first time. It was a time of great academic freedom, and students could pursue their own interests. I developed a series of brief courses dealing with such topics as sexual education, sexual deviance, alternative lifestyles, and the history of sexuality. I also became a local chair of the Dutch Association for Sexual Reform, a large organization that had been very active in promoting contraception, in particular condoms, in the period after World War II. This was a controversial issue in a society dominated by Protestant and Roman Catholic religions. At the end of the 1960s, with the emergence of the sexual revolution, the Dutch Association for Sexual Reform became a mass movement aimed at changing the existing sexual morale. For a while, I took an active role in this movement.

The sexual revolution seemed to be characterized by rapidly shifting views of what was considered normal. It is particularly noteworthy how much changed during a relatively brief period of time. Premarital sex was still disapproved of when I started college in 1965. My parents taught me to believe it was wrong (I could never understand why feminists claimed men were raised to be sexual!). The whole idea of nonmarital cohabitation did not even occur to me as a possibility. To give an example of the times, it was considered progressive and liberal to approve of marriage between students. Just a few years later, students started to live together in large numbers and to experiment with all kinds of lifestyles. Behaviors that challenged the traditional sexual morality of the heterosexual monogamous marriage, such as open marriage, having multiple relationships simultaneously, nudism, and living in communes, were discussed and sometimes tried out.

Characteristic of this period was a general feeling that sexually the sky was the limit and that what one wanted to change could be changed. There was a general optimism about societal progress, including changes in marriage and the family. Feelings such as jealousy were considered to be culturally determined, and thus easy to eliminate. Possibly there had never before been such a strong conviction that humans could change the world, and their very natures. However, I had seen many people engage in experiments with open relationships; it struck me that jealousy was not so easy to overcome as many proponents of "alternative lifestyles" were suggesting. Therefore, after I got my master's degree in 1971, I became interested in jealousy, in particular sexual jealousy. Were some people more jealous than others? What role did characteristics of the rival play? What was the influence of other situational factors? By coincidence, I came into contact with a publisher, who asked me to write a book on jealousy. I started exploring the literature, and I also interviewed a number of men and women about their jealousy experiences. A number of things still surprised me in rereading this book for the preparation of this chapter. Most importantly, it struck me that even during the "sexual revolution," jealousy was a very intense experience. As one of the interviewees expressed it, "I could drop a nuclear bomb out of jealousy."

Until a few years ago, there were no programs of graduate education like those in the United States in the Netherlands. Obtaining a Ph.D. was usually done by writing a dissertation while being employed as a junior lecturer. Thus, I began working on my dissertation on jealousy as a junior lecturer at the University of Groningen in 1971.

In 1975, I moved to the University of Nijmegen, where I was expected to finish my dissertation within four years. But I had a choice: I could continue with the topic of jealousy, or research a different topic. I chose jealousy primarily because it was an important real-life issue. I also expanded the topic to include the broader issue of extradyadic sexual relationships, in particular, their nature, the motives behind them, and their long-term effects on the primary relationship.

Social Psychology, Sex, and Close Relationships

I see myself primarily as a social psychologist. I may attend a thousand sexology conferences, but I would never define myself primarily as a sexologist. Therefore, when I started my research on jealousy and extradyadic sex, I wanted to study these topics from a social psychological perspective. By doing so, I hoped not only to get a better perspective on jealousy and extradyadic sex but also to contribute to the development and application of social psychological theories. But social psychology seemed far removed from real-life issues in close relationships. Little could be found in social psychology that seemed directly relevant for understanding close relationships in general and jealousy in particular. Nowadays, social psychologists regularly publish laboratory studies examining processes in close relationships, but when I became interested in close relationships, the strong emphasis on laboratory experiments seemed a barrier to studying such relationships. There was a blossoming research tradition on interpersonal attraction, but most of this research focused on attraction in general, more or less ignoring the idea that sexual attraction might be quite different from friendship. Moreover, most research was done on undergraduate students, and I strongly felt, and still feel, that the processes between partners in a long-term marriage are, to put it mildly, quite different from those between students who are just getting to know each other.

However, the times seemed to be changing. I remember my excitement when I first learned about Berscheid and Walster's theory of passionate love that was based on Schachter and Singer's work on social influences on emotion. Here I found a theory that was firmly rooted in social psychology that acknowledged the special nature of romantic attraction. According to Berscheid and Walster, passionate love requires two components; first, a state of physiological *arousal,* due to either positive emotions such as sexual gratification and excitement or negative emotions such as frustration, fear, and rejection; and second, romantic love, which consists of *labeling* this arousal as "passion" or "being in love." Whether such labeling occurs depends on a number of factors, including general notions about what one should feel in the case of passionate love, beliefs about what constitute appropriate partners and circumstances, knowledge about which situations produce which emotions, and self-perception as a romantic person. Nevertheless, despite my enthusiasm about the theory, it bothered me that this theory ignored the basis of the arousal, because it did not explain why people got aroused in the first place. I felt this situation was typical of a lot of social psychological work on attraction: it simply did not get to the basic issues of sexuality and attraction. Fortunately, at the time when I became interested in close relationships, many other social psychologists did too.

Jealousy and Extradyadic Sex

There were many issues that I had to resolve to study extradyadic sex and jealousy. The first problem was: How would one define and measure jealousy? In retrospect this seems to be an easy question, but it was one with which I struggled for quite a while. I began with defining jealousy as a negative emotional response to an attraction between one's partner and a third person. I was not interested in clinical, paranoid, or obsessive forms of jealousy but in jealousy that occurred in response to actual erotic and sexual involvement of a partner with someone else. Because there were no existing measures for jealousy, I developed a number of scales myself. The first was called the *anticipated jealousy scale*. It contained just five items, assessing how people felt they would respond if their partner engaged in specific behaviors with a third person, that is, having a long, established sexual relationship, being in love, having sexual contact, making love occasionally, and flirting. I deliberately did not use the word *jealous* because it had a negative connotation, especially among those who were involved in open marriages. That is, I was not interested in whether individuals would label their feelings as jealousy, but whether individuals did not like their partner's involvement with someone else. The scale is quite reliable, and has proved useful in a number of studies.

The second issue was: What did I really want to know? There was no existing research. All questions were open. That was precisely the problem: How could these questions be narrowed? What would be the most important question to study? This was a particularly problematic issue because, as noted above, there were no social psychological theories of jealousy. Fortunately, when I came across the emerging literature on group sex and mate exchange, I encountered an interesting phenomenon: many people seemed not to be jealous when they were engaging in mate exchange (or "wife swapping" as it was sometimes called before it was politically incorrect to do so). Thus, it seemed that if people had extramarital affairs themselves at the same time their partners had affairs, jealousy was neutralized. Amazingly, given that sexual jealousy can be such an intense emotion, apparently it was possible for people to accept the temporary adultery of their spouses if they had a simultaneous affair themselves. It also became clear, however, that for these same individuals, affairs carried on independently by their spouses would evoke serious jealousy.

The possible neutralizing effect on jealousy of having an extradyadic involvement oneself made a social exchange perspective on jealousy quite relevant. In one variant of social exchange theory, *equity theory,* it is assumed that individuals are concerned with fairness in their relationships, that they want equitable relationships, and that both feeling deprived (e.g., one's partner has an extradyadic affair, but one has not) and feeling advantaged (e.g., one has an affair oneself, but one's partner has not) was associated with distress. Thus, I assumed that because of considerations of reciprocity, people will react with less jealousy when they themselves feel a need to engage in extradyadic sexual behavior. In such a case, it will be felt unfair to manifest jealousy, even when this emotion is felt. By the same token, someone who refrains from extradyadic sex will react more jealously when the partner does engage in such behavior, because the norm of reciprocity is violated.

I collected data by selecting a heterogeneous sample of individuals chosen at random from the telephone book of Nijmegen. These individuals were approached at home. I also recruited participants by giving lectures for various groups, including people active in an ecumenical church and members of the Dutch Federation for Sexual Reform, some of whom had actually been involved in extradyadic sex. I also collected data from college students. My hypothesis was that reciprocity would govern extradyadic behavior. I found indeed that individuals who were open to extradyadic sex themselves were also more willing to tolerate similar behavior by their partners. Of course, this could be a rationalization. Individuals might feel that they would have to be consistent within the same questionnaire by not allowing themselves freedom in contact with the other sex that they would deny to their partners. I therefore contacted the participants again three months later. This follow-up showed that the individuals who scored high on the jealousy scale when they were questioned for the first time scored low on the scale for intended extradyadic involvement when they were questioned three months later, and vice versa; those who scored low on the extradyadic scale when they were questioned first, scored high on the jealousy scale three months later.

However, there is another possible explanation for the "reciprocity effect." Individuals with extradyadic sex experiences may have partners who are similar in this respect. Thus, having a partner who has had extradyadic sex experience in the past could be responsible for a lower level of jealousy because people may gradually get used to it. I found that the more often one's partner had engaged in extradyadic sexual and erotic behaviors, the less jealous one was. However, the data showed that this could not at all account for the reciprocity effect: even when statistically controlling for the number of extradyadic relationships of one's partner, the association between intended involvement and jealousy remained the same. Thus, the reciprocity effect seemed to be a robust phenomenon.

Equity theory has played an important role in my research ever since. Although I moved away from research on close relationships and sexuality when I became a senior lecturer in work and organizational psychology in Nijmegen in the mid-1980s, I have done a number of studies on equity in organizations and in the relationships between supervisors and co-workers. Fortunately, at the same time that I moved into work and organizational psychology, I received a grant from the Netherlands Organization for Scientific Research for a project on justice in close relationships. This made it possible to hire a research assistant, and one of my first graduate students, Nico VanYperen, with whom I developed a productive collaborative relationship. One of the papers that came out of this project was done with Karin Prins on equity and extradyadic sex. The respondents for this study were obtained from an announcement in a newspaper, accompanied by an interview with me. The study was not described as dealing with extradyadic sex. The results were fascinating. Men were, in general, more interested in extradyadic sex, more or less independent of the state of their relationships. Women, however, were more interested in extradyadic sex when they were in inequitable relationships: not only when they felt deprived (putting more into the relationships and receiving less in return than their partners) but also when they felt overbenefited (putting less into the relationship and receiving more in return than their partner). One possible explanation for the finding that overbenefited women were more open to extradyadic sex is that women find it difficult to respect men who are "too good" to them.

Through the collaboration with Karlein Schreurs on her Ph.D. project, equity brought me back to where I started my work on sexology—research on homosexuality. In fact, the papers with Karlein on lesbian relationships were the first I published on homosexuality. To my own surprise, equity appeared to be very important in the intimate relationships of lesbian women. As we expected on the basis of what had been written on lesbian relationships, satisfaction in such relationships appeared to be highly dependent on factors such as the degree of intimacy and dependency. However, we found that independent of such factors, the most satisfying relationships were those in which both partners perceived the relationship to be equitable, emphasizing the importance of equity for understanding intimate behavior.

The Consequences of Extradyadic Relationships

Studying the impact of extradyadic relationships requires finding individuals or their partners or both who had been involved in such relationships. This sounds easier than it was; there is no way to get a representative sample of individuals who are having or have had an extradyadic sexual relationship. One has to rely on a sample of convenience. So, for the major study for my dissertation I again gave lectures for members of the Dutch Association for Sexual Reform and placed announcements in various magazines, stating that I was seeking individuals who, within the past two years, during their marriage or cohabiting relationships, had a sexual relationship with someone else. It worked. Soon, more than 300 individuals had responded. Some did not fulfill the criteria, and during the research process a number of others had to be excluded, but I had a total sample of 250 individuals. Thanks to a grant from the Netherlands Organization for Scientific Research, I had a team of interviewers who went to the homes of the respondents and administered questionnaires. Most participants were couples, and spouses were questioned separately.

The central issue that emerged was the impact of the "most significant" extradyadic relationship upon the marital relationship. In most cases, this relationship had lasted longer than one month. More often than not, the spouse and the extradyadic partner were friends. About 25 percent appeared to feel guilty while having the affair. An interesting discovery was the existence of various ground rules to counter the potentially negative impact of extradyadic relationships upon the primary relationship. I had come across some of these in my reading of the small literature on open marriages and had included a questionnaire to assess them. I could identify a number of different patterns. For instance, some individuals had the agreement that they always had to put their marriages first, others agreed always to consult each other in advance. Still others had different rules: extradyadic relationships were allowed, provided one was discrete about them and did not tell too much. I had devised a questionnaire containing the perceptions that might play a role in jealousy in response to real extradyadic sexual relationships. I emphasized cognitive rather than emotional factors in jealousy. The most important perceptions involved in jealousy appeared to be a feeling of receiving less love and affection than before, competition with the rival, being excluded from the partner's life, and insecurity.

A major issue in this study was how conflicts surrounding the affair were handled. On the basis of theories of conflict management, five types of conflict resolution were distinguished: *pushing-aggression* (forcing one's own interest with little respect for the feelings of the spouse), *avoidance* (physically or emotionally withdrawing from the situation, being unwilling to discuss the situation), *compromise* (trying to find a fair solution, involving concessions by both partners), *soothing* (trying to prevent an open conflict, covering up differences between both partners), and *problem solving* (open and direct communication, exploring causes of the conflict, clarifying misunderstandings). In general, the more jealousy individuals felt, the more they engaged in pushing-aggression, and the less they engaged in problem solving. Jealous men, more than jealous women, engaged in avoidance (emotional and physical withdrawal from the situation), possibly because they were embarrassed about their own jealousy. Especially when the husband had an affair, sex differences in communication were apparent. In this situation, wives reported pushing-aggression as well as problem solving, with husbands showing avoidance and soothing. The way in which conflicts were managed was strongly related to the self-reported effects upon the relationship. The main effect upon the marriage seemed to be an intensification of the marital relationship resulting in an increase in quarrels and conflicts as well as an improvement in satisfaction. These findings are consistent with social psychological research that shows that arousal—whatever its source—can intensify romantic attraction.

Because our information was collected at a single point in time, it might, in part, reflect the desire of participants to present themselves and their marriage in a positive light and be just a passing episode in the marital relationship. To obtain more reliable findings on the impact on the relationship, I did two things. First, I employed a control group design to study how couples who had stayed together after or during the affair differed from couples who had broken up. In this study, I had 44 people who had broken up, and I matched them with 44 people who were still together. Those in the breakup group reported a higher level of relationship dissatisfaction, attributed their own and their partners' extradyadic sexual relationships more to motives of aggression and deprivation, and mentioned a higher level of conflict generated over these relationships than did those who stayed together. However, the two groups did not differ in the number of extradyadic relationships, or in the degree of involvement in the most significant extradyadic relationship. Interestingly, men tended to blame the breakup on their partners' extradyadic sexual relationships more than women did, a result remarkably similar to that found by Kinsey and his colleagues decades earlier.

The second thing I did was to approach a subsample five years later to see what had happened. Had these couples become less jealous? Had they become more open to extradyadic affairs? Remarkably, although attitudes towards extradyadic sex had hardly changed, jealousy had increased and relational satisfaction had decreased. Those who had developed a more negative attitude toward extradyadic sex were less satisfied with their relationship five years earlier, in a general as well as in a sexual sense. Those who had adhered to ground rules that emphasized giving priority to the marital relationship, were now the most happy—in general, they seemed to be able to deal better with the impact of extradyadic sexual relationships.

My dissertation came out in 1980 and was simultaneously published as a book. It generated a lot of media attention. In those days, I was quite naive and responded happily to requests to give interviews for various newspapers. I soon discovered that journalists are not primarily interested in scientific accuracy. Findings were distorted, as was information about my personal life. For instance, one reporter (who had not even interviewed me) published a biased article about the main findings and also stated that my wife and I had often practiced mate exchange. As I was not married at that time, and never had engaged in the behavior, I found these allegations quite annoying. More surprising, however, were some responses from my colleagues. Although the Netherlands is a liberal country, my dissertation evoked considerable controversy. It seemed that treating extradyadic behavior as a topic for scientific investigation and discussion implied that one approved of such behavior. I never felt I did, although it is true that I did not feel the strong moral objections against this behavior that intensely religious people seem to feel. What I did underestimate at that time is that most individuals have instantaneous moral and emotional responses to the topic of extradyadic sex.

The AIDS Crisis: Legitimating Research on Extradyadic Sex

Then came AIDS. Everyone who has been involved professionally with sexology can attest to the dramatic shift from the sexual revolution to the AIDS crisis. In some ways, this was a strong experience for me. As may have become clear, doing research on sexual behavior, especially behaviors such as extradyadic sex, was not explicitly condemned but was still viewed with some suspicion by mainstream social psychologists, even in the Netherlands. Why would one study that? What could be the theoretical and practical significance of it? Why not study a "real" topic such as coalition formation or attitude change that would lend itself to experimental investigation? Suddenly with the AIDS crisis, one did not have to defend oneself any longer for studying sexual behavior; and even promiscuity became a legitimate topic of research. All kinds of issues—how many people had affairs, how many affairs did they have, why did they have them, and did they use condoms while having them—became topics of self-evident relevance.

The AIDS crisis provided funds to study sexual behavior, and because of a number of grants from the Ministry of Health and the Prevention Foundation, we have been able to do a large number of studies on factors affecting safe sex, while studying sexual behavior. One issue Arnold Bakker, a research assistant on this project, and I became interested in was whether the determinants of extradyadic sex before and after the AIDS crisis had stayed largely the same. In the previously mentioned study of jealousy and extradyadic inclinations, I had examined factors affecting the willingness to become involved in extradyadic sex. Arnold and I decided to try to replicate the finding that a facilitative social context was an important predictor of extradyadic sexual behavior.

Because we were fortunate to have collected data in 1977 on the perceived prevalence of extradyadic sex in the reference group (the group one feels one belongs to, whose opinions one feels are important), we were also able to shed light on a theoretical issue in social psychology that had emerged in the period between both studies. In attitude-behavior models in social psychology, norms are usually conceptualized in terms of what one perceives that others in the reference group think one should do. In other words, social norms are defined in terms of social pressure and approval of others who are important to the individual. These are called *injunctive* norms, and are primarily based upon sanctions from the group when deviating from the prevailing group standards. However, even in 1977 I thought that a different type of social influence might play a more important role in extradyadic sex. That is, it may not be as important what others are perceived to *approve,* but rather what others are perceived to *do.*

We reanalyzed the data from 1977 and analyzed the data from a sample questioned in 1992 as part of a study on safer sex. Both samples included a substantial number of individuals who had been involved in extradyadic sex. We explored the normative determinants of the willingness to engage in extradyadic sex should the occasion present itself. We found that the perception that one's friends engaged in extradyadic sex (1977) and that one's friends would engage in extradyadic sex (1992) were strongly related to one's willingness to engage in extradyadic sex.

I had found that individuals, even those who were explicitly open to extradyadic sex, took precautions to reduce negative effects of their behavior upon their primary relationship. The involvement of one's partner in an extradyadic sexual relationship already evokes strong negative reactions in most individuals and is often perceived as a sufficient reason to end the relationship. However, the threat of AIDS has added a new dimension to the impact of extradyadic sexual relationships upon the primary relationship: it makes extradyadic sex of one's partner a potential threat to one's life. In another study, Arnold Bakker and I assessed a number of behavioral responses that might occur when individuals find out that their partners have had unprotected extradyadic sex. First, we assumed that a substantial number of individuals would be so angry and upset that they would turn away from their partners, and may consider ending the relationships. We referred to this response as *angry retreat.* Second, an individual might respond with *accommodation,* that is, adapting to the partner by expressing loyalty and by trying to understand the partner's behavior. Third, an individual might exhibit an *assertive* response, such as by taking precautionary measures such as demanding condom use within the relationship, requiring that the partner take an HIV-antibody test, and demanding that the partner refrain from unprotected extradyadic sex in the future.

Equity theory was again one of the theoretical frameworks that guided the study. However, new directions often arise from coincidental events. At a conference on close relationships, I met Caryl Rusbult, who had given an invited address on her investment model, which, like equity theory, was based on social exchange theory. Caryl had found that high commitment promotes a willingness to accommodate, possibly by inhibiting impulses to react destructively, and by responding constructively when the other partner engages in a behavior that is potentially destructive to the relationship. This led to our hypothesis that when one's partner engaged in unprotected extradyadic sex, accommodation would be particularly characteristic of individuals highly committed to their relationships. The study was conducted with 249 heterosexual adults in the Netherlands and included a substantial number of individuals who had had unprotected sex with a new partner. As we predicted on the basis of equity theory, angry retreat was found among individuals with a low intention to engage in extradyadic sex themselves, whereas assertiveness was common among those with a high intention to use condoms with new sexual partners themselves. Thus, in both cases, individuals expected a similar behavior from their spouses as they had done or would do themselves. As we had predicted, accommodation was characteristic of those high in commitment. Commitment was also the only psychological predictor of the intention to use condoms in extradyadic sexual contacts.

Sex Differences in Jealousy: The Power of the Evolutionary Perspective

Over the years, my research has revealed many sex differences in jealousy. I had done cross-cultural research in seven different nations with Ralph Hupka of California State University. We found that men anticipated being more upset than women if their partners might have sexual fantasies about others. In my research in the Netherlands, I had found that men and women also coped differently with their jealousy. Women were more inclined to feel disappointment and to engage in self-doubt when their partners would have affairs; this was especially true for women with low self-esteem. Women were also more motivated than men to try to get their jealousy under rational control. Moreover, whereas the jealousy of men was unrelated to the number of extradyadic sex partners their wives had had, women seemed to be able to adapt to their spouses' infidelities; they indicated less disappointment in each new instance of adultery. Also intriguing was the finding that cohabiting women were more jealous than married women, a pattern not found among men.

It was Donald Symons' book *The Evolution of Human Sexuality* that put everything in place for me. For me, it became completely clear that an evolutionary perspective could explain most sex differences in sexual behavior. In our evolutionary past, men and women have differed in their sexual strategies to ensure reproductive success. Men could be reproductively successful by impregnating multiple sexual partners, which could explain the stronger male preference for casual extradyadic sex. A more successful strategy for women, who could have only a limited number of offspring, would be cautious and selective mate choice to secure males who would be willing to invest in them and their offspring. This would explain the greater jealousy among cohabiting as opposed to married women. In addition, for men it would have paid off to prevent cuckoldry, as in that case they would prevent investing in offspring that were not their own. This explained my finding that men were more upset when their partners' infidelity was motivated by a desire for variety, and the consistent finding that men were more upset by sexual fantasies by their partners. Moreover, it could explain why women seemed to adapt more easily to the infidelity of their spouses.

Although I was, and still am, fascinated by the evolutionary perspective, at first I found it quite hard to derive empirical studies from this perspective. I found it predominantly an excellent explanation of a plethora of phenomena that could not be explained otherwise. Psychologists such as Doug Kenrick and David Buss have had not only the courage to introduce evolutionary thinking into psychology but also derived testable predictions from evolutionary theory and developed clever paradigms to test these hypotheses. I feel very fortunate that I am collaborating with both of them. David developed a simple paradigm by giving people the choice of what would upset them more, if their partner would have an intense sexual affair with someone else, or if their partner would become emotionally attached to someone else. As evolutionary theory would predict, men were more upset than women about the sexual aspect, and women more upset than men about the emotional aspect. I replicated this finding in the Netherlands.

The evolutionary approach led to another line of research that was consistent with my interest in social comparisons. It struck me how important issues of rivalry, status loss, and competition were to jealousy. Individuals felt they were jealous because the rival was outperforming them on important dimensions, such as being a good listener, and this was especially strong when the primary relationship was falling short on that dimension. Social comparison theory would seem to be an important perspective to understand jealousy, but, unfortunately, because of its vagueness and its central concern with the way individuals evaluate their abilities, this theory was of little direct relevance to jealousy. The emphasis was particularly on comparison choice after having learned one's own score on a test, not on the effects of various kinds of comparisons as they may occur in real life. This last topic has received much more attention recently, and social comparison is now increasingly used to study jealousy. However, social comparison theory is an "empty," "content free" theory. It cannot make predictions about what features of a rival would evoke the most jealousy. And that is where evolutionary theory comes in. In a recent study that was the subject of the master's thesis of Pieternel Dijkstra, we reasoned that as dominance is a more important criterion for mate choice among women than among men, men would evaluate their rival particularly in terms of dominance. On the other hand, as physical attractiveness was more important for men, women would pay particular attention to the attractiveness of the rival. We did an experiment in which volunteers were presented with a hypothetical rival who was, as shown in a picture, either very or moderately attractive and either high or low in dominance. Participants were asked to imagine their partner and the rival flirting with each other. The results were in line with the hypotheses: women's anticipated jealousy was affected by physical attractiveness and men's jealousy by the dominance of the rival. I was excited and amazed about these findings. We are now planning a series of follow-up studies—and I am curious what we are going to find.

A Concluding Note

Thus far, I have found my life as a scientist in general to be very rewarding and fulfilling. Research is often a journey where one does not know the destination, and the journey itself is what makes it worthwhile. And it is a journey that one cannot make on one's own. Writing this chapter made me realize how my professional life has been closely connected with important developments in society and in social psychology—the sexual revolution, the AIDS crisis, the emergence of the field of close relationships within social psychology, and the shift from sociocultural to evolutionary explanations of intimate behavior. It also made me realize how much I have learned from collaborating with many others in the Netherlands and the United States over the past decades, and how much joy this collaboration has brought me. I look forward to the years to come and to working on the many interesting issues generated by the evolutionary perspective.

Suggested Readings

Bringle, R. G., & Buunk, B. (1985). Jealousy and social behavior: A review of personal, relationship, and situational determinants. In P. Shaver (Ed.), *Review of personality and social psychology* (Vol. 6, pp. 241–264). Beverly Hills: Sage.

Buss, D. M. (1994). *The evolution of desire.* New York: Basic.

Buunk, A. P. (1986). Husbands' jealousy. In R. A. Lewis & R. E. Salt (Eds.), *Men in families* (pp. 97–114). Beverly Hills: Sage.

Buunk, B. (1987). Conditions that promote breakups as a consequence of extradyadic involvements. *Journal of Social and Clinical Psychology, 5,* 271–284.

Buunk, B. (1995). Sex, self-esteem, dependency, and extradyadic sexual experience as related to jealousy responses. *Journal of Social and Personal Relationships, 12,* 147–153.

Buunk, B., & Hupka, R. B. (1987). Cross-cultural differences in the elicitation of sexual jealousy. *The Journal of Sex Research, 23,* 12–22.

Buunk, B. P. (1982). Anticipated sexual jealousy: Its relationship to self-esteem, dependency, and reciprocity. *Personality and Social Psychology Bulletin, 8,* 310–316.

Buunk, B. P., & Bakker, A. B. (1995). Extradyadic sex: The role of descriptive and injunctive norms. *The Journal of Sex Research, 32*(4), 313–318.

Buunk, B. P., & Van Driel, B. (1989). *Variant lifestyles and relationships.* Newbury Park, CA: Sage.

Hendrick, C. (Ed.). (1989). *Close relationships.* Newbury Park, CA: Sage.

McKinney, K., & Sprecher, S. (Eds.). (1991). *Sexuality in close relationships.* Hillsdale, NJ: Erlbaum.

Prins, K. S., Buunk, B. P., & VanYperen, N. W. (1993). Equity, normative disapproval and extramarital relationships. *Journal of Social and Personal Relationships, 10,* 39–53.

Salovey, P. (Ed.). (1991). *The psychology of jealousy and envy.* New York: Guilford.

Schreurs, K. S., & Buunk, B. P. (1996). Closeness, autonomy, equity, and relationship satisfaction in Dutch lesbian couples. *Psychology of Women Quarterly, 4,* 577–592.

Symons, D. (1979). *The evolution of human sexuality.* New York: Oxford University Press.

Chapter **10**

"Not Now, Darling, I'm on the Pill": Researching Oral Contraceptives

Cynthia A. Graham

Cynthia A. Graham (Ph.D., McGill University) is Clinical Assistant Professor of Psychiatry and Adjunct Assistant Professor of Psychology at Indiana University. Dr. Graham has been a member of the International Academy of Sex Research since 1994 and has published in the areas of premenstrual changes, menstrual synchrony, and the behavioral effects of steroidal contraceptives. She worked on a World Health Organization project on the effects of oral contraceptives on women's well-being and sexuality. Her clinical work has been mainly in the areas of sex therapy, HIV/AIDS, and premenstrual complaints. She, her husband, and their daughter Rosie (pictured above) enjoy traveling and music.

As a politically active undergraduate involved in women's issues, I was appalled at the lack of attention to women's reproductive health long before I did any research in the area. When my interests became more academic, it was my political and feminist beliefs that most influenced my choice of research topic. The first research I designed was on the effects of social factors on the menstrual cycle. My interest in the effects of oral contraceptives on women's mood and sexuality developed when I was a graduate student in clinical psychology searching for a "clinically relevant" topic to study.

Looking back at my early career goals, I remember that I wanted to be a clinical psychologist from the age of 15. I really had no idea what clinical psychologists *did*, but I had an uncle with whom I was particularly close who was a clinical psychologist. My undergraduate degree was a joint honors B.A. in psychology and philosophy from the University of Stirling in Scotland. This combination was frowned upon by some of the more experimental psychologists in the department. I remember the professor who taught physiological psychology telling me that because I was missing one of his lectures each week (to attend a philosophy seminar), I would probably fail his course! In fact, I found psychology relatively easy and did well (especially in physiological psychology!); philosophy was for me a much more difficult subject.

In the final year, honors students in psychology were required to carry out a research project and dissertation, which was an important part of the overall degree "class" awarded (the equivalent of a GPA). At this time, however, my ambition was to obtain a good honors degree to gain a place on a postgraduate course in clinical psychology, and then to work as a clinician. I believe that if my early research experience had not been so positive, I would have done just that. I was fortunate enough to have excellent research supervisors both for my B.A. (Bill McGrew) and my Ph.D. (Barbara Sherwin): approachable, constructive in their criticism, and very conscientious in their roles as advisers. Both always appeared genuinely interested in what their students were doing, and their encouragement and support were very important to me.

For my undergraduate research project, I looked at the effect of social interaction on the timing of the menstrual cycle, known as menstrual synchrony. Synchronization of menstrual cycles among women occurs when their dates of onset of menstruation shift progressively closer together in time. I first heard about Martha McClintock's study of menstrual synchrony among female college students in a developmental psychology lecture given by Bill McGrew. I became fascinated by this phenomenon and by the possibility that human pheromones might be the underlying mechanism. I wanted to replicate McClintock's findings (her study had been the only one published on human menstrual synchrony), and also to look at the effects of social contact with males on the length of the cycle. I had originally planned to study female prison inmates and had gained permission to do so, but just around the time I was due to start collecting data, the governor of the prison changed her mind; I was told that there was already enough research being done at the prison. After some initial panic, I decided to look at undergraduate students living in residence on a coeducational campus. This was my first experience of collecting prospective menstrual data; the 79 women who took part kept menstrual diaries over four months. A trend toward synchrony was found for close friends, but not for neighbors or randomized pairs, suggesting that the significant factor in menstrual synchrony was the amount of time that individuals spent together, and not similar living conditions. Once my honors thesis was completed, Bill encouraged me to write a paper for publication (something I would *never* have done otherwise). I learned a great deal from working on that first paper with him, and I remember feeling very excited when the paper was accepted by *Psychoneuroendocrinology* (with fewer revisions required than for any paper I've submitted since!).

After working for a year as a research assistant, I was accepted into the postgraduate clinical psychology course at the University of Glasgow. For my dissertation, I carried out another study on menstrual synchrony, this time using a sample of nurses. My aim was to determine whether any relationship existed between menstrual synchrony and (1) the amount of time spent together by close friends, or (2) the use of perfume and deodorants. Similar to my earlier study, the menstrual cycles of close friends were again more synchronized than the cycles of neighbors or randomly chosen pairs of nurses. No relationship was found between the time spent with close friends and the degree of synchrony shown, though almost all of the women spent at least two hours each day with their closest friends. Unfortunately, it wasn't possible to test the hypothesis that perfumes or deodorants influenced synchrony because more than 93 percent of the women reported using deodorants or perfumes at least once daily. The (all male) clinical psychologists who ran the course in Glasgow were extremely disinterested in my research topic. In retrospect, I suspect that they were also embarrassed about it as they were always joking about my "women's" study. But fortunately, Bill McGrew acted as my unofficial supervisor and we later cowrote a chapter based on the results.

Before starting the Ph.D. program in clinical psychology at McGill University, I had already completed postgraduate clinical training in Britain. I had also done two years of clinical work in England, primarily seeing patients presenting such problems as anxiety or depression. In my clinical work, I frequently saw women who reported that their symptoms worsened around the time of menstruation. In reviewing the research literature, I discovered that studies of medical treatments for premenstrual syndrome (PMS) had produced very inconsistent and inconclusive results; moreover, there seemed to be very few controlled studies of the most commonly used therapies (such as the pill).

I was also struck by the fact that so little research had been carried out on the general effects of oral contraceptives (OCs) on well-being and sexuality. In a fascinating biography about John Rock, the man who became known as the "father of the pill," Loretta McLaughlin described the early field trials of the pill carried out in Puerto Rico. According to her account, women in these trials were warned that they might experience side effects such as nausea and headaches during the first few months of pill use, but most of them felt such discomforts were minor compared to the alternative of another pregnancy every year. This suggests a possible reason why so little research was focused on what were regarded as troublesome, but "trivial," side effects: the immense impact that the pill had on the lives of women and the immeasurable positive effects that having an effective, reversible contraceptive method (over which women had control) must have had. However, when one considers that the pill fundamentally alters a woman's hormonal cycle, (not to mention the obvious link between birth control and sexual activity!), it is surprising how little research has investigated possible effects on sexuality. More than 30 years after the pill was introduced, with millions of women using steroidal contraceptives worldwide, most of what we know about their behavioral effects is derived from studies using pills that are no longer in use. Interestingly, although the male contraceptive pill is still in the "development" stage, very early on there were studies designed *specifically* to examine possible effects on (male) sexual interest and functioning. In research carried out into the acceptability of new contraceptive methods for men, there has been an emphasis on possible side effects related to sexuality. I believe that the reasons for this discrepancy are clear: it is considered less important if women experience loss of spontaneous sexual interest, whereas it is assumed that any sexuality-related side effect would not be tolerated by men.

Most of the early studies on OCs, done in the 1960s and early 1970s, assessed contraceptive efficacy and tolerance of the pill (usually defined in terms of tolerance of changes in bleeding patterns); very few set out to study possible behavioral effects. As a consequence, assessment of side effects was often superficial, sometimes restricted to the woman's spontaneous comments. These early investigations suggested that a proportion of women (between 10 and 40 percent) reported adverse changes such as depression and loss of sexual interest after starting the pill; many authors assumed the causes were psychogenic rather than hormonal. Women who complained of "loss of libido" on the pill were said to be characterized by "poor sexual adjustment," an initial negative attitude to the pill, and underlying guilt about practicing birth control. This was only rarely based on any empirical evidence; for example, one paper, published in the early 1960s, suggested that loss of sexual desire might be due to psychological factors because "the female of the species is less predictable and logical, her reactions less subject to exact explanation, and the instinct for motherhood is strong." (Dickinson & Smith, 1963) As a feminist, I was outraged by assumptions such as these, and I remember feeling a kind of missionary zeal about doing research in this badly understudied and socially important area.

Few of these early studies on contraceptive efficacy involved any systematic evaluation of the effects of OCs on menstrual cycle–related symptoms, but nonetheless many reported a "dramatic" improvement in premenstrual symptoms associated with pill use. However, there was usually a subgroup of women who either reported no change or a worsening of PMS. There was seldom any attempt to differentiate between subtypes of premenstrual change or to find predictors of differential response to OC administration. Assessment of symptoms was by retrospective questionnaire or interview, often carried out only at the end of the study period. Another major methodological shortcoming was that none of these studies selected women on the basis of premenstrual complaints, and indeed, pretreatment levels of symptoms were seldom assessed. Finally, a consistent finding in treatment studies of PMS has been a high rate of placebo response (i.e., improvement in response to an inert tablet). Despite this, only three studies on OCs and premenstrual symptoms had been placebo controlled. Indeed, some investigators argued that it was impossible to use placebos in this area because of the ethical problem of exposing women to the risk of pregnancy; others pointed out that placebo controls could be instituted, provided the drugs are not being relied upon for contraceptive purposes.

In addition to the methodological problems in these studies, the early formulations of the pill contained approximately 3 times the amount of synthetic estrogen and 10 to 20 times more progestogen than modern, low-dose OCs. However, research into the early-use effects (i.e., the first few months of pill use) of currently used OCs is extremely sparse, so these early studies, while of questionable relevance, provide the best available evidence.

Ater I identified all of these methodological shortcomings in previous studies, in particular the lack of placebo control and of prospective assessment, the first study I did was an *uncontrolled, retrospective* comparison of the perimenstrual changes reported by pill users and nonusers. However, the aim of this pilot study was to pretest some of the measures to be used in the prospective treatment study I hoped to carry out, as well as to examine possible relationships between subtypes of premenstrual change and variables such as menstrual cycle characteristics and expectations about the pill's effects.

As an idealistic graduate student, I wanted to design a study that would avoid *all* of the above methodological difficulties. There had been no previously published studies that had assessed premenstrual changes prior, and subsequent, to OC use in women whose symptoms are confirmed on prospective (daily) ratings. Most of the recent studies on OCs, involving lower-dose pills, simply compared the incidence of premenstrual symptoms in women who were *established* on the pill with nonpill users. However, this type of study is of limited value because women whose symptoms are exacerbated by OCs or who develop other adverse effects are more likely to discontinue the pill and will have selected themselves out of the "established pill user" group. Because of this (and the likelihood of a significant placebo response), it was important that the study be placebo controlled. I also wanted to increase the probability that any changes seen after OC administration would be due to direct hormonal effects of the treatment. Virtually all of the available evidence on the effects of OCs on premenstrual changes derives from studies in which the pill was being used for contraceptive purposes. As the study I was planning would involve women using nonhormonal methods of contraception, the pill could be introduced as a low-dose hormone rather than as a birth control pill. The purpose of this was to minimize the symbolic effects of taking birth control medication, that is, the knowledge that the pill effectively prevents pregnancy and the sociocultural beliefs about the pill's effects. I was also interested in recruiting only women seeking treatment for moderate to severe premenstrual symptoms. As a number of researchers had demonstrated that retrospective measures tended to inflate the severity of premenstrual symptoms, prospective confirmation of the severity of premenstrual symptoms was important. I decided to use daily ratings of mood and physical and behavioral symptoms (completed throughout the study), and also to include some standardized measures of mood and perimenstrual changes. Finally, the treatment phase had to be a minimum of three months and the pretreatment phase at least one complete menstrual cycle. My aim was to recruit 100 women, so I reckoned that the data-collection phase would take at least 18 months.

I remember very clearly that when I told my adviser, Barbara Sherwin, of my plans she sensibly pointed out that it would add a year onto my Ph.D. But she said this without in any way discouraging me from doing it (and she *was* right about the time it would take!). I wanted to finish my Ph.D. within a reasonable time; part of graduate student lore were horror stories about students taking up to 13 years to complete their theses. I did not want to join their ranks, but I also very much wanted to do this study.

The main aim of this study was to evaluate the effects of a triphasic OC in women seeking treatment for premenstrual complaints. Triphasic OCs were designed to mimic in a crude way the normal menstrual cycle: the ratio of the progestogen to the estrogen is not fixed (as in monophasic pills) but is made to change at least once during each 21-day course of pills. A second aim was to relate the response to OC administration to different subtypes of premenstrual change; if predictors of response to OCs could be identified, this would provide empirical guidelines for treatment.

After a telephone screening interview and a gynecological examination to rule out any contraindications to OC use, women attended an initial interview, during which questionnaires on their menstrual history and perimenstrual changes were completed. They then made daily ratings of mood, physical, and behavioral changes for at least one menstrual cycle before they were randomly assigned to receive three months treatment with either the triphasic OC or the placebo. The study was double-blind, that is, neither the woman nor I knew which treatment was administered until the final debriefing session. Women were required to make monthly visits to the research unit, where they completed various standardized mood questionnaires. During the last month, they gave blood samples, which were tested for estrogen and progesterone levels.

I learned a lot about doing clinical research in this area from carrying out this study. I became aware that the women taking part experienced significant distress and saw their premenstrual symptoms as having a substantial impact on their lives. While recruiting women, I discovered the importance of being accessible at different times of the day and on weekends. This became even more important after a woman was entered into the study, because of the need to schedule appointments at certain times in their cycle and to be available in the event a woman was experiencing worrisome side effects. Interviews often needed to be in the evening because of women's jobs. Frequent personal contact (e.g., telephone reminders about appointments or to send diaries in) was important to maintain interest in the study and increase compliance.

There were practical issues regarding the placebo preparation; as the study was double-blind, the active pills should have been identical in appearance to the placebo. However, the triphasic formulation we were using contained pills of different colors, corresponding to the different dosages. The pharmaceutical company that supplied the OCs was willing to provide the placebo tablets, but only of *one* color. To preserve the double-blind protocol, we had to distribute the pills to the women in sealed brown envelopes; otherwise, I would know whether a woman was receiving the active or inert tablets. The placebos were packaged identically to the active preparation, and because women received either all placebo or all active tablets, there was no way for them to be aware of the difference in color.

Recruitment for this study was originally to be carried out in association with the university's Department of Obstetrics and Gynecology, where the doctors had agreed to pass out information sheets to patients who met our selection criteria. This initially worked well, but after a few weeks, the number of women referred decreased. Despite reminders to the doctors, it became clear that they were not giving out information about the study to their patients. I learned from this that one should not rely upon doctors working in busy clinics to recruit research participants! Any method that directly appealed to women (e.g., posters in gynecology outpatient departments) seemed to work better. In addition, I had to look at other sources of recruitment: public notices, newspaper articles about the study, and some advertisements. As I was looking for a highly selected group of women and had a number of exclusion criteria (e.g., current medical or gynecologic disorder, irregular menstrual cycles), it was necessary to screen a large number. A total of 212 women who were interested in participating underwent an initial telephone screening interview and, of these, 82 women were entered into the study; recruitment took 14 months. Although the attrition rate was fairly high (23 women dropped out, 14 of these because of side effects), this was consistent with previous treatment studies on PMS.

After the data collection was under way, I quickly learned the importance of being organized when running this type of study. Daily ratings of symptoms, kept over a number of months, produce a huge data set that can be quite overwhelming. Thanks to my adviser, I was fortunate enough to have the help of a very competent undergraduate, Natalie Rubin, who worked on the entry of data. Barbara used some of her grant money to pay for this and also for the technicians' fees for blood sampling and the costly hormonal assays. I learned how to use a centrifuge (my contribution to the hormone assays), which made me feel very scientific; after all the subjective self-report assessments, an objective measure! However, after a few months of spinning down blood in the lab at 10 p.m., the glamor wore off. Also, for this particular study, the self-report data were far more informative than the hormonal data.

Briefly, the main treatment results for the study were that there was an overall beneficial effect of *both* treatments on all symptoms; in general, the OC was no better than the placebo. The only two symptoms that showed a greater reduction in the OC group than in the placebo group were bloating and breast pain. The other (unexpected) finding from this study was that women who received the triphasic pill reported decreased sexual interest after starting the pill. This finding was particularly interesting, given that there was no evidence of any adverse effects on mood; in fact, the predominant effect of both the OC and the placebo on mood was one of improvement. Previous studies had pointed to a close link between feelings of well-being and sexuality; these findings suggested that mood and sexual desire were to some extent independent of each other. Also, the fact that the women in our study were not aware that the treatment was an OC suggested that this may have been a direct hormonal effect of the OC on women's sexuality. The possible mechanism for such an effect was unclear, but one possibility was that decreased free testosterone induced by the pill might have had a dampening effect on sexual desire.

One of the other unexpected outcomes was the media attention these findings received when the first article from the study was published. By this time, I was back in Britain and completing my clinical internship. An article appeared in *New Scientist,* a reputable publication, but this was followed by a number of newspaper articles (in the United Kingdom and in North America), and in women's and health magazines. At this stage in my career I was *extremely* naive about the tactics of the British tabloid press. I assumed that journalists would request an interview before writing an article that included direct quotes, and that they would allow me to see a copy of the article before it went to press. The first occasion that a journalist from one of the national newspapers contacted me, I am embarrassed to say that I was flattered and excited about this media attention and chattered on for some time about our research findings. After a lengthy conversation, I asked this journalist if he was considering writing an article; he replied that it would appear in the next day's paper. After this article appeared, other newspapers picked up the story; it seemed to me that each one that came out was more misleading than the last. In our report, we had stressed that the negative effect on sexual interest was a tentative finding (the numbers were small and the sample was a group of women with premenstrual symptomatology), so I was horrified by the sensational headlines (some examples were "Warning! The Pill can ruin your sex life," "Not now, darling, I'm on the pill," and "New safe birth control pill turns you off love"). Apart from making me determined not to speak to journalists from certain British tabloid newspapers ever again, this experience also made me understand how the media focuses on negative information about the pill. None of the articles mentioned the beneficial effects of OCs on the two physical symptoms that we had reported.

After finishing my Ph.D. in Canada, I returned to Britain to live, in part because I missed Scotland but also because after four years in a long-distance relationship, I missed my significant other. I moved to Edinburgh, where I started a full-time clinical job in HIV/AIDS treatment, working in a clinic for sexually transmitted diseases. Although I enjoyed this job and learned a lot, I soon began to miss doing research. I had kept up with the literature in the area and had become more interested in the broader area of the general effects of OCs on women's well-being. I had decided to start looking for another job, and I was keen to do further studies on OCs, but I knew the chances of finding a research position in this area would be slim. Just then a vacancy for a research psychologist to work on a World Health Organization–funded project on OCs came up. This would be a double-blind, placebo-controlled study of combined and progestogen-only OCs on well-being and sexuality of women from two contrasting cultures: Edinburgh, Scotland, and Manila, Philippines. The study design was very similar to my Ph.D. study, and it was exactly the area I had hoped to do postdoctoral research in. There was one big problem: the principal investigator for the project was my significant other, who was by then my husband. I knew that I was well qualified for the job, but I nonetheless spent weeks agonizing over the decision about whether to apply. I had no worries about working with John (in fact we work well together), but I was concerned about how other people would view this and apprehensive about how members of his research team would react to me. Around this time I thought (not for the first or last time) how much I wished that John worked in another research area. The fact that he is quite senior to me makes it more difficult. However, there are benefits to sharing similar research interests, such as being able to discuss ideas and ask for *honest* feedback on drafts of papers. Besides, we would never have met if we didn't work in the same area. In the end I could not resist applying; the fact that this was only a two-year post made my decision easier.

Our aim in this study was to distinguish between the direct hormonal effects of steroids and the psychological reactions to OCs as a method of fertility control. To achieve this, it was necessary to involve volunteer women who had either been sterilized or whose partners had been vasectomized, so that no placebo control was possible. Also, women would not be taking the steroids as a contraceptive, so factors such as personality characteristics, which affect the choice of contraceptive method, attitudes toward contraception, and so on, would not be involved. Women were randomly assigned to one of three treatment groups: low-dose "combined" OC (these contain both a synthetic estrogen and progestogen), progestogen-only OC (containing no estrogen), and placebo. Low-dose combined OCs are the most commonly used type of pill and we chose to study progestogen-only pills because although they are widely used in developing countries, there has been virtually no research on their behavioral effects. The study procedure also was similar in many respects to my Ph.D. study. Before starting on pills, the women were comprehensively assessed for a minimum of one menstrual cycle to provide a baseline, and treatment continued for four months. We were interested in relating any adverse effects to pill type and to prepill characteristics of the women (such as history of perimenstrual mood change or of depressive illness). A combination of daily self-ratings, questionnaires, and interview responses were used. One of the most important measures was a detailed interview of sexual functioning, assessing not only activity and enjoyment but initiation, arousal, sexual difficulties, and so on. Women kept diaries to record any sexual activity and rated their spontaneous sexual interest.

One of the first problems I encountered, only weeks into the job, involved the training period organized for the research workers in Edinburgh and Manila. The Manila research group visited Edinburgh for two weeks, during which all aspects of the procedure and measures were reviewed and practice interviews were done by both research groups. Although the protocol stated that the research psychologist in Edinburgh would organize this training, my impression was that the Manila researchers expected the senior, male, medically-trained member of our group (my husband) to take charge of this. I found this difficult because I had spent a lot of time working on these training sessions. In hindsight I think that I should have anticipated that the huge cultural differences between our research groups would have an influence on our collaborative research. For example, communicating with the Manila group was fraught with difficulties: trying to send faxes was an exercise in frustration tolerance, and anything sent by mail took weeks. Being quite organized and a little obsessional, I found their more relaxed attitude in responding to my efforts at communication quite trying. Since the study has been completed, I have learned a little more about the Filipino culture and realize that I was more than a little intolerant of the cultural differences.

In the study protocol, two main difficulties were anticipated. First, we were concerned about the likely selection bias that would result from our use of volunteers willing to take OCs when they had no need for contraception. The specific concern was that women who had experienced any difficulties taking OCs in the past would not participate in the study. Although we have no way of knowing how many women declined to enter in the study for this reason, we did obtain details about previous OC use. Of those women who had previously used the pill, there were sizable proportions of women who reported that they had either changed to a different type of OC or discontinued the method because of side effects. A small percentage of past pill users also reported a worsening of premenstrual symptoms on OCs.

Another major worry at the start was that we wouldn't be able to persuade women to take part; in fact some members of the World Health Organization (WHO) steering committee were extremely skeptical about our ability to recruit sufficient volunteers in the time available. Asking women who had been sterilized to take a contraceptive pill for five months, keep daily ratings and menstrual records, and complete questionnaires and lengthy interviews (on four occasions) did seem a lot to ask. Moreover, many of the assessments involved sensitive questions; there was the detailed sexuality interview, and daily ratings included items on masturbation and sexual interest. In Edinburgh most of the recruitment of women who had been sterilized took place immediately poststerilization (actually on the hospital ward). The reason for this was that in Edinburgh women admitted for sterilization did not normally attend any preoperative or postoperative appointments. This was in contrast to the procedure followed for men requesting vasectomy, where a prevasectomy counselling appointment, involving the man's partner, was routine. I initially felt apprehensive about approaching women as they lay in their hospital beds, in the hour or two after they had surgery (although at this time women were only given an information sheet about the study and asked for permission to contact them in two to three weeks time). However, women seemed to find this a welcome distraction and were often eager to talk. Many had questions about the sterilization procedure and its aftereffects, which they had not had the opportunity to ask.

Despite the initial concerns, recruitment proceeded well in both centers, and I was impressed by the motivation of the women who participated in the study. Although there was a financial incentive provided, it was clear to me that the majority of women took part for altruistic reasons; some mentioned their belief that there should be more research carried out in this area, others wanted to "improve the pill for future generations of women." Other frequently cited reasons for participating we classified into a "benefit to self" category; these included responses such as "found it interesting" and "helps you to understand yourself." The motivation of these women was reflected in the conscientious way most of them kept the daily ratings and questionnaires. I believe that many researchers underestimate people's motivation to help with research and also their interest in finding out more about themselves and discussing topics that are usually taboo. Providing time is available for establishing rapport, the justification for asking intimate questions made clear, and confidentiality assured, I think that most people welcome the opportunity to talk about issues important to them, but which they rarely discuss with others (such as their sexual relationships).

Our request to recruit an additional 30 women (15 in each center) presented us with another obstacle. We were required to submit a progress report to the WHO steering committee. The study had been proceeding well, and recruitment had been under way for nine months, so we were not apprehensive about the outcome of this meeting. But one new male member of the steering committee, who had not been involved in the initial funding of the study, expressed the view that the study was "unethical" and should be immediately discontinued. His reasoning was that there were risks involved in taking OCs and no benefit to the women from taking part. We appealed by pointing out our careful screening procedures: prior to a woman entering the study, we had to receive a letter signed by her doctor confirming her eligibility. Then, at the initial screening interview, we completed a detailed checklist to identify women for whom OCs would be contraindicated and took a blood-pressure reading. In Edinburgh we also decided to exclude all women over 35 years of age who smoked, whereas this is usually deemed a relative (rather than an absolute) contraindication. Although the behavioral effects of OCs have been neglected, research into their *physical* effects, and the risk factors associated with them, has been extensive. None of the women who were entered into the study had any contraindications to pill use. As far as we were concerned, it was ethically doubtful to have allowed millions of women to use OCs, many for much of their reproductive lives, without careful evaluation of short- and long-term effects on mood and sexuality. Also, it seemed to us that women should have the opportunity to be altruistic if they have been informed of the very small risks involved.

In the end, our request to recruit additional women was approved. Recruitment continued until 75 women had been entered in each center (i.e., 150 in total). To obtain these numbers, a total of 436 women were approached and asked to take part; the primary reasons for this were exclusions at the initial screening (e.g., medical contraindications, currently breastfeeding).

Most of the interviews in Edinburgh were completed in the women's homes; the only exception was when conditions of privacy could not be ensured. There were occasional awkward moments—for example, when a woman's husband was at home and didn't seem inclined to leave the room when the interview began. I was faced with the dilemma of whether to ask him to leave his own living room, or hope that this wife would suggest that we go elsewhere to do the interview. I completed all the (300-plus) interviews. Many of the interviews took place in the evening and involved traveling up to 60 miles around southeast and central Scotland, where I frequently got lost. Many of the women lived in working-class "housing estates"; these are low-cost, state-owned housing schemes, often with significant drug and crime problems. I often wished I had a car phone.

The importance of personal contact with women taking part was again underlined by our experience in this study. In both centers, daily diaries were collected at two-week intervals. In Edinburgh, if we did not receive diaries from a woman, we would telephone to remind her. All of the women were encouraged to contact us in the event they had queries or anxiety about any changes experienced. Although the study was double-blind, it was important that this did not deter any woman from calling us if she had side effects that concerned her.

Of the 150 women who started the treatment phase, there were only four dropouts. A number of women who completed the study *had* experienced negative side effects (particularly bleeding irregularities in the group receiving the progestogen-only pill). I believe they persisted because they considered the research was important.

At the completion of the 16-week treatment, all women were told which treatment they had received, but before they were told they were asked to guess whether they had taken an active pill or a placebo. The occurrence of side effects with OCs (particularly effects such as breakthrough bleeding) can make it difficult to preserve the double-blind aspect of the study. The majority of women who received an active pill did guess correctly, but of the placebo group, 36 percent in Edinburgh and 20 percent in Manila believed that they had received an OC. Early on I learned the importance of sensitive debriefing. The first couple of women who completed the study had experienced an improvement in various physical symptoms (such as migraine headaches) after they started on treatment. They were convinced that they had been taking an active pill for four months; I had to tell them that in fact they had received a placebo. Understandably, these women initially felt quite embarrassed and also puzzled about the reason for the improvement in their symptoms. It was important to spend time with women during the final interview to discuss the importance of placebo response in other areas of medicine, and also to check back with them over the following few weeks. For example, I discussed some of the medical conditions in which placebo effects have been observed, such as angina, hypertension, rheumatoid arthritis, and pain symptoms. Although a placebo response is often understood as a "psychological" response, I would point out that there is evidence that biological mechanisms might be involved, such as placebo-induced release of endogenous opioids, which relieve pain.

Once the data were analyzed, I was responsible for writing a full report for WHO. Because of the volume of data, this was not dissimilar to writing a thesis. A number of interesting results came from the study. The baseline comparisons between the Edinburgh and the Manila women produced some striking differences, particularly in various aspects of sexuality. The majority of Edinburgh women described enjoyable sexual relationships, associated with relatively high levels of sexual interest, preparedness to initiate lovemaking, and feeling "close and comfortable" with their partners during lovemaking. The Manila women, while reporting a somewhat higher frequency of sexual intercourse, were less likely to initiate, had less sexual interest, enjoyed lovemaking less, and were less likely to feel "close and comfortable" with their partners during sexual activity.

The most striking treatment effect involved sexuality, in particular sexual interest. There was a negative effect of the combined OC (COC) on sexual interest, but confined to the Edinburgh women. Twelve of the 25 women in the COC group in Edinburgh reported the side effect of reduced sexual interest. There was also some suggestion of negative mood change in this pill group, which was evident in both Edinburgh and Manila. The progestogen-only pill was associated with no negative effects on sexuality and some improvement in well-being in both centers. In presenting these results, we had to attempt some explanation of the discrepancy in the effects of the COC between the two centers. One possibility was the substantial differences between the two centers in their reported sexual experiences in the baseline month: there was simply more scope for negative change in the Edinburgh women. However, we also had to consider whether the methods of assessment may have been less appropriate and less valid for the Manila women. I would speculate that there were real differences between the two samples. The average level of sexual interest in the Manila sample was equivalent to the lowest level of interest reported by the women in the Edinburgh COC group who experienced a significant drop in sexual desire. Clearly, there were cultural differences in gender roles and relationships between Scotland and the Philippines, with relationships more male dominated in Manila and women less likely to take the initiative in sexual relations.

We were excited by these interesting and potentially important results, but the WHO Steering Committee—now with a completely different membership than the one sponsoring the study—were very worried that a great deal would be made out of the results, in particular that they would receive the kind of media attention that my earlier study had. My own feeling was that they also did not like the results, in particular the finding that during the baseline, women in Edinburgh appeared to have more enjoyable sexual relationships than their Manila counterparts. They were also concerned about the generalizability of these findings (even though this study was the largest of its kind). In writing the results for publication, we were very cautious in our conclusions. For example, we pointed out that because we were interested in assessing the direct hormonal effects of the OC, we should not assume that similar results would be found in women who are starting on OCs for contraceptive purposes. However, given the fact that the highest discontinuation rates for OCs are in the first few months of use and that the proportion of women who stop because of side effects is not known, we also believed that possible adverse effects on sexuality warranted further attention.

Since the completion of the WHO study, there have been a number of major changes in my personal and professional life. In 1995 our daughter, Rosie, was born; when she was two months old, John and I both left our respective jobs in Scotland, sold our flat, and moved to Bloomington, Indiana (all my students in Edinburgh warned me about my high life-events score). We have now been living in the States for one year and are probably just getting over the culture shock. I recently started work at Indiana University (as clinical assistant professor in the Department of Psychiatry and adjunct assistant professor in the Department of Psychology). I plan to continue research in the area of OCs and sexuality and will also be teaching a new Human Sexuality course, which I am excited about. I am currently a coinvestigator (in collaboration with colleagues from the Kinsey Institute) on a study assessing prepill characteristics (such as sexual experience and attitudes, contraceptive history and risk taking, motivation for parenthood, etc.). The aim of this study is to see if these characteristics of women predict acceptability of and continuation with the method. In the protocol for the WHO study, there were two research studies outlined: one on the direct hormonal effects of OCs, and the second on the psychological effects of using this type of contraceptive method. The aim of the second study is to assess carefully the psychological, sexual, and menstrual-cycle characteristics of women starting on OCs for the first time. We will monitor their reaction to and continuation with these methods over the first few months of use. This is the objective of the current study being carried out.

To conclude, there has recently been a swing toward greater concern about many aspects of women's reproductive health. In spite of this, the attention paid to sexual aspects of fertility control in women has been minimal, and even today relatively little work is being done in this area. Yet this is an issue of worldwide importance. One of the major obstacles to world population control, particularly in the developing countries, is the low level of acceptance of available contraceptive methods, rather than the lack of a suitable technology. So my mission remains as important now as when I first started.

Acknowledgements

I thank my husband, John Bancroft, who (as always) provided useful suggestions and feedback on earlier drafts of the chapter.

Suggested Readings

Bancroft, J., & Sartorius, N. (1990). The effects of oral contraceptives on well-being and sexuality. *Oxford Reviews of Reproductive Biology, 12,* 57–92.

Dickinson, J. H., & Smith, G. G. (1963). A new and practical oral contraceptive agent: Norethindrane with Mestranol. *Canadian Medical Association Journal, 89,* 242–245.

Graham, C. A., & Sherwin, B. B. (1992). A prospective treatment study of premenstrual symptoms using a triphasic oral contraceptive. *Journal of Psychosomatic Research, 36,* 257–266.

Graham, C. A., & Sherwin, B. B. (1993). The relationship between mood and sexuality in women using an oral contraceptive as a treatment for premenstrual symptoms. *Psychoneuroendocrinology, 18,* 273–281.

Graham, C. A., Ramos, R., Bancroft, J., Maglaya, C., & Farley, T. M. M. (1995). The effects of steroidal contraceptives on the well-being and sexuality of women: A double-blind, placebo-controlled, two-centre study of combined and progestogen-only methods. *Contraception, 52,* 363–369.

McLaughlin, L. (1982). *The pill, John Rock, and the church. The biography of a revolution.* Boston: Little, Brown.

Chapter **11**

Preventing Sexual Violence

Gene G. Abel

Gene G. Abel (M.D., University of Iowa College of Medicine) is a clinical Professor of psychiatry. He was for many years a tenured Professor at Columbia University School of Medicine and currently teaches at both Morehouse School of Medicine and at Emory University School of Medicine. He is a past President of the Society of Behavioral Medicine, a Fellow of the Academy of Behavioral Medicine Research, and a Fellow of the American Psychiatric Association. Dr. Abel was honored with the 1990 Society for Sex Therapy and Research Masters and Johnson Award and the Association for the Treatment of Sexual Abuse's 1991 Significant Achievement Award.

Dr. Abel is the inventor of the Abel Screen, a diagnostic test that discriminates between people who have a high sexual interest in children and adolescents and those who do not. He has directed six National Institute of Mental Health research projects that have uncovered new information about the evaluation of sexual deviancy problems. Through these federal research projects he has developed effective treatment methods. Dr. Abel has published more than 100 medical articles in scientific journals.

I am a physician who practices a limited amount of medicine and a psychiatrist who practices a limited amount of psychiatry. Primarily I am a science practitioner who evaluates and treats child molesters and other types of sex offenders. I often wonder how, as an individual raised in the conservative state of Iowa, I ended up in a career dealing with sexual violence. There were no physicians in my family and I had no early life ambition to become a physician. I suspect it was curiosity and my love of science that led me to this career.

While a freshman in high school, I developed an interest in chemistry and began what might be called an independent study of the subject, especially how to make explosives and how to grow plants without soil (hydroponics). While in college, I took one of the large, introductory courses in psychology and found it exceedingly interesting, but it was too easy. I therefore took the study of psychology off my list of potential careers since my perception was that a career requires hard work and suffering. I studied chemical engineering, botany, and of all things, Greek tragedies. In my senior year, without much reason (other than it was a difficult course of study), I applied to medical school. I enjoyed medical school because it was so difficult and seemed to be a practical application of science. I intended to become an obstetrician-gynecologist until I took a required elective on psychiatry while a medical student. I found it fun and, at the last moment, reluctantly switched from obstetrics and gynecology to a psychiatry residency. Psychology had been so easy for me that I was cautious about continuing a psychiatric residency, since it appeared to lack the scientific rigors of other specialties.

A fortuitous set of circumstances led me into research involving sex offenders. Homosexuality at the time was viewed as a psychiatric illness, and a resident one year ahead of me was doing group treatment of male homosexuals. I was relegated the responsibility of evaluating and treating all other clients who had sexual problems. I was being supervised by a faculty member who allowed me great freedom in pursuing the assessment and treatment of sex offenders. One offender was a man in his 30s recently released from Joliet Prison after serving time for the sexual molestation of a young girl. He told me he had been cured of his sexual interest in young girls because of the negative consequences of incarceration.

Psychiatric residents generally are not very knowledgeable about the factors that contribute to a complex behavior, such as molesting a child, so I searched the literature, which was mostly psychoanalytic. I ignored most of it because it lacked scientific rigor, and instead began investigating the literature on measuring sexual interest in sex offenders using a penile transducer, a mercury filled tube that encircled the client's penis. By presenting depictions of sexual interactions, the scientist can objectively measure clients' erection responses by quantifying their changes in penile circumference. Here I saw the application of science to the investigation of a significant psychiatric problem.

Motivated by my basic philosophy of "I must do everything myself," I went to the biophysics department, gathered up the materials, and made a penile transducer by hand. A technician built me an amperage meter for $25 to allow a means of monitoring the changes in penis size measured by the transducer. I tested it on myself by fantasizing sexual images while wearing it. I was fascinated by the objectivity that such measurement might bring to the study of internal thought—in this case, sexual thought.

Having only a rudimentary knowledge of child molesters, I assumed that because the majority of people were aroused by touching and fondling whomever they were attracted to, child molesters must be similar. I had the child molester wear the device while I described his touching of a young girl. To my surprise he easily developed a partial erection to my description. But the most critical aspect of this experiment was when I asked him whether my description was arousing to him; he flatly denied any sexual arousal to the description.

The patient's self-report appeared genuine, but his measured erection response seemed more genuine. I decided to ignore the molester's self-report and, instead, let my next description be guided by his erection responses to the first description. Looking closely at the amperage meter, it was relatively easy to see that some descriptive words were followed by marked accelerations on the amperage meter while other descriptors were not. I expanded on those descriptors associated with larger erection increases, such as the child's smooth skin, smallness of the child's breasts, the absence of pubic hair, and her young age, and dropped those descriptors not associated with prompt erection responses. The end product was a description guided entirely by the patient's erection responses. I concluded that it was possible to record internal sexual thought objectively, assuming that erections reflected internal sexual thought. This research strategy has been the basic paradigm of my research for the last 28 years: trying to objectify sexual interest in individuals who may be attempting to conceal that interest.

This experiment had a profound effect on my career. Being able to objectify internal thought allowed me to justify remaining in psychiatry because I saw the potential for psychiatry to become more scientific, more rigorous and, therefore, an acceptable career for me.

There are some principles of research I learned from this early experience. First, research the population clinically available to you or put yourself into a specific clinical setting so you can identify potential research issues. Second, naïveté has its advantages. I would have been less likely to pursue a research career investigating paraphiliacs (or sex research in general) had I been aware of the tremendously negative attitudes that my peers and colleagues had toward research on this population. Third, seize the moment. Life has a way of putting you in circumstances such that, if you act on your innate curiosity and use the experiences immediately before you, good things are more likely to happen.

The Research Milieu

Psychiatrists, in general, are poorly trained to do research. My solution to this deficit was to put myself in an environment surrounded by colleagues who were intensely engaged in research. The University of Mississippi's Department of Psychiatry, whose chairman was Stuart Agras, was a center for academic excellence in research using the behavioral model. The University of Mississippi had the added advantage that it was a relatively small medical school. Smaller medical schools are more likely to offer opportunities for young researchers, whereas larger schools have a more rigid structure with fewer opportunities for young staff.

A further problem in conducting sex research relates to one's own personality. I had viewed myself as a rather practical, science-oriented individual who had a knack for innovation. I appreciated my lack of political skills in negotiating many of the complex issues involved in sexual research, especially in the investigation of sexual violence. Changing one's personality is not an easy undertaking and takes time. An alternative is to collaborate with someone whose personality and skills fill in for your deficits. I subsequently began collaborative research with Judith V. Becker, a sensitive, caring individual who was exceedingly adept at negotiating the political problems of conducting sex research in a world where the victimization of females was becoming a politically hot issue. To compensate for my limited knowledge of research design and statistical analysis, I began collaborative research with Ed Blanchard, a seasoned, hard-working researcher. These collaborative efforts brought a balance to our joint research efforts. Our combined efforts became greater than the sum of their parts.

The political climate in the United States had progressively shifted after the National Organization for Women declared the reduction of sexual violence a priority. The federal government established the Center for the Prevention and Control of Rape through the National Institute of Mental Health in Rockville, Maryland. If you are going to do research, you must have funding to pay for the necessary staff, space, equipment, statistical analysis, and subject acquisition. This translates into submitting grant applications.

I would like to say that it was a search for truth that motivated me to write my first grant application, but I suspect a stronger motivator was the necessity of differentiating myself from the many excellent researchers already productive in my department. I suspect that it is this need to differentiate myself from others that has always contributed to my developing new methodologies and treatments. This need for personal recognition has been an asset as I pursued research ideas less encumbered by the critiques of others; however, it is also one of my greatest deficits. The obvious drawback is that a researcher gains skills by working with and listening to the ideas of other researchers. My attempt to differentiate myself from others led to my submitting a 125-page research proposal that took six months of very hard work to write and a relatively short period of time to be rejected by the funding agency.

While at the University of Mississippi Medical Center, a second case provided another turning point in my research career. I was treating a 40-year-old minister with a history of exhibitionism. During an outpatient appointment, he reported that the night before he had broken into a woman's home and attempted to rape her. At that time there was no published literature regarding the use of descriptions of sexual assaults as a means of investigating a patient's proclivities toward rape. Because descriptions of child molesting had been effective in earlier years, I assumed that descriptions of rape could be used to evaluate rapists. I generated three tapes: a two-minute description of a sexual rape, another description of consensual sex, and a third description of a physical, nonsexual assault of a woman. The rapist responded with erections to the explicit description of the sexual rape and the description of a mutual consenting encounter but not to the description of physical nonsexual assault. These results, obtained from a single patient, opened up a series of research studies of sexual violence in rapists and nonrapists and the differentiation of child molesters who used physical force to molest children from molesters who did not.

Research to identify sexually violent individuals matched the government's funding priorities for research on sexual violence. Our next grant application was funded. A major problem, however, was that there was a low rate of reported rapes in Jackson, Mississippi (less than 110 total rapes per year), and, without an adequate number of rapists and child molesters to evaluate and treat, our research project was destined to wither. At the same time, Memphis, Tennessee, had one of the highest rape rates in the country. The demands of needing to evaluate and treat a large number of child molesters and rapists ultimately led to moving our research team to Memphis.

Our research on the measurement of sexual interest began to expand as the team became more aware of the literature on sexual violence, the treatment needs of victims, and how to work with biomedical technicians in the development of assessment instruments. Our research focus extended from working with perpetrators to also working with victims of sexual assault. James Geer published information on the vaginal photoplethysmograph, an instrument that measures blood-flow changes in the outer third of the vagina during sexual arousal. We developed modifications of this device and began measuring women's responses to sexual stimuli.

A third patient led to further expansion of our research. A young woman in her 20s had been brutally gang raped as a teenager in the backseat of a car by three adolescent males. Her presenting symptoms included a lack of sexual interest and problems reaching orgasm. The literature reported accounts of women using descriptions of rape to become sexually aroused. We subsequently developed audiotaped descriptions of a variety of sexual assaults as well as descriptions of consensual heterosexual encounters. This patient displayed marked vaginal responses to detailed descriptions similar to her own sexual assault, a very puzzling result.

We subsequently developed a research protocol, based on this assessment methodology, to evaluate and treat rape victims and, in our naïveté, advanced the research protocol to Washington. This turned out to be a political blunder. In essence, we were asking for grant monies to investigate a highly politically charged issue, women's possible sexual responses to descriptions of rape. The application had gone to a subcommittee that, in retrospect, was probably vehemently opposed to any such research. Our observation of rape victims having vaginal responses to descriptions of sexual violence was, no doubt, an example of the tremendous impact violent acts can have on an individual's physiologic responding. The patient's responsiveness to such stimuli was probably a marker for the attack having occurred and had nothing to do with sexual enjoyment of such descriptions. The potential interpretation of such results would be a political minefield.

Our grant application for this study was not funded, but our preliminary study had confirmed physiologic responding of rape victims by the use of vaginal photoplethysmography. We agonized about what to do with our preliminary research findings. If we published our findings, we anticipated we would incur the wrath of the feminist movement and funding agencies. Furthermore, such information could be easily misinterpreted, especially at a time when we, ourselves, were unclear regarding its meaning. Science does not exist in a political vacuum. We decided not to publish these results; they still lay buried in the unpublished dissertation of a collaborator. Instead we chose to use our experience with the photoplethysmograph technology and apply it to a less controversial area to determine if women have vaginal responses during rapid eye movement (REM) sleep similar to men's erection responses during REM sleep. Men without erectile disorders get four to six erections during the night during the dream phase of sleep, called REM sleep. Men with organic erectile disorders fail to get the same REM erections and this characteristic can be used to differentiate psychogenic from organic erectile disorders in males. It seemed natural to assume that women would have similar vaginal engorgement responses during REM sleep.

Bill Murphy joined our research group. Due to his excellent technical skills and tolerance of staying awake while female subjects slept during such assessment, we were able to demonstrate that women do indeed get vaginal engorgement during REM sleep, similar to men's penile engorgement that leads to erection. Unfortunately we were unable to recruit enough women with failure to obtain vaginal engorgement as a clinical symptom to determine if vaginal-REM response could be used to differentiate psychogenic from organic problems in women. In my experience, science does not follow a clear, unwavering path but progresses more often as a result of serendipitous findings.

The Department of Psychiatry at the University of Tennessee College of Medicine (Memphis) was an ideal setting for researching child molesters and rapists. The city was large enough to have an adequate number of sex offenders available to study, and the Department of Psychiatry was small enough that an individual researcher could flourish without being encumbered by an extensive administrative structure. Our research group had a wonderful blend of assets. I continued to see my role as that of innovator. But as a physician, I had also been taught to get things done. The varied strengths of our research team were all focused on gathering needed information on sex offenders.

Once our next grant application was submitted, the National Institute of Mental Health program officer attached to our grant, James Breiling, advised that we include monies for training postdoctorate psychologists or psychiatrists and that we organize national meetings bringing together sexual violence researchers located throughout North America. This led to the publication of a newsletter (the *Sexual Aggressive News*) to foster better communication regarding the research efforts of various research centers. At the time, there were only 62 centers that could be identified as focusing on sexual aggression; now there are hundreds.

A major focus of our research grant was to develop a system in which information could safely be gathered regarding sexual assault without jeopardizing the source of that information—the sex offender. If offenders provide information that is accessible by the criminal justice system, they in essence provide information to bring about their own arrest and felony conviction. If the criminal justice system could access such information, sex offenders would not participate in research, and, therefore, less would be known regarding how to evaluate and treat this population.

We subsequently developed an elaborate system for protection of the research participants. First, we applied for and were granted a certificate of confidentiality that specified that no city, county, state, or federal agency could access information regarding the research participants. Second, all research participants were identified only by a code number. The code identifying each participant's name was held by the participant and also by an individual outside the United States not attached to the research grant. If the criminal justice system attempted to access this information, the individual holding the code outside the United States would ask whether the request for the identification number was at the initiation of the criminal justice system. If the answer was yes, they would simply hang up. A third measure regarding security was that members of the team were encouraged to make no attempts to remember any identification numbers. The charts held in the Department of Psychiatry had no names associated with them, only identification numbers. When the participant came to the research center, he would give us his identification number, we would pull the chart with that number on it, and we would proceed with evaluation and treatment using that record.

The protection of participants' data is critical when acquiring information on sex offenders. Information regarding sex offenders, at the time, had been primarily obtained from incarcerated offenders who reported an exceedingly low number of sex crimes. After we had completed the research and gathered information regarding the self-reported sex crimes of offenders under this system of data collection, it was apparent that sex offenders carry out many more offenses than was suggested by the available literature. We found that the median and mean numbers of sex acts for those molesting girls outside the home were 1.4 and 23.2; for those molesting boys outside the home, 10.1 and 281.7; for those molesting girls in the home, 4.4 and 81.3; and for those molesting boys in the home, 5.2 and 62.3. On hearing the results of the research, many individuals were opposed to our protection of the data. Instead, they believed that child molesters who reported such crimes unknown to the criminal justice system should be reported so that they could be arrested and prosecuted. Reporting such research participants would break the ethical guidelines of human investigation and would have terminated the research project, so the field would still be naive regarding what sex offenders actually do.

A second problem arose when the data began to be used for political purposes. The marked differences between the medians and the means indicates that there are some child molesters who perpetrate a large number of child molestations (thereby raising the mean), while other child molesters molest a fewer number of times (thereby the median being considerably less than the mean). The culture was moving away from a focus on treatment to a punishment mode. Those with political aims therefore ignored the medians, and quoted the means as representative of how frequently child molesters had acted. They were not at all concerned about why there was a great discrepancy between the medians and the means of this population. Scientific data can easily be manipulated by those with political motives to support their political position, and our research data was not immune to such manipulation.

Many researchers, and certainly the general public, believe that those attempting to stop sexual violence fall into two camps: those providing services to victims and working to incarcerate offenders, and those who work with offenders. In actuality there is only one group; all of us are attempting to stop sexual violence.

With our acquisition-data system in place, we began accelerating the number of sex offenders evaluated. We examined these data and discovered that the most frequent sex offense involving physical contact with the victim was not rape but the molestation of children. From this point on, our research efforts began centering on preventing the sexual molestation of children. Memphis had been a very good environment for conducting our research, but we had not been able to access a significant number of research participants to complete our study. It became apparent that we had to move to an even larger city to gather an adequate participant population in the limited amount of time available to complete the grant. After considering a number of large metropolitan areas, we decided on New York City.

The College of Physicians and Surgeons of Columbia University provided an ideal setting for completing our research activities. We completed our research study on rapists in New York and prepared multiple grants involving the evaluation and treatment of child molesters, evaluation and treatment of diabetic males and females with organic sexual problems, and the evaluation and treatment of victims of sexual assault.

Although the chairman of the Department of Psychiatry, Edward Sacher, was receptive to our research, other researchers at Columbia were less than overjoyed with our arrival. I presented our research to faculty and staff of the Department of Psychiatry at the College of Physicians and Surgeons of Columbia University. The auditorium bubbled over with the audience's emotional response on learning that an evaluation and treatment program for sex offenders was to be moved to the institution. In retrospect, I believe they feared that in a city already known for violence, their risk of being attacked increased because their workplace would house a center that invited sex offenders. In actuality we provided treatment for sex offenders already at large in the city, and thereby reduced the risk of the staff's being attacked. During the course of the grant work in New York, there were no sexual assaults on the staff or faculty by our research participants.

A sex researcher should not expect to be favorably greeted by colleagues at a research institute. Professionals have minimal education and training in the evaluation and treatment of sex offenders. Sex research with perpetrators is frequently perceived as a dirty business. Professionals have the same attitudes that the general public has about working with sex offenders. That is, if offenders are bad, so are those who treat them. The public is of the opinion that if sex offenders are incarcerated or fear incarceration, somehow the consequences of arrest and incarceration will serve to stop their deviant behavior. Furthermore, the public believes that if these individuals are incarcerated, they will stay incarcerated, and, if they are released, they will be doubly fearful of carrying out a subsequent sex crime. This erroneous thinking of the public also extends to the average professional.

While we were in New York City, scathing articles were written about our program, suggesting that we were giving "sex lessons to rapists." Other professionals at Columbia wrote letters to the editor regarding the inappropriateness of treating sex offenders. When the "Take Back the Night" program was initiated in New York City to chase pornography off 42nd Street, we received threats that protest marches by this group would be conducted at Columbia University because of our research there. What allowed us to endure these attacks was the realization that the only other existing system attempting to stop sexual violence, the criminal justice system, was able to act only after a victimization had occurred. It was, and is, our belief that it is preferable to prevent sexual perpetration so that individuals are not victimized in the first place. In numerous talks around the country, we attempted to ascertain whether audience members were satisfied with the preventive measures that were currently being employed to stop sexual victimization. Caught up in their anger toward the sex offender, the public frequently loses track of the goal of stopping sexual victimization.

By the late 1980s, a series of events occurred that had a profound effect on research with sex offenders. The media across the United States had become increasingly focused on the issue of sexual violence. Programs like "Good Touch, Bad Touch" were being implemented and rape crises centers had expanded their emphasis not only on preventing violence against adult females, but also on preventing violence against children. Treatment programs for juvenile sex offenders had become increasingly common; with them came attempts to assess adolescent sex offenders.

A treatment program in Arizona was evaluating juvenile sex offenders using penile plethysmography. Most of these juvenile offenders had been adjudicated and were under the supervision of the courts. A family member of one of the juveniles became upset with the plethysmography assessment that her adjudicated sex-offending son had undergone. This issue subsequently became the centerpiece for more than ten articles in the state paper on the evaluation and treatment of juvenile sex offenders.

A legislative investigation was subsequently initiated to evaluate the use of plethysmography with adolescents, the appropriateness of showing nude slides to adjudicated adolescent sex offenders, and whether the cognitive-behavioral treatment offered these adolescents was appropriate. Penile plethysmography had long been the most objective means of assessing sexual interest in males. However, to accomplish this assessment, the adolescents had to be shown sexual stimuli during the penile measures that reflected their possible sexual interest that may have led to their committing sex crimes.

The legislature was also investigating whether cognitive-behavioral therapy was appropriate. The scientific literature identified two forms of treatment for adolescent sex offenders. In the more severe cases, treatment involves reducing sexual drive by the use of a serotonin reuptake inhibiting antidepressant medication that, as a side effect, reduces sex drive and decreases obsessiveness. The use of the more invasive antitestosterone drugs was precluded in treatment of adolescents because they inhibit bone growth and this side effect would reduce the child's height.

The second form of treatment is cognitive-behavioral, with a strong relapse-prevention component. This involves identifying faulty thinking (cognitive distortions) that some adolescents have that molestation does not harm the victim, identifying the chain of events or antecedents leading to sex offenses so that early behaviors heading toward sex offending can be disrupted, victim empathy training to help the adolescent perpetrator appreciate the consequences to the victim of being sexually abused, uncovering drug and alcohol misuse that may be antecedent to the sexual abuse, identifying the adolescent's own sexual victimization that may be a contributor to the adolescent's victimizing others, and the development of a relapse-prevention plan that minimizes the factors leading to abuse and maximizes positive behaviors that would preclude the necessity of perpetrating against others. Some therapists in Arizona were not familiar with the literature regarding the effectiveness of cognitive-behavioral treatment and endorsed older treatments that had proven ineffective in the treatment of sex offenders.

The controversy regarding the use of plethysmography extended to Texas, where other centers were using an identical methodology for assessing adult and juvenile sex offenders. The investigation also extended to the Federal Food and Drug Administration; it was questioned whether penile plethysmography was a medical device and therefore necessitated a medical license to prescribe it. The FBI was also concerned about the proliferation of child pornography, and these inquiries extended to the use of slides depicting nude children during plethysmography assessment.

Sexual violence researchers across the United States needed to compare their research results with one another. The only way this could be accomplished was by the researchers all using the same sexual stimuli during plethysmography assessments. Virtually all treatment programs employing plethysmography used slides depicting nude children and nude adults. The only source for a standard set of slides in the United States was the Farrall Instrument Company in Grand Island, Nebraska, which also manufactured plethysmographs and provided slides to clinicians. The company subsequently came under the scrutiny of the attorney general's office in Nebraska and eventually closed, being unwilling to go through the long and costly legal process of dealing with these issues.

The closing of Farrall Instrument has had a profound effect on research involving male sex offenders. The major advances in sex-offender research have been made at a few universities in North America. Common to most of these centers has been the use of plethysmography to assess the sexual interest of sex offenders. Those researching the evaluation and treatment of sex offenders are primarily concerned about preventing sexual violence. We believe sexual violence is of epidemic proportions and needs to be stopped. Sexual violence is so common that it constitutes a public health problem. Public health problems have never been stopped by treating the problem after it has already occurred. The way to eliminate a public health problem is to attack the pathogen, the etiologic agent, the cause. The cause of sexual violence is the perpetrator. To stop the perpetrator we need to understand what leads the perpetrator to commit sexual violence and what needs to be done to prevent these sexual acts.

A number of positive results came from these events. These included: (1) a greater understanding that the type of sexual stimuli presented to adolescent sex offenders should match the extent of the sexual violence the adolescent has perpetrated; (2) the conclusion that in assessing adolescent sex offenders under 15 years of age, an advisory board (not associated with the assessment team) should be consulted regarding the appropriateness of penile plethysmography; and (3) the public developed a greater appreciation that if individuals have been guilty of committing a sex crime, they require serious assessment to identify their treatment needs to preclude relapse. Some negative consequences resulted as well, including the following: (1) in the United States there is no longer a standard set of visual stimuli to use during penile plethysmography assessment of sex offenders, and (2) the absence of this standard has made comparison of assessment and treatment outcome across states very problematic.

Being a principle investigator on a federal grant has many advantages. The funds allow the investigator to pay the cost of statistical analysis, participant acquisition, and provide work space and personnel for the project. The status of having obtained a federal grant also provides credibility for the project. Universities seek out researchers who are able to obtain grant funding, because overhead costs are provided to the university housing the federal grant, in addition to the direct cost of the funded study. Universities may receive as much as a 60 percent overhead rate, which means that for each grant dollar brought to the university, there is an additional 60 cents given to the university to cover overhead costs. However, as the researcher becomes more and more successful at obtaining such grants, the relationship with his or her department becomes less important, since the principal investigator becomes more attached to the grant funding agent and less attached to the department.

In my case, the most important connection between my research and the university was the university's mainframe computer. For years it had been impossible to do adequate statistical analyses involving large numbers of participants on any system other than a mainframe computer. With the advent of microcomputers, their increased storage capacity, and the development of statistical software packages for microcomputers, mainframe computers were no longer critical.

In 1987 I resigned my tenured position at the university to expand my research studies with sex offenders, anticipating that I could finance research in the private setting through evaluating and treating sex offenders and could analyze their data on microcomputers. Although federal grants have been exceedingly helpful in establishing my career as a researcher of sex offenders, for me there have been two major drawbacks. The first is that the process is too slow and too unreliable. Federal research projects take at least three months to write, and, if they get funded, up to two years may pass before these funds are received. Unfortunately, with the reduction of research dollars, the number of grants which receive funding has also been markedly reduced.

A further complicating issue has been the increasing conservatism in the country, the greater criminalization of sexual behavior, and the retreat from treatment of sex offenders to a more punitive approach. The general public has failed to appreciate that if child molestation is to be prevented, it is necessary to identify and stop those with proclivities to commit sex crimes. The public holds the general opinion that a more punitive incarceration approach will be more successful. The major problem with this approach is that, before incarceration can occur, someone must first be victimized. This I believe is wrong; victimizations should be stopped before they occur.

The Private-Practice Setting

I would have liked to say that the decision to break away from a 20-year career in academic psychiatry to do research in a private setting, funded by the private practice, was well thought out, based on weighing the pros and cons and making a well-reasoned choice. As a scientist, I should have made such a well-thought-out, calculated decision. In actuality, my decision was probably motivated by the same personality characteristics that have always motivated me as a researcher, namely curiosity, optimism, and a strong desire to personally have an impact on reducing sexual violence. Such a decision was not for the weak of heart. It was a decision that I could make only after years of grant applications that were either "sink or swim" investments of time. In the academic setting, you always have academia to fall back on should your grant application fall through. In the private setting, successful research must be supported by the success of your private practice.

A major factor that has allowed my research in the private care setting has been the standardization of the patient evaluation methodology I employ. For years I have used the same type of evaluation whether I was evaluating private patients or research participants. In this way, data I have gathered in the private setting are compatible with data gathered in the research setting. The result is a very large database.

A critical aspect of research in the private setting is attaching oneself to an organization or institution that has a human investigation committee, so there is always supervision from others regarding the ethics of the research that one is doing. Furthermore, statements of informed consent must be obtained from all research participants, indicating that they agree to participate in the study and agree to allow their data to be used for research purposes.

The Search for a New Methodology

In 1969, as a psychiatric resident, I had read a paper by my departmental chairman, Paul Houston, who had studied the time that depressed patients versus nondepressed patients spent sorting small symbols related to depression (symbols of a cross, church, knife, casket, etc.). Houston had found that individuals' internal mood or concerns had an impact on their sorting time. I later investigated whether visual reaction time (time looking at slides) could be used to identify sexual interests, assuming that a similar sorting test would be applicable to evaluating sexual interest. In the first week of this research it became obvious that this assumption had great promise. If research could demonstrate that visual reaction time could be as effective as plethysmography for identifying sexual interests, we would next study whether slides of nonnudes used with this new methodology would yield similar results to those obtained with slides of nudes. About two years later, the FBI became more vigorous in prosecuting individuals who transported slides depicting nude children across state lines. This action, of course, provided further impetus to eliminate the use of slides of nudes.

My repeated desire to differentiate myself from others, to be first to develop the system ahead of others, continued to play a part in my study of visual reaction time. For the next three years, I found myself caught in the position of researching a new methodology that was effective for identifying sexual offenders' sexual interest. At the same time, I was reluctant to publish data regarding its reliability and validity because this would require disclosure of the methodology. Staying ahead of other researchers remained important to me.

I first presented this work in 1990, at the annual meeting of the International Academy of Sex Research. This was followed by a series of studies demonstrating that visual reaction time was a valid, reliable methodology that could be used effectively without the necessity of using slides of nudes. This was a tremendous breakthrough in sex-offender research methodology. This methodology may also extend to any kind of sex research, because it affords the opportunity to evaluate sexual interest in both males and females, in adults and adolescents. The following are examples of how this methodology assists in clinical decisions.

Deacon Smith was a single male in his early 40s referred by his bishop after being accused by an adolescent parishioner of molestation. The deacon had denied any inappropriate behavior, saying that he had actually been providing religious counseling and drug counseling to the boy and his family. The deacon reported that this accusation was made because he confronted family members about their drug abuse. To further complicate matters, the deacon, who had finished his seminary training, was to be ordained as a priest in six weeks, and his bishop wanted to know if he should proceed with the deacon's ordination.

The deacon was shown slides of males and females in three age groups: under 14, 14 to 17, and adults. His visual reaction time to these slides was then compared to visual reaction times of sex offenders who had been involved sexually with young or adolescent boys or girls. The deacon's results clearly matched those who had molested adolescent boys. Our recommendation to the bishop was to hold off on the ordination. Within three weeks, a second allegation of child molestation of an adolescent boy by the deacon was provided by a family unaware of the previous accusation against the deacon. Putting off the ordination had prevented the bishop from ordaining someone whose subsequent behavior would have proved terribly problematic for the church.

Mrs. Brown was a married mental health worker employed to care for intellectually impaired children and adolescent boys and girls. She had an extensive history of a variety of sexual activities, including masturbating while inserting objects into her rectum, developing a masochistic arousal pattern in which she could climax only by injuring her body, being involved in bestiality, having oral and vaginal intercourse with her preteenage brother, and being involved in various swinger clubs since her marriage. She was referred because of depressive symptomatology and a comment to her husband that he should watch her to prevent her from molesting their young son.

We were unable to identify whether she had actually molested her young son. But using visual reaction time, we investigated her sexual interest to see if she had specific interests toward young or adolescent boys or girls, since she was a caregiver in an institution dealing with that population. We subsequently measured her sexual interest using the categories of stimuli we had applied in the case of Deacon Smith. Her visual reaction time showed she was sexually interested in boys under age 14, adolescent males age 14 to 17, and females age 14 to 17 but not interested in females under 14. Relying on her visual reaction time, we subsequently confronted her with our findings. During the course of that confrontation she admitted sexual interest in all four categories and admitted she had been sexually abusing adolescent and younger boys and girls for years. These victims were so profoundly intellectually impaired that they were unable to communicate her behavior to others. She was subsequently reported to the appropriate child protection services, who removed her from her position with children.

The practice of psychiatry was in chaos in 1994; the entire system of health care insurance was contracting, with profits in treating psychiatric patients declining along with my opportunity to continue privately funded sex research. In that year, I reversed my decision and disclosed to the scientific community that I was measuring visual reaction time. I also packaged and began selling the methodology and software I had developed along with questionnaires I had been using to evaluate potential sex offenders. My new goal was to establish sites in North America, using this methodology, that would assess large numbers of sex offenders and to develop an equation that would predict which child molesters would reoffend and if they did reoffend, which sex offenders would use force with the child. In this way, I could help to integrate the field at the national level, for the purpose of stopping child molestation. My concomitant goal was to change my role from that of an individual researcher to that of a facilitator of research regarding the prevention of sexual violence. The only significant obstacle to overcome was the same as it has always been: my narcissistic desire to stay ahead of others, which needed to be replaced with assuming the role of facilitating the research efforts of others.

Screening for Sexual Interest in Children

The development of visual reaction time as a methodology for identifying inappropriate sexual interests has allowed a unique opportunity to prevent child molestation by screening applicants to volunteer organizations, organizations whose primary responsibility is the education or care of children. Because the methodology is noninvasive and does not affront the public by employing slides of nudes, and because it is exceedingly rapid, it can be used as a screening instrument. Our studies to differentiate those who have actually molested children from those who have not resulted in discriminant analysis equations that accurately identify individuals whose scores match the scores of those who have molested girls under 14, boys under 14, girls 14 to 17, or boys 14 to 17. Here is a needed tool to address a major social problem, violence against children. The scientific problems, however, began to be replaced with political and constitutional issues. Is such an assessment an invasion of privacy? Who would be allowed access to the results of such an assessment? Would volunteer organizations incorporate such an assessment methodology into other screening methods or would they rely on it exclusively to remove such applicants from their application pool without attempting to provide guidance or counseling to the applicants? Which needs are greater, the protection of children from child molestation or the protection of adults from possible invasion of privacy?

The Future

One should never attempt to predict the future, unless it is in retrospect. In spite of this cautionary note, I believe that a reasonable estimation can be made regarding the investigation of sexual violence for the next 10 or 20 years. Microcomputers have forever changed the landscape of sex research. The concentrated efforts of a few now can have a profound impact, because methods of research are becoming increasingly accessible. The liberal-to-conservative pendulum will continue to swing toward the more conservative, punitive approach to sex offenders, until it is forced back because of the cost of incarcerating offenders. The biggest threat to research with sex offenders is the lack of training for young researchers and the continued attitude that research with sex offenders is dirty. As long as the lay public continues to label those working with sexually violent offenders as bad, universities will not be inclined to look favorably on educating students regarding the evaluation and treatment of sex offenders. I continue to believe that my own efforts to bring greater coordination to the field will be productive. Accessing the resultant database will allow individual sites to research subtopics and test hypotheses from a large common database. This will bring further clarity to subgroups of offenders who in the past have been lumped together in a heterogeneous group. This will allow the development of specific assessment and treatment individualized to subgroups of offenders. And what will happen to my own research? It will be covered over by the new research of others who are also interested in stopping sexual violence and preventing victimization.

Suggested Readings

Abel, G. G., Barlow, D. H., Blanchard, E. B., & Guild, D. (1977). The components of rapists' sexual arousal. *Archives of General Psychiatry, 34,* 895–903.

Abel, G. G., Becker, J. V., Mittelman, M. S., Cunningham-Rathner, J., Rouleau, J. L., & Murphy, W. D. (1987). Self-reported sex crimes of nonincarcerated paraphiliacs. *Journal of Interpersonal Violence, 2,* 3–25.

Abel, G. G., Becker, J. V., Murphy, W. D., & Flanagan, B. (1981). Identifying dangerous child molesters. In R. Stuart (Ed.), *Violent behavior: Social learning approaches to prediction, management and treatment* (pp. 116–137). New York: Brunner/Mazel.

Abel, G. G., Blanchard, E. B., Barlow, D. H., & Mavissakalian, M. (1975). Identifying specific erotic cues in sexual deviation by audio-taped descriptions. *Journal of Applied Behavior Analysis, 8*(3), 247–260.

Abel, G. G., Blanchard, E. B., Becker, J. V., & Djenderedjian, A. (1978). Differentiating sexual aggressiveness with penile measures. *Criminal Justice and Behavior, 5,* 315–332.

Abel, G. G, Lawry, S. S., Karlstrom, E. M, Osborn, C. A, & Gillespie, C. F. (1994). Screening tests for pedophilia. *Criminal Justice and Behavior, 21,* 115–131.

Abel, G. G., Murphy, W. D., Becker, J. V., & Bitar, A. (1979). Women's vaginal responses during REM sleep. *Journal of Sex and Marital Therapy, 5,* 5–14.

Cunningham-Rathner, J., & Abel, G. G. (1984). Psychophysiologic measurement of sexual arousal in females. In M. Ficher, R. E. Fishkin, & J. A. Jacobs (Eds.), *Sexual arousal: New concepts in basic sciences, diagnosis, and treatment* (pp. 70–87). Springfield, IL: Charles C. Thomas.

Chapter 12

A Few Minutes with Venus,
A Lifetime with Mercury

William W. Darrow

Bill Darrow (Ph.D., Emory University) is a Professor of Public Health at Florida International University (FIU). He continues to conduct research and to publish on the social and behavioral aspects of AIDS and other sexually transmitted diseases, and serves South Florida as a member of the Dade County HIV/AIDS Prevention Community Planning Group, the AIDS Prevention Task Force, and the South Beach AIDS Project Advisory Committee.

Before accepting a position at FIU, Dr. Darrow served as Chief of the Centers for Disease Control and Prevention's Behavioral and Prevention Research Branch of the Division of STD/HIV Prevention, National Center for Prevention Services. He has published more than 100 scientific papers in professional journals, books, and research monographs. In addition, he has presented more than 100 scientific papers at professional meetings, and has consulted with many professional and service organizations, including the World Health Organization and the European Union.

Dr. Darrow was recognized for his lifetime contributions to science and humanity by his hometown of Norwich, Connecticut, in 1992 when he was presented with its Native Son Award. In 1993 he received the Award for Sociological Practice from the Society for Applied Sociology. He received the Sociological Practice Award in 1994 from the Sociological Practice Association. In the same year he accepted the Thomas Parran Award from the American Venereal Disease Association. In 1996, he was chosen for the Distinguished Alumni Award by the Alumni Association of his alma mater, the University of Connecticut.

When I was a senior in high school, a staff member for the year-book handed me a self-administered questionnaire the size of a large index card and asked me to fill in my name, academic major, activities, interests, and plans after Norwich Free Academy. Without much thought, I completed the form and returned it as requested. As a consequence, in the upper right-hand corner of page 71 of the 1957 *Mirror* you will find the black-and-white photograph of a very young looking boy—with a very short crew cut and very tweed jacket—and the caption, "Will probably become a doctor, lawyer, or psychologist."

As it turned out, I became none of those things. Yet, at various times in my life, I have been all of those things, and even a few things else. Let me tell you about my experiences as a venereal disease investigator, public health adviser, research sociologist, and a few things more.

Who Can Meet the Challenge?

By the time I was a senior in college, I was quite certain that I had learned everything I needed to know to find a satisfying job that paid well and would be intellectually rewarding. So one typically chilly day in the winter of 1961, I walked over the icy sidewalks of the campus in Storrs to the University of Connecticut placement office. A kind counselor invited me into his warm office and started asking me a few questions about my career plans.

I admitted that I had changed my academic major at the beginning of each semester until I ran out of options. After a fraternity brother told me economics was interesting, I declared economics to be my major. "My mind is completely open to do anything you might suggest," I said, "but I am certain of one thing after studying premedicine, prelaw, and introductory psychology: I don't want to be a doctor, a lawyer, or a psychologist."

John F. Kennedy had just been sworn in as our thirty-fifth president, and I thought he was talking to me when he said, "Ask not what your country can do for you, but rather ask what you can do for your country." The counselor apparently was not impressed with my idealism and advised me to do a little window shopping. "Why don't you browse the bulletin board for job listings to see who will be visiting us next week and sign up for a few interviews for jobs that you would never be interested in?" he advised as he rose to walk me to the door. "That way you'll be able to get the practice you need to impress interviewers for the jobs you would really like to have."

Among the scores of multicolor, glossy brochures tacked on a crowded bulletin board, I found a tattered, faded, and off-center mimeographed announcement for health representatives to work for the New York City Department of Health. The description of duties was so vague that I had no idea what I would be doing. A huge grin crossed my face when I read the starting salary: $4,490 a year. "They've got to be kidding," I thought to myself. "I'm signing up for this one."

When the appointed hour came, I entered a brightly lighted room to find a bespectacled, middle-aged Mediterranean-looking man with dark hair, an ebony mustache, and a dark suit facing three students who looked like they were rushing Animal House, as in the famous scene from the movie where Flounder introduces himself as "a legacy." I pulled up a chair to join the fun. The man was saying, ". . . and the backseat of the automobile has taken the place of the whorehouse. Here is your chance to make a difference. Join us in our humanitarian effort to rid our nation of syphilis. We want very capable and eager young men just like the four of you to work with us. Now, which one of you can meet the challenge?"

Start Me Up

On the day after Labor Day, September 1961, I walked into the office of the man, Joe Giordano, at 93 Worth Street in downtown Manhattan to report for duty. His assistant greeted me with a friendly smile and firm handshake. "Hi, I'm Ferd Tedesco." "Pleased to meet you, Fred," I said. "No, the name is Ferd: F-E-R-D," he spelled it out for me. Shortly thereafter he introduced me to my eventual supervisor at Chelsea Clinic, Frank Di Giovanni, and to a local employee who would be showing me around lower Manhattan, Tony Bellatoni. "Great reward for earning a bachelor of arts degree in economics at UConn," I thought to myself, "Next they will ask me to burn my contract as they order me to recite, 'If ever I should break the sacred code of silence, may my body burn in hell as this worthless piece of paper burns in my hands.'"

Of course there would be a year of training before I could be admitted to "the Program." Ed McKenna would teach us how to interview patients for their "sex contacts," and someone would take us into "the field." The Program would send me and "other VDIs [venereal disease investigators] from across the country" to the Fulton County Health Department in Atlanta for two weeks of "more intensive" training, but I was particularly fortunate. I had been selected to attend the "World Forum on Syphilis and Other Treponematoses" to be held in Washington, D.C., in December. If I performed all my tasks up to the high standards of the Public Health Service, I could join an elite cadre of (nontechnical) public health advisers. I could become "a venereal disease investigator." Wow!

The Bum on the Bench

After completing my training with Ed McKenna in New York City and Bob Stewart and Jim Simpson in Atlanta, I was assigned to the Social Hygiene Clinic at 303 Ninth Avenue in New York to interview patients diagnosed with early syphilis about their "sexual partners, cluster suspects, and associates." I knew how to apply the "modified direct approach" to discover the patients' most intimate secrets and to elicit information from them about other people who might be infected with syphilis. Everybody "in the Program" seemed quite impressed with my abilities to identify and locate people living on the West Side of Manhattan, the area that quickly became my territory (many of my colleagues had resigned as the weather grew colder and the work became more monotonous).

Late one cold winter day in 1962, Frank Di Giovanni entered my small office in the basement of the clinic with a medical chart and other forms of various hues attached. "Bill," he began, "there's a gentleman from New Jersey upstairs who has just been diagnosed with secondary syphilis. I want you to interview him. Here are his records. Note that this is his first visit to our clinic. His number is 31, but you will immediately recognize him. He is the bum on the bench."

I climbed the stairs to find an unshaven white man with a dirty face in his late 30s dressed in layers of old, torn clothes sitting alone on a cold steel bench outside the waiting room. I greeted him as I was trained to do by giving him my name and asking him if he was number 31. After I confirmed that the gentleman was indeed the man I was seeking, I invited him to accompany me on a short trip back down the stairs to my office so we could talk about his diagnosis and the implications of his infection for himself and others.

The first part of the interview was designed to review demographic and other personal information about the patient. Number 31 told me he was single, never married, and lived with his mother, a disabled widow, in Hoboken. He was employed by a large chain of parking garages as a parking attendant in Queens. His usual working day was spent riding public transportation from Hoboken to Queens and then returning for a warm supper with mom and a quiet evening of situation comedies and game shows on television.

The second part of the interview was designed to inform the patient of his diagnosis and to educate him about the natural history of the disease. I looked number 31 in the eye, told him he had been diagnosed with secondary syphilis, and told him he was very wise to come to the clinic today because the doctors in the clinic could treat him for his infection. But there were others in the community who might not be as wise and observant as he. I asked him to help me find those who were still infected and possibly spreading syphilis to others, so they too could be treated.

The third part of the interview was designed to establish the patient's pattern of sexual activity and to elicit the names, addresses, and telephone numbers of those who had exposed or been exposed to the patient during the period when he acquired and might have transmitted syphilis. Following the modified direct approach, I said, "The only way you could have acquired syphilis was by having sexual intercourse with someone who was infected. Sexual intercourse includes vaginal, anal, and oral sex. In your lifetime, would you say that you have had a thousand or more than a thousand sex partners?" I asked.

The gentleman who was introduced to me as "the bum on the bench" looked perplexed, so I repeated the question. After a long silence, he responded, "Five, perhaps." "Oh no, I don't mean in the last week, but in your whole lifetime," I said. "I am sure you started your sexual activity in your early teens, just like most Americans. Now you are 38, so in the last 25 years or so, how many different people have you had sex with, a thousand or more than a thousand?" I asked in a stern voice. Again confusion and a meek reply. "Maybe six."

I was growing impatient with this man who did not fit the profile of the typical gay man with multiple partners who was diagnosed with syphilis at our clinic in the early 1960s. And so I began to intimidate him by showing him gruesome pictures of syphilitics with their distorted faces covered with lesions and by lecturing him on how he should be honest with me if he cared at all about other people who were less fortunate than he.

Then "the bum on the bench" taught me a lesson that cold winter day in the basement of a social hygiene clinic in New York City that has remained with me throughout my career in public health. He did the only thing a sensitive and caring person would do in the face of an obnoxious bureaucrat. He started crying. He didn't say a word. He just cried, quietly. I can still see those large crystal-clear tears rolling unevenly down his sad, dirty, and unshaven face, reflecting an image of Bill Darrow as an arrogant and abusive bureaucrat, an image from that day forward I have tried to live down, thanks to "the bum on the bench."

Red the Painter

With the summer of 1962 came a fresh crop of college graduates. Some were assigned to work with me to learn how to conduct field investigations. A young Polish American dressed in an inexpensive plaid jacket from J. C. Penney's and rumpled khaki trousers brought with him a pink copy of the Public Health Service Form 0.2936.

The name at the top of the form was "Red," last name "Unknown." He was described as a recent contact to an "S-20" (a case of syphilis in the secondary stage)—a short, muscular man with a receding hairline, believed to be in his late 30s or early 40s. His occupation was listed as "painter." His address was given as a suite of three rooms on the top floor of a hotel on the northeast corner of Lexington Avenue and East Twenty-Ninth Street in Manhattan.

A note written in carefully constructed printed letters appeared on the back of the form. It said that Red was a client of prostitutes and "very dangerous." The writer of the note wanted us to know that Red could become belligerent. We should approach him "with extreme caution."

I turned to my young colleague and asked with a grin, "Are you ready to meet the challenge?" "I guess so," he responded, with an apprehensive tone in his timid voice. Off we went in our gray Chevrolet with the words "For Official Use Only" stenciled on the side doors to find our man, "Red the Painter."

It was late afternoon on a hot and humid day in July when we arrived at the hotel. Fortunately, we found a vacant parking space across the street, locked the doors, and headed up a few stairs into a lobby, where we found a clerk busy making notations in a registration book. "Is Red in?" I asked without stopping. "Yeah, he's up there," my young colleague and I heard him reply just before the automatic elevator doors closed behind us.

All the way to the top we went, found the room number we were looking for, and knocked. "Hi, Red, it's Bill Darrow from the Health Department. Could I speak with you for just a few minutes?" A short, stocky man with a sunburned face speckled with variegated housepaints partially opened the door and muttered, "What's this all about?" "If you let us in, Red, I'll be glad to tell you." Reluctantly, Red slowly opened the door wide enough for us to enter a large dank room with a kitchen sink, cutting board, dining table, sofa, and a few chairs.

"Red, I am here to tell you that we received some important information concerning your health. You may have been exposed to an infectious disease, and that disease is called syphilis. It is too late today for you to come to our clinic for a free checkup, but we would be happy to schedule an appointment for you tomorrow. Would the morning or afternoon clinic be better suited for you?" I asked, trying to display my very best diplomatic skills in front of my junior colleague who was experiencing the first week of his first job after graduating from a small liberal arts college in western Pennsylvania.

"Neither one. I ain't goin' to your clinic," was Red's reply.

"OK, Red, if you want to visit your own doctor, that's fine with us. Just give me your doctor's name and I'll call him to provide him with the information he will need to test you for syphilis," I said as I began to notice that strange objects covered the cutting board next to the sink, the dining room table, and even the sofa and chairs in the foul-smelling room where we were standing.

"Naw, I ain't gonna visit no doctor," Red said.

"Well then, here's what we can do. We have a blood-testing kit with us, Red, and with your permission, we can draw a specimen of your blood. That specimen will be tested for antibody to see if you have any evidence of infection with the spirochete that causes syphilis. If so, we'll see to it that you get treatment." As my eyes began to adjust to the dim light in Red's room I could tell that he had been carving a carcass of meat just before we arrived. Thick slabs of carrion seemed to cover every inch of elevated space in the room where we stood at arms' length with a "very dangerous" man. Red's hands, arms, and old torn T-shirt were still covered with rich, red blood.

"I ain't gonna give you guys any of my blood," Red said, as he turned to pick up a large stainless steel cleaver off the dining table, "but I'm gonna get some of yours."

My young colleague and I quickly retreated to the door, hurriedly turned the handle, and slammed the door behind us as we fled. Red came after us, glistening cleaver in hand. To avoid the oppressive heat and humidity, a disheveled man had opened the door to the fire escape and was quaffing his last taste of Thunderbird wine when my colleague and I hurdled over him and his precious pint. Red stumbled over the startled man, just enough so his lunging cleaver only grazed my colleague's plaid jacket. We made it safely down 14 flights of grated metal stairs, across the street, and out of harm's way.

My young colleague refused to enter the gray Chevrolet with the words "For Official Use Only" stenciled on the sides and headed off on his own as I fumbled with my keys. I drove slowly to my apartment in New Jersey, parked, walked to the neighborhood grocery store, bought three quarts of Iron City beer for 99 cents, and fell asleep sometime after midnight with the last quart still half full by my side.

The next morning I called Ferd to report the incident. He said he knew all about it. The young lad from Pittsburgh told him about it as he submitted his letter of resignation. The boy had booked a seat on Allegheny Airlines and was on his way home. He couldn't meet the challenge.

Blowin' in the Wind

The eradication of syphilis was a worthy goal for the Public Health Service (PHS) to pursue in the 1960s. Penicillin was now relatively cheap and widely available to treat infections, morbidity had been decreasing since the PHS began to count cases in 1919, and there was a mood of optimism in the United States about solving longstanding social problems. Martin Luther King Jr. was preaching social justice from the pulpit and protesting in the streets, a Peace Corps was forming to provide services to people in need overseas, and the Communicable Disease Center (CDC) had employed more than 500 public health advisers just like me who were willing to risk our lives to find persons in need of a shot of long-acting penicillin G.

The Task Force on the Eradication of Syphilis made six recommendations for achieving this admirable goal. One of them was to establish a social and behavioral sciences unit at the CDC to conduct studies of adolescent sexual attitudes, beliefs, and behaviors as they relate to the problem of veneral disease (VD). The chair of the Sociology Department at the University of Maine, a speaker at the "World Forum" I had attended a year earlier, was recommended to establish a Behavioral Research Activities Unit within the VD program. He accepted the job and moved to Atlanta in 1962. His name was Raymond Forer, and Ray Forer inspired me to be a social scientist.

At the time I met Ray, I was working with Stuart Kingma in the Field Services Unit as national recruiting coordinator. My job was to direct national recruiting services through PHS regional offices and state and local health departments. A staff of eight young men assisted me by visiting college campuses, state employment offices, and other sites where we might find capable men interested in VD control. When I was recruited at UConn, the job of a venereal disease investigator was thought to be too dangerous for women and too difficult for men

Venereal disease education in the 1960s supported national efforts to eradicate syphilis as a public health problem, as illustrated in the pamphlet panels shown above.

of color. I was given an opportunity to challenge at least one of these myths and recruited the first African American men to join the program, several of whom enjoyed more successful careers as civil servants than I.

Apprenticeship

The Behavioral Research Activities Unit began by supporting a few small studies of adolescent sexuality in New York City, one through the American Social Health Association (ASHA) and the other through Columbia University. In 1965, Ray was asked to develop two major studies, one on the attitudes of private physicians toward reporting cases of VD to health authorities and another on the VD contact interview. With a shortage of resources and staff to carry out these studies, Ray turned to his colleagues at the ASHA and the National Opinion Research Center in Chicago for help in designing and conducting these two projects. He also asked a couple of public health advisers in Atlanta to assist him. Don Scheer was recruited from the information and education office; I was recruited from Field Services.

Don began before me and took the lead in guiding Ray through the bureaucratic maze and helping him meet the people at the CDC who could facilitate behavioral research. Some people welcomed the opportunity to work with and learn from a behavioral scientist. Others resisted. They were skeptical, threatened, or oblivious to the social, economic, and political problems associated with VD. As much as the syphilis task force saw the urgency to address the underlying problems of sexuality in American society in order to confront the continuing problem of VD, important and powerful biomedical scientists, bureaucrats, and others at the CDC and elsewhere within Government saw otherwise. It was Don's job to charm them.

I was assigned to work with Ray and the staff in the New York City Health Department on the VD contact interview study. My job was to coordinate research activities in New York through an office at the ASHA. Four major variables were to be investigated: (1) the characteristics of the patient, (2) the characteristics of the interviewer, (3) the exchange (the interview), and (4) the setting (the place where the interview was to be conducted). This was to be a large, complex, and ambitious study. It sought to provide answers as to how patients should be interviewed to identify by name and locate all of their recent sex partners. I was eager to help, full of enthusiasm, and empty of biases. I had no research experience when I accepted this job. I had not even taken a course in the principles of sociology. But believe me, I was prepared to meet the challenge!

Novice Sociologist

The VD Contact Interview Study was a disaster. Bob Swank, the Army nurse who had developed the "modified direct approach" to contact interviewing and had talked Ray Forer into conducting the study, died of a heart attack in his office at CDC midway through the study. His replacement didn't share Bob's enthusiasm for social science and withdrew support for the investigation. Attempts were made to undermine the integrity of the study and sabotage preliminary findings that questioned the modified direct approach as the sine qua non of VD interviewing.

Long-haired hippie former drug addicts and other "weird people" we had hired on an experimental basis in New York City were not to become program representatives. At one meeting I attended in Atlanta, the principals involved had to be restrained by force from punching each other out. Needless to say, the study was cut short, no scientific reports were ever written, presented, or published, and business was conducted as usual.

Although my first experience with research did not have a happy ending, I sure learned a lot. First, there were the books, research monographs, and journal articles that I was asked to read. They opened a whole new world to me—a new way of looking at things. I knew that syphilis would never be eradicated on a case-by-case basis as we were attempting to do in New York City, but I did not know why until Ray Forer introduced me to the concept of "social forces."

I wrote a paper for Ray on the "Oswalds" of the world in which I tried to describe the assassin of my heroic president in terms of psychological traits. His frank criticism of my essay convinced me that there are social forces, that these forces shape human responses to events, that humans often have little volitional control over these forces, and that social forces must be understood and tamed if we are to understand human behavior and control the apparently fanatical behavior of an assassin like Lee Harvey Oswald. I was stung by Ray's criticism, then grateful to him for forcing me to search for a better answer. It was the beginning of my transition from a research assistant to research sociologist.

Another valuable lesson I learned had to do with the scientific process of inquiry. There were people like Bob Swank who wanted to have his best ideas challenged by scientific research. There were also people like his successor who were quite comfortable with the current state of the art and did not want to have their sacred beliefs challenged by an outsider who had not been initiated by the system. Too many people in government were like him, I thought. They start on a certain course of action and continue down that path, refusing to see signs of danger and failing to make corrections for their mistakes. It was people like him at CDC who refused to take responsibility for unconscionable acts and allowed a "study of untreated syphilis in the Negro male" to continue until it and the program for the eradication of syphilis were brought to an abrupt end just five years later, when a venereal disease investigator in San Francisco, California, told a reporter in 1972 about the infamous Tuskegee study.

The Golden Road

Don Scheer joined the Behavioral Research Activities Unit in 1963; he returned to school to study sociology in 1965, one year before I. Don enrolled at the University of North Carolina in Chapel Hill, earned his master's degree, and decided not to continue his career as a sociologist. I learned from Don's experiences, matriculated at the University of New Hampshire in September 1966 to follow a more applied course of study, and convinced my superiors at CDC that I should continue my formal studies at Emory University after I was awarded my master's degree in sociology. By the time I returned to Atlanta in August 1967, my mentor had resigned and taken an academic position in upstate New York. With a master's degree in hand, I became the acting chief and sole member of the Behavioral Research Activities Unit of the VD program.

How did I manage to work full-time for CDC and fulfill the requirements of a full-time graduate student pursuing a doctorate in sociology at Emory University? By studying and conducting library research on the social and behavioral aspects of VD control. For each course, I would somehow manage to bring in a problem we were dealing with at CDC. In most cases, it worked fairly well. I passed all my courses, passed my comprehensive examinations, and began pondering a problem that I could address in my doctoral dissertation. That problem was given to me by the associate director for science for VD control, Dr. Jim Lucas.

One spring day in 1970 Jim knocked on my door and asked to speak with me for a few minutes about something that he assured me I would be interested in. "Sure, Jim," I said, as he eased himself into the other wooden chair in my small office. "Bill," he began, "no one has ever examined the role of the condom in venereal disease prevention. Now is the time. Someone around here has to do it. And you're our man."

"Fine, Jim, I'll do my best, but what kind of help can you offer?" I inquired.

"I'm glad you brought that up, Bill, because resources are very scarce around here," Jim acknowledged. "I wish I could offer some money, some staff, and a site to conduct this project, but I can't. However, you're a very resourceful guy." He smiled as he rose from his chair and headed for the door. "I'm sure you can meet the challenge."

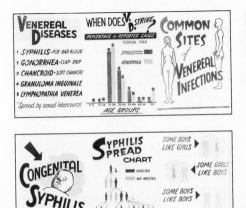

Venereal Disease control efforts in the 1970s included screening (premarital and prenatal testing), contact tracing, and other case-finding measures designed to identify untreated persons in the community, as shown above.

The Sacramento Special Study

I had heard that the director of VD control in California was interested in condoms. I arranged to get an invitation from him to address the state VD control conference and was fortunate to find the regional sales representative for Youngs Drugs Products Corporation in the audience. I met with Lew Brenner, convinced him that we needed empirical data to prove the efficacy of the condom in preventing venereal transmissions, and asked Lew to arrange for me to meet with the president, chief executive officer, and owner of Youngs, John MacFarlane. My research on the use, acceptance, and use-effectiveness of the condom as a VD prophylactic, my resulting doctoral dissertation "Innovative Health Behavior," and my earliest publications were accomplished through the cooperation and support of 2,358 public health clinic patients in Sacramento, California (the eventual site), private industry (Youngs), an academic institution (Emory), a state and local health department, and a federal health agency.

What did we learn? First of all, not too many young people were using condoms in the early 1970s. That fact—combined with generous amounts of sexual experimentation with multiple partners—greatly contributed to sudden increases in reports of gonorrhea and other sexually transmitted diseases (STDs). The contraceptive pill had recently become available for sexually active women. Only 82 (5%) of 1,686 men and women in Sacramento reported using condoms as their current method of contraception when they came to the VD clinic in 1971.

The next thing we learned was that few young people were interested in using condoms for VD prevention. To test the popularity of condoms, we offered free samples of regular and lubricated Trojans to patients when they visited the clinic during a 13-week study period. Twenty-five percent of clinic patients accepted the offer; 36% of the men and 18% of the women left with samples of condoms to try.

Finally, and most importantly, we obtained very little evidence for the effectiveness of condoms in preventing the spread of gonorrhea, genital herpes, and other STDs in the community. Young people who reported always using condoms were less likely to be infected at follow-up than those who sometimes or never used condoms, but even the few who said they always used condoms included two who were infected with gonorrhea. Both admitted to foreplay and insertive sexual activities with sex partners that could have led to their infections. Our findings suggested that a major health promotion effort would be required to overcome the social forces that seemed to be driving the gonorrhea epidemic among young Americans in the 1970s.

My doctoral dissertation and defense were accepted by the review committee and I was awarded a doctoral degree in sociology by Emory University in 1973. At the reception for graduates, I was given a large, folded, hand-drawn card that cited unusual scientific accomplishments. To mark my achievement, a cartoon was included as the final panel. It showed a colorful sketch of me drawing a diploma out of a natural skin condom and the caption, "Bill Darrow, the first human being to pull a sheepskin out of the cecum of a sheep."

AIDS Research

Many opportunities to engage in significant research followed. In 1976 I joined a team investigating the source and spread of penicillinase-producing *Neisseria gonorrhoeae* (PPNG) in the United States. That work required me to study prostitutes and their sex partners. In 1977 I joined a team looking at the prevalence, incidence, and prevention of hepatitis B by vaccine among homosexual men in five cities. In 1981 I was invited to serve on the Task Force on Kaposi's Sarcoma and Opportunistic Infections, and I helped design and train interviewers for a national case-control study of AIDS. A follow-up study I conducted with my colleagues at CDC led me to Patient 0, a man who told me about 71 of his estimated 2,500 sex partners from many different parts of the world.

The story of my encounter with Patient 0 has been told by Randy Shilts in his best-selling book about the first five years of the AIDS epidemic, *And the Band Played On*. My character was portrayed by actor Richard Masur in the Emmy Award–winning movie of the same name. But many other stories about the AIDS epidemic remain to be told, including one about my attempt to contact some of those 71 sex partners Patient 0 told me about.

Some of the sex partners Patient 0 named had been reported as persons with AIDS, but others had not. I was interested in contacting those who had not been reported with AIDS to inquire about their health. If they subsequently developed AIDS, it might add further weight to our working hypothesis that AIDS was not caused by a toxic agent or a genetic flaw but by an infectious agent that was being passed from one man to another through unprotected sexual activities. Because many of these recent 71 sexual partners of Patient 0 were living in New York City, I sought permission from the New York City Department of Health to contact and interview these men and a few other men diagnosed with AIDS who might be linked with Patient 0. Permission was granted but under the condition that an escort would be assigned to accompany me on my travels around the city.

The young woman assigned to work with me in New York was a venereal disease investigator who was familiar with my work with prostitutes. She had worked on a screening project in lower Manhattan to test for PPNG Asian women working in brothels. We talked about our mutual interests in promoting STD control and the problems we had encountered as we prepared our schedule for the week. She agreed to pick me up in front of my hotel at 9 A.M. on the next morning to take me to the West Side for our first interview.

We arrived at our destination on Riverside Drive a few minutes late, parked her black Plymouth with the words "For Official Use Only" stenciled on the side, and spoke with the uniformed doorman about our appointment. He allowed us to enter and instructed us to take the elevator to the penthouse suite. A frail but handsome gray-haired man in his late forties answered our ring as he held his index finger to his pursed lips and allowed us to enter. "They are playing one of my pieces on WQXR," he whispered. The melodious sounds of a romantic etude by Claude Debussy resonated throughout a luxurious room overlooking the Hudson River and the rusty sandstone cliffs marking the New Jersey shoreline to the west.

"I prepared a fresh pot of tea," the man quietly announced. "Will you join me in taking a cup?" he asked. As he departed for the kitchen to prepare our libations, I studied the magnificent twin grand pianos that dominated his living room. "Now what can you tell me about this rare skin cancer my doctor tells me I've got?" he asked as he returned with a tray of colorful cups and saucers. "And what can you tell me about my musician friend who lies near death in New York Hospital? Has the CDC figured out yet what's going on?"

I did my best to explain to him what we knew and what we didn't know, and why it was important for me and others at the CDC to gather as much epidemiologic information as we could to direct the laboratory scientists in their efforts to isolate the causal agent. Once the cause was identified, diagnostic tests, treatments, and vaccines could be developed and tested. To speed up this process, I asked the distinguished gentleman sitting across from me on a small sofa in his West Side apartment to answer my questions candidly and as completely as possible.

Without raising his eyes from his tea cup, he answered, "I'll do my best to cooperate, but I want you to know that I have never talked about my sex life in front of a woman." My partner insisted that there was some paperwork that she simply had to do right away and excused herself to find a quiet place where she could work. He began to relax as she left the room. I carefully launched my interview into the most intimate sexual activities of this renowned concert pianist and could tell from his reactions how difficult it was for him to talk about such things.

When the interview was over and we departed, my colleague asked if we could go to a coffee shop and talk privately for a few minutes. She confided in me how distressing this "gay-related immunodeficiency disease" was for her because she had worked with a medical mission in central Africa after graduating from college. From reports she was receiving, it appeared that some people in the African villages where she had worked, including some who were very close to her, were developing similar symptoms and dying from the same disease that was striking gay men in the United States.

"Could the two problems be related?" she asked. "Could it be an infectious agent that is spread through heterosexual as well as homosexual activities? And that despondent, wonderful man we just met, he's dying, isn't he?" I answered "yes" to all three of her questions. As we gathered up our belongings and prepared to leave the coffee shop she said, "That man we just met reminded me so much of my father. I could not have interviewed him as you had to, Bill. I was so glad when he gave me an opportunity to leave the room."

The concert pianist died of AIDS at the age of 53. His obituary in the *New York Times* failed to mention the cause. The venereal disease investigator from the New York City Department of Health who accompanied me to his apartment in August 1982 died of AIDS at a much younger age. I don't know where she died or where she is buried, if an obituary was written about her short life, or if the cause of her death was attributed to the terribly lethal virus that causes AIDS.

The Stop AIDS project in Switzerland promoted condom use for HIV prevention in the 1990s by using familiar images of a milkmaid, cows, and a freshly picked bouquet of wildflowers, as shown in this poster: Ohne? (without?) Ohne mich (without me).

To Unlimited Devotion

When I retired from CDC in April 1994, my friends and colleagues held a farewell roast in my honor at a Chinese restaurant in suburban Atlanta. I plied myself with mai-tai cocktails as speaker after speaker recounted the many embarrassing experiences I had brought upon myself during my 33 years of civil service. Many laughs were shared—and very few tears shed—on that delightful night of reflection and celebration.

A young colleague helped carry my goodbye gifts to my thrice-restored 1970 Karmann Ghia. As we packed the odd-shaped plastic bags into the back seat he asked, "Bill, I don't want to ask you why you decided to retire at this stage of your career, but I do want to know why you chose to stay at CDC for so long." I smiled as I closed the door behind me and pulled the damp seatbelt across my chest to snap it shut. "Someone had to do my job," I explained to him as I started the ignition, "for the bum on the bench." Then I drove off through the tall Southern pine trees down a dark, dewy Georgia highway into the next stage of my life.

Suggested Readings

Auerbach, D. M., Darrow, W. W., Jaffe, H. W., & Curran, J. W. (1984). Cluster of cases of acquired immune deficiency syndrome: Patients linked by sexual contact. *American Journal of Medicine, 76,* 487–492.

Brandt, A. M. (1985). *No magic bullet: A social history of venereal disease in the United States since 1880.* New York: Oxford University Press.

Darrow, W. W. (1976a). Approaches to the problem of venereal disease prevention. *Preventive Medicine, 5,* 165–175.

Darrow, W. W. (1976b). Social and behavioral aspects of sexually transmitted diseases. In S. Gordon & R. W. Libby (Eds.), *Sexuality today and tomorrow: Contemporary issues in human sexuality* (pp. 134–154). North Scituate, MA: Duxbury.

Darrow, W. W. (1981). Social and psychological aspects of sexually transmitted diseases: A different view. *Cutis, 27,* 302–320.

Darrow, W. W. (1988). Behavioral research and AIDS prevention. *Science, 239,* 1477.

Darrow, W. W. (1989). Condom use and use-effectiveness in high-risk populations. *Sexually Transmitted Diseases, 16,* 157–160.

Darrow, W. W. (1991). AIDS: Socioepidemiologic responses to an epidemic. In R. Ulack & W. F. Skinner (Eds.), *AIDS and the social sciences: Common threads* (pp. 83–99). Lexington, KY: University Press of Kentucky.

Darrow, W. W. (1992). Assessing targeted AIDS prevention in male and female prostitutes and their clients. In F. Paccaud, J. Vader, & F. Gutzwiller (Eds.), *Assessing AIDS prevention* (pp. 215–231). Basel, Switzerland: Birkhauser Verlag.

Darrow, W. W. (1996). Evaluating behavioral interventions for HIV prevention. *AIDS, 10,* 346–348.

Darrow, W. W., Barrett, D., Jay, K., & Young, A. (1981). The gay report on sexually transmitted diseases. *American Journal of Public Health, 71,* 1004–1011.

Darrow, W. W., & the Centers for Disease Control Collaborative Group for the Study of HIV-1 in Selected Women. (1990). Prostitution, intravenous drug use, and HIV-1 in the United States. In M. A. Plant (Ed.), *AIDS, drugs and prostitution* (pp. 18–40). London: Routledge & Keegan Paul.

Darrow, W. W., Gorman, E. M., & Glick, B. P. (1986). The social origins of AIDS: Social change, sexual behavior, and disease trends. In D. A. Feldman & T. M. Johnson (Eds.), *The social dimensions of AIDS* (Chapter 5). New York: Praeger.

Darrow, W. W., & Valdiserri, R. O. (1992). New directions for health promotion to prevent HIV infection and other STDs. In H. Curtis (Ed.), *Promoting sexual health* (pp. 39–54) . London: Chameleon.

Etheridge, E. W. (1992). *Sentinel for health: A history of the Centers for Disease Control.* Berkeley: University of California Press.

Forer, R. (1965). Behavioral science activities in a venereal disease program. *Public Health Reports, 80,* 1015–1020.

Garrett, L. (1994). *The coming plague: Newly emerging diseases in a world out of balance.* New York: Farrar, Straus & Giroux.

Jones, J. H. (1981). *Bad blood: The Tuskegee syphilis experiment.* New York: Free Press.

Shilts, R. (1987). *And the band played on: Politics, people, and the AIDS epidemic.* New York: St. Martin's.

U.S. Department of Health, Education, and Welfare. (1963). *Who can meet the challenge?* [Brochure]. Washington, DC: U.S. Government Printing Office.

U.S. Department of Health, Education, and Welfare. (1964). *Proceedings of the World Forum on Syphilis and Other Treponematoses* (Public Health Service Publication No. 997). Washington, DC: U.S. Government Printing Office.

Chapter 13

Breaking In to Prison: The Story of a Study of Sexual Coercion of Incarcerated Men and Women

Cindy Struckman-Johnson

Cindy Struckman-Johnson (Ph.D., University of Kentucky) is Professor of Psychology at the University of South Dakota in Vermillion, where she has worked since 1980. Cindy has been recognized as one of USD's outstanding teachers and is best known for her popular courses Understanding the Sexes and Psychology of Sexuality. She and her partner, David Struckman-Johnson (pictured above), conduct research on sexual coercion, sex roles, contraception and condom use, and traffic safety. Each semester, a team of undergraduate students joins Cindy in her latest research projects. Away from work, Cindy enjoys reading, mountain hiking, traveling to art museums, and spending time on the family farm.

In November 1992, I was working in my office in the Department of Psychology at the University of South Dakota when I received a phone call from Michael Stevenson, book review editor of *The Journal of Sex Research*. Dr. Stevenson said that he was aware that I was one of the few people in the country doing research on sexual coercion of men and asked if I would be interested in reviewing an edited book on the subject by Gillian Mezey and Michael King from the United Kingdom. Shocked to hear from a prominent psychologist, I told Dr. Stevenson that I had no experience writing book reviews and that I could not do a suitable job. As this awkward conversation ended, Dr. Stevenson urged me to reconsider. I pondered my lack of courage for several hours and then called Dr. Stevenson back and agreed to do the review. And so began my unanticipated foray into the realm of research on prison rape.

Several days later, a slim volume entitled *Male Victims of Sexual Assault* arrived in the mail. In the meantime, I had asked Dr. Peter Anderson at the University of New Orleans to cowrite the review. As Peter and I were in the initial stages of coediting a book on female sexual coercion of men, I saw this as an opportunity to introduce ourselves to the readership of *The Journal of Sex Research*. It was incredible to read an entire book about a topic in which almost no one in America seemed interested. As I moved through the chapters, it became clear that it was not easy to study or write about sexual coercion of men in the UK. Social stigmas against male victims, public disbelief, homophobia, punitive antihomosexual laws, and reluctance of boys and men to reveal sexual exploitation were recurrent themes.

Some of these problems resonated with my own difficulties in conducting research on sexual coercion of college men. In 1985, I accidentally discovered that men, as well as women, are sometimes forced to have sexual intercourse with dating partners. I distributed a campus survey to assess students' opinions and sexual practices. As an applied social psychologist, my main interest was students' use of contraception. But because of the national publicity about date rape of women that year, I included the question, "In the course of your life, how many times have you been forced to engage in sexual intercourse while on a date?" I was amazed to find that 16% of male respondents said that it had happened at least once. Unable to fathom how men could be forced, I returned to half of the respondents and requested more data from victims. This clumsy but necessary research maneuver yielded information from 22 men. They explained in written comments that women had "forced" them into sex with psychological pressure, use of alcohol, and some use of physical restraint. When I presented this information at a research conference in 1987, reactions varied from humor to skepticism to hostility. Newspapers carried stories of "strange happenings" in South Dakota, colleagues thought that the men had to be lying, and some researchers argued that I was trivializing the rape of women. Fortunately, Dr. Elizabeth Allgeier, then a decision editor for *The Journal of Sex Research,* took the results seriously and published the study in 1988.

Following this experience, I vowed to find more convincing evidence that men could be sexually exploited. In 1990, I conducted a second survey using an improved questionnaire. Adopting a strategy used by Dr. Susan Sorenson at UCLA, I asked men if, since the age of 16, they had ever been pressured or forced to have sexual contact (touching of sexual parts of their body or sexual intercourse). Those who answered yes were asked to give details about the most recent incident. Because several of my male students had told me about narrow escapes from sexually aggressive men, I asked about same-sex as well as other-sex forced encounters. I found that 34% of more than 200 predominantly heterosexual men had experienced sexually coercive contact—24% with a woman, 4% with a man, and 6% with initiators of both sexes.

This study profoundly changed my understanding of how men respond to sexual coercion. I attached a note to surveys inviting any participant to come to my office for a confidential interview about his sexually coercive incident. I offered a token payment of $5. Within a few days, I was contacted by nine men, most of whom were familiar to me from my classes. I learned that one man lost his job when he refused to have sex with a co-worker at a fast-food restaurant. Another man could not tolerate being physically touched years after a girlfriend and a male acquaintance tried to pressure him into a sexual threesome. A heterosexual man was humiliated for months by a heterosexual teammate who fondled his testicles during high school wrestling practice. A heterosexual man said that he felt ashamed for more than a year after a homosexual roommate sexually touched him, and a gay man dropped out of college because an older male graduate student pressured him into sex. After these interviews, I understood that a young man's life can be significantly altered by even a brief, nonviolent episode of coerced sexual contact.

My 1990 survey was eventually published in the *Archives of Sexual Behavior*. By this time, several other social scientists had presented or published accounts of sexual coercion of men, including Charlene Muehlenhard, Ilse Lottes, and my colleague Peter B. Anderson. Taking our work together, we offered reasonable evidence that men can be pressured and forced into unwanted sexual experiences. Our findings, however, appeared to be having little impact on the zeitgeist of sexual coercion research. Throughout the early 1990s, nearly all articles on sexual coercion in mainstream journals continued to focus on the victimology of women or children, not men. For example, a 1992 special issue of the *Journal of Social Issues* on "Adult Sexual Assault" discussed male victims in only one of 12 articles. Thus, I considered Mezey and King's book to be a major breakthrough in the cultural silence surrounding this issue.

A Conversation with an Authority on Prison Rape

As I outlined the review, I offered praise for every chapter except one on "Male Rape in Institutional Settings." I was dismayed that only four of the seven pages were devoted to prison sexual assault and that most of the references were from the 1970s and early 1980s. I remembered reading an article by Stephen Donaldson on prison rape that kept me awake nights thinking of the horrors that prisoners may be experiencing every day. I suggested in the review that Donaldson's work should be cited in this chapter. Needing an up-to-date citation, I made call after call until I reached the elusive Donaldson at his home in New York City. Although he was quite surprised that I was able to locate him and that South

Dakota is indeed inhabited, Donaldson agreed to send me his most recent essay on prison rape. He said that his work only summarized statistics from dated surveys of prison rape, and that if I really wanted new information, why didn't I go to a prison and get it myself? Somewhat bewildered, I replied, "But I don't do prisons!" I thanked him for the information and promised to send him a copy of the review.

Peter and I finally completed the Mezey and King review, which was published in *The Journal of Sex Research* in May 1993. During the spring months, I kept thinking about Donaldson's suggestion. I did a literature search and found that only a few surveys had ever been conducted on prison rape. In the late 1960s, Alan Davis, a district attorney, exposed an "epidemic" of sexual assault of young men processed through the Philadelphia jail system. Based upon interviews with more than 3,000 persons, Davis estimated that over a 26-month period, approximately 2,000 of 60,000 men (about 3%) were sexually assaulted. In the 1970s, Daniel Lockwood interviewed a random sample of 89 inmates from a New York state prison. He found that 28% were the target of sexual aggression, although only one inmate (1.1%) reported a completed rape. In the early 1980s, Peter Nacci and Thomas Kane documented that only 2% of a sample of 3,300 inmates interviewed in federal prisons had experienced sexual assault. In contrast, Wayne Wooden and Jay Parker distributed anonymous surveys to a sample of several hundred inmates in a California state prison and found that 14% had been sexually assaulted. Unfortunately, these divergent rates could not be reconciled because no surveys had been conducted since 1984.

While reading *Male Rape: A Casebook of Sexual Aggressions* edited by Anthony Scacco, I came across "A Punk's Song: A View from the Inside" written by Robert Martin under the pseudonym of Donald Tucker. The essay told of Martin's experience in 1972 when he was arrested with fellow Quakers while demonstrating against the Vietnam War outside the White House. Martin irritated the Washington, D.C., jail staff by refusing to pay the $10 bail as a matter of principle. In apparent retribution, the jailers moved him into an unsupervised cell block with violent prisoners. Over the next two days, Martin was beaten and brutally raped more than fifty times. He managed to escape by the third day and was eventually taken to a hospital for surgery to repair his rectum. Tucker called a press conference and became one of the first persons publically to reveal prison rape. As I pieced together several articles, I realized that Robert Martin later adopted the writer's name of Stephen Donaldson. I now understood why Donaldson was so adamant about the need for new research on prison rape.

The Approach to South Dakota Prisons

It began to bother me that no one seemed to be investigating prison sexual assault. Stephen Donaldson wrote that, based upon the most conservative estimates of incident rates (i.e., 1% to 3% of prison populations), more than a hundred thousand men in America's overpopulated prisons are raped each year. How could social scientists ignore such a problem? In my opinion, the lack of research reflected prejudice against an activity that involved prisoners, male victims, and "homosexual" acts. One spring afternoon I decided that I would do my own survey. I called colleagues in the Criminal Justice Department and discovered that a friend, Dr. Lila Rucker, was preparing to submit a proposal to the South Dakota Department of Corrections (DOC) to do a survey on the prison environment. Lila is a spirited and courageous professor who initiated the alternatives-to-violence programs for inmates in our local prisons. She agreed to my suggestion to combine our two surveys into one proposal to the DOC. If the study were accepted, I would help Lila with data coding and analysis.

Over the next several weeks, Lila and I developed a proposal to administer an anonymous survey to all male and female inmates incarcerated in South Dakota prisons. To compare inmate with staff perspectives, we planned to give the same survey to a select sample of prison employees. The inmate and staff survey forms contained (1) a demographic inventory, (2) Kevin Wright's scale for assessing perceptions of the prison environment, (3) estimates of the level of sexual coercion occurring in the facility, and (4) ideas for preventing such incidents. In the inmate survey, a fifth section assessed incidence of sexual coercion in prison and details of the victims' most harmful incident. We decided that the least disruptive way to administer the survey would be to deliver it through the prison mail. Our biggest concern was how to have the inmates *return* the surveys in a way that protected their confidentiality. We thought it would be safest to have respondents mail their surveys directly to us in postage-paid envelopes.

We submitted the proposal to the DOC in June 1993, knowing that fate and timing were not on our side. A few months earlier, inmates at our local penitentiary had rioted and caused considerable damage to the building. DOC staff were stressed and uneasy with the status of an acting warden. Lila's contacts, however, were encouraging, and the proposal made it through the first several hoops. In late June, a prison official raised a major objection to "obscene" and "unprofessional" words used in the sex survey. In the question in which we asked inmates to indicate the sexual outcome of the incident, we used simple but graphic terms to define anal sex ("in the butt"), vaginal sex ("in the pussy"), and oral sex ("give head"). I sent a letter to the DOC explaining that inmates had to understand which sexual acts we were talking about. The end result was that we had to remove the offensive word *pussy* but were allowed to keep the other terms!

By late July we were given the impression that the study was going to be approved, and we began to prepare in earnest for an early-September administration of the surveys. We knew that we had to get our data and leave before a new warden was hired in October. By late August, we finalized the informed-consent issues with the DOC and the USD Human Subjects Ethical Review Committee. I was just on the verge of sending the questionnaire to press when Lila called and said that the study had been put "on hold." There seemed to be no single explanation or person behind the decision. DOC officials recommended that we check back with them after the new warden was in place and a better climate had been reestablished in the prison—perhaps in six months to a year. Lila and I were sick at heart. There was no way to make an appeal; we were simply shut out. When it finally hit me that our project could be permanently on hold, I grieved over our lost work and the possibility that my sex survey had doomed approval of Lila's original study.

Going South to Nebraska

I recovered by throwing myself into teaching classes and returning to my research on televised promotions for condom use.

Later that fall, I called Stephen Donaldson to tell him that I had "almost" done a prison. Stephen asked if I had considered going to a smaller facility such as a local jail, where it is easier to get access. Our local jail, I told him, held two or three persons maximum—not a great sample. Stephen then asked if Nebraska had a large enough jail or prison. I had never considered going out of state. By chance, a few weeks later Lori Lundquist, one of my former undergraduate researchers now attending graduate school in Nebraska, called for a USD update. When I raised the question of Nebraska prisons, Lori volunteered the help of a good friend, Kurt Bumby, who happened to work as a clinical psychologist at the local prison. I called Kurt, who enthusiastically agreed to join our research team and help gain approval of the study. With growing excitement, I reassembled the South Dakota proposal into the Nebraska plan. Kurt hand delivered the proposal to the Nebraska DOC.

It was now early January and I expected a wait of many months to hear the status of the proposal. To my amazement, Kurt informed me that the Nebraska DOC liked the proposal and that an approval was likely within three to four weeks! I bowled Lila over with the news that she might get her prison environment data after all. The weeks stretched into February, but the news from Nebraska was consistently promising. I was now in regular contact with Steve King, a manager from the state's Office of Research, Planning, and Accreditation. We negotiated over the informed-consent form and discussed the easiest ways for prison officials to administer the survey. I poured over the questionnaire with my partner, David Struckman-Johnson, who found numerous ways to improve the clarity of the questions for an inmate population. I put my team of undergraduate research assistants on alert. In March 1994, I received official approval to proceed with the study. We had permission to administer surveys to a large sample of staff and the entire adult prison population of Nebraska housed in one minimum-security and two medium-maximum-security facilities for men and one small facility for women.

After so many months of anticipation, I went into overdrive to get the study started. I was exuberant yet fearful that the project would suddenly be put on hold. In a moment of excitement, I imprudently told the Nebraska DOC that I would be ready to deliver the surveys in two weeks. This proved to be one of the most enormous tasks I have ever mounted. In fact, we almost didn't make it on time. I ordered a ten-page questionnaire and consent forms to be printed for 1,800 inmates and 700 staff. My assistants, Lila, and I took command of an entire staff room in the Psychology Department and filled it with thousands of sheets of paper. Nine undergraduate research assistants—Chad, Damon, Ericka, Mike, Jay, Jill, Julie/"Ed," Julie P., and Skye—joined us in shifts to collate, staple, stuff, and label survey packets. The department secretaries, Lois Norling and Pam Jorgensen, volunteered to help during spare moments. As the deadline drew closer, I called up a sorority house and the campus gay student group and asked if they would help their adviser out in an emergency. They supplied ten more helpers and we finished hours before the delivery date.

I loaded the surveys into my car and made the three-hour trip to prison facilities in Omaha and Lincoln, Nebraska. My niece Stephanie, sensing my own irrational fears, cautioned me not to be taken hostage during a prison riot. With Kurt Bumby as my guide, I had my first experience inside medium-maximum-security prisons. Towing huge boxes of surveys, we were escorted by intimidating officers through a series of locked doors and gloomy hallways. However, after we reached the mail rooms, we found friendly staff ready to help with the study. They assured me that they would deliver the surveys within two days and distribute our postcard reminders within eight days. Now it was just a matter of waiting for the returns.

I expected the first wave of return surveys to arrive at my office by the fourth day after delivery. However, by day five I had received only a few surveys from staff. I began to think that the inmates had refused to take the survey. I castigated myself for not making the questionnaire shorter and easier to take. Just as I approached the panic stage, I received a huge box full of hundreds of inmate surveys. The mail room staff had decided to hold the surveys and send them in batches! I had several encouraging mail days until I noticed that inmates from one of the medium-maximum facilities were writing their names on the outside of the sealed envelopes. Why would they identify themselves when they had been guaranteed anonymity? Then I opened a letter from an inmate who asked me if I knew that the prison staff in his facility were enforcing the rule that no one could send a letter unless they put their return address on the envelope. I was on the phone in minutes to the Nebraska DOC. They explained that there was a little "mix-up" for a few days, but now the staff were letting the surveys be mailed confidentially. I wondered how many inmates refused to return their surveys because their names were demanded by staff.

Coming to Terms with the Results

The surveys kept coming in and surpassed my 20% expected return rate. Within four weeks, I had received more than 500 surveys from inmates (a 30% return rate) and more than 250 from staff (a 39% return rate). Every day I opened and reviewed the surveys for my logbook. Reading the inmates' responses, comments, and attached letters was an education in itself. Some told us that other inmates would not take the survey because they thought we must be in "cahoots" with the DOC. A few told us to "fuck off" and mind our own damn business. Several told us that we asked naive questions about something we didn't understand—which was close to the truth. The majority of inmates, however, indicated that they welcomed a survey on this topic. They said that they didn't like the idea of anyone getting raped, even if it had never personally happened to them. Some of the "longtimers" wrote lengthy accounts of ways to prevent prison rape. One inmate said that the survey had motivated him to propose a program in which older inmates would teach new arrivals at prison how to protect themselves from sexual exploitation.

One of the hardest parts of conducting the study was reading the responses of inmates who had been sexually victimized. Contrary to my expectation that Nebraska prisons would have a low incidence rate, 20% of responding inmates said that they had been pressured or forced into sexual contact against their will while in prison. The percentage of "target" inmates who reported sexual victimization for each facility is shown in Table 13.1. Also shown are the rates of sexual coercion estimated by all responding inmates and staff for each facility. Overall, 12% of the inmates who returned a survey had been forced to have sexual intercourse (anal or oral sex). Another 8% had experienced less severe incidents such as being verbally pressured into intercourse or having their genitals forcefully grabbed or fondled. Two thirds of the targets reported that it had happened more than once—the average was nine times, the most common number was three.

It was very disturbing to read about the high frequency of incidents, the ugly tactics used by perpetrators, and the scope of the negative consequences suffered by victims. Many of my undergraduate research assistants, including two men who were initially unsympathetic to prisoners, said that they felt physically ill when they coded the victim data. Below are some examples of descriptions from male inmates. Their writing style has been left unchanged.

> I was 19, young and a good looking guy—They wanted to have sex with me. I told them to get lost & they pulled me into a room (cell) that was one of theirs and held me down and raped me, after I checked into p.c.!

> I was in my room. 6 guys rushed me. They stabbed me in the back and raped me. They left. I told the guard. He laughed and walked away.

> It was about my first week in the Prison System and the administration put me in the hospital . . . Well, they put this one guy in the same room as I was in as he was just back from the hospital down town as he was stabbed. Well, he told me that to give up some of my ass or we are going to fight. I was scared to death and wasn't sure if he had a knife as he had guys coming in to see him & passing him things. A few days later it happened again.

> I was ordered to move into a cell with another inmate twice my age & size & within a week he sodomized me & the prison hasn't done Jack Shit about the incident . . . I'm so angry I'd like to kill many people for allowing this to happen. I'm so messed up I don't think I'll ever fully recover from this nightmare.

> When I was at _____ 2 black dudes approached me with verbal threats of rape, It was a serious situation, They were about to pull me into a cell, however a respected white friend came to my side and got the situation ended. There is a high incidence of sexual assault here.

> A male guard grabbed my penis after a shower and told me if I said something I'd loose in the end! The next time he grabbed my butt at the same time rubbing my butt and chest than I pushed him away! And

Table 13.1 Comparison of Reported Sexual Coercion Rates to
Rates Estimated by Inmates and Staff

		Respondent Estimates	
Facility	Reported Rate	Inmates	Staff
Men's maximum security A	23%	19%	19%
Men's maximum security B	22%	26%	16%
Men's minimum security	16%	16%	11%
Women's facility	7%	3%	8%
All	20%	19%	15%

Source: Reprinted from *The Journal of Sex Research,* published by
The Society for the Scientific Study of Sexuality; P.O. Box 208;
Mount Vernon, IA 52314-0208 USA.

he tryed it again but I grabbed both his arms and told him Id hurt him if
he did it again! He just laughted & said he'd get me before it over
with—blew me a kiss and left.

The futility of the inmates' situations was very clear. If the victims managed
to fight off the perpetrators, they could be "written up" for causing a distur-
bance. If they turned themselves in for "protective custody," they lived in isola-
tion while the perpetrators enjoyed full privileges. If they turned in the perpetrators, they faced retribution for being a "snitch." The following victim summed
up the options:

In 1989 three cats fuck this one guy, they split his asshole apart, he had
to get stiches. Do you think he was willing? Ya, he was willing to have
his ass split, Not! If a person is kind small, has long hair he usually has a
choice #1 he can fight #2 he can find a Daddy for protection #3 go to
p.c. If he fights he still might get fucked, but for the most part get left
alone. What it is-is this take all the little cats and keep em away from rest
of the population. Also a person got to have some heart, heart, thats the
biggest thing. Only the strong survive in here so it don't matter what
they try to do to stop sex assult, its still gonna happen. I have learned to
look the other way when Im not involved. I came here by myself and Im
leaving by myself.

However, many staff who replied to the survey reported their own sense of
futility in preventing prison sexual assault. They wrote about severe under-
staffing, poor communication between inmates and staff, relentless predators
who avoided punishment, and inmates' refusals to tell staff what was happening.
One wrote:

In my opinion, it is difficult to prevent all sexual assaults in prison, when
staff is outnumbered 15 or 20 to one we cannot be everywhere. When

inmates want to accomplish something we do our best to prevent it, but in my opinion, we are only successful occasionally.

Conflict with the Prison Administration

Soon after data collection started, there were several bumps in our relationship with the Nebraska DOC. In the consent form, inmates were told to contact us if they had concerns about the study. At least 15 inmates wrote me letters requesting more information about prison rape. A few said outright that they were victims having trouble coping with the incident. I wrote each of them back and sent a copy of a prison rape trauma-treatment program edited by Stephen Donaldson. To my knowledge, it is the only existing program of its kind. I encouraged the men to send away for free audiotapes for surviving prison rape that accompanied the program. I made the mistake of not clearing the audiotapes with the Nebraska DOC. In early May, I received a curt letter from Steve King telling me that the audiotapes were viewed as contraband and that I was to stop communicating with inmates unless I had DOC approval. I apologized for suggesting the tapes but said that I was ethically bound as a researcher to respond if an inmate contacted me.

In the early summer months, David and I rushed through the data analysis to get a summary of results to the inmates and staff as soon as possible. I had promised feedback in the consent form as a way of thanking respondents for revealing their opinions and experiences in the survey. As past chair of the USD Human Subjects Ethical Review Committee, I have developed a strong sense of ethical obligation to provide results to people who participate in my studies. Therefore, I was taken aback when the Nebraska DOC delayed my request to present feedback to the inmates. Steve King said that they were extremely busy and had to have time to review my five-page summary. I waited and called regularly, from August through October, without receiving approval. In the meantime, several inmates wrote to ask why I had let them down by not sending the results. I felt very frustrated and could not make myself work on the study until this issue was resolved.

To complicate matters, Stephen Donaldson, or "Donny" as he prefers, began to call me regularly asking for the results. I now knew that Donny was the president of Stop Prisoner Rape, a small organization dedicated to education, legislation, and research on prevention of sexual assault in prisons. I told him that I had an agreement with the DOC to release information only in a professional context such as a research conference or journal article. Needless to say, my relationship with Donny and the DOC suffered during these months.

A breakthrough happened in November. Steve King said that DOC officials would approve the summary if I qualified some of the findings. For example, they wanted me to emphasize that the figure regarding inmates who said they had been forced into sexual contact did not reflect a "prison rape rate" and that the data were based upon inmate reports, not established facts. The advice was reasonable, and I modified the summary accordingly. In January 1994, the Nebraska DOC posted my comprehensive summary of the study for several days in every participating facility. I felt that I had won a small victory for inmates' access to information that they had contributed to my research.

Then the media entered the picture. Apparently, several inmates mailed copies of the summary to a local newspaper, which ran a story on the topic. I could only imagine the displeasure of the Nebraska DOC. They had allowed me to do the study because they ran a progressive prison and were willing to look at this difficult problem. Dramatic news stories on the results of my study, however, made them look like the "prison rape capital of the world," as one my friends put it. I began to receive calls from reporters who wanted me to comment on the study. I tried to explain that the rate found in Nebraska was most likely lower than in states with larger, more crowded prisons, but this was speculation on my part. The only person happy with the press outbreak was Donny, who finally got his long-sought statistics.

Presenting the Paper and Meeting Donny the Activist

In the midst of the press hoopla, I received word that my paper on sexual coercion in prison had been accepted for presentation at the Midwestern Psychological Association meeting in Chicago in May. Finally, I could present the results of the study to my colleagues with proper context and qualification. Donny flew to Chicago to meet me and receive a copy of the paper. My paper presentation was timely for a Chicago news event. Several weeks earlier, an inmate in an Illinois prison announced that he was suing the state for failing to protect him from prison rape. He had medical evidence that he became HIV positive after a series of gang rapes. State Representative Cal Skinner was calling for action by the prison administrations to get sexual assault and the spread of HIV under control. Donny was in the middle of all these activities and wanted me to accompany him to meetings the morning before I gave my paper.

It was a day of unforgettable experiences. Although I had a two-year telephone relationship with Donny and had read much about his colorful history, meeting him was still a trip. I knew he had a prison record, practiced the Hindu religion, had started the first bisexual student group in the nation, and had an IQ of 170. I was not quite prepared for Donny's regalia, which included a Lincolnesque beard, punk-rock buttons and boots, and clothing that he proudly declared was from Goodwill barrels. Now approaching celebrity status, Donny was shadowed by a newspaper reporter who scribbled down every conversation. We walked to consecutive meetings with the powerful editorial boards of the *Chicago Tribune* and the *Chicago Sun-Times* to discuss the issue of prison rape. The editors' bemused expressions at the first sight of Donny changed quickly as he eloquently described how prison rape affects men and society. Our study was offered as evidence that the problem is real. When the editors asked what could be done, Donny listed practical and inexpensive solutions, such as cell-mate screening and educational programs for staff and inmates. After attending a press conference with the newly formed Mothers Against Prison Rape, my paper presentation seemed anticlimactic. The day was topped with a dinner with Cal Skinner, who dazzled me with an offer to help me conduct surveys of sexual assault in Illinois prisons.

Paying My Dues to the Wardens

I returned to South Dakota with a sense of anxiety. The Nebraska DOC had finally summoned me to give a briefing on the sexual assault study. Although I can stand up for what I believe, I have few debating or confrontation skills. Would I be able to defend my study? I forwarded copies of the 40-page paper presented in Chicago to the Nebraska DOC and traveled to Lincoln in mid-May. My first face-to-face meeting with Steve King was inspirational. In our 16 months of phone conversations, I had learned that the Nebraska DOC struggled daily with underbudgeted, understaffed, and increasingly overcrowded prison conditions. Steve worked with a group of people who are devoted to running a good prison regardless of the constraints. Steve personally was committed to conducting research and evaluation of programs as a means for finding the most effective way to solve problems. Hence, he supported my study even though he knew that the results could upset some people and cause political problems.

Steve escorted me to a locked, unventilated conference room at one of the medium-maximum-security prisons. I will never forget how cold the room felt even though the temperature must have approached 90 degrees. At the table were the head administrators and wardens from the facilities surveyed in my study. I was allowed to give a half-hour overview of the major findings before questions started. The first reaction was positive. Results of the study indicated that the women's facility had an excellent prison environment and a low incidence of sexual coercion. The cheerful warden of this facility stood up and took an apologetic bow! The other wardens, however, were furious. They bombarded me with questions about my lack of experience with prisons and the validity of survey data. They believed that the inmates were lying to make the prison look bad. In the past few years, only a small number of inmates had reported sexual assaults to prison authorities. The wardens were most upset with the finding that 18% of the victimized inmates reported that prison staff were involved in the incident. This was impossible—their staff was recruited and trained with the best of procedures.

I responded that although I had no experience with prisons, I had expertise in measuring sexual coercion. I agreed that the return rate was only moderate and that we will never know how 70% of the inmates would have responded to the survey. However, I thought that my results were valid for many reasons. By using an anonymous questionnaire, I gave inmates the freedom to discuss a sexually humiliating event that they normally would not reveal to anyone. (Half of the inmate victims said that they had not told anyone about the incident until the survey.) In my judgment, the inmates gave consistent and reasonable answers to a long series of questions about one incident. I had excluded data from several inmates whose answers did not seem credible. Moreover, the fact that I had found similar incident rates for the two medium-maximum facilities supported the validity of the results. Perhaps my best evidence, I argued, was that prison staff estimates of sexual coercion almost matched the actual reported rates. (Look back to Table 13.1 for the numbers.) The wardens had difficulty refuting the opinions of their own staff.

Regarding staff involvement in sexual coercion of inmates, I said that I was as surprised as the wardens were about the findings. The descriptions of victims suggested that perhaps only a few staff were responsible for the exploitation of many inmates. I told them that I had actually received a letter from a female prison guard who said that she had participated in sex with male inmates. My defense did not calm anyone down, but I felt that I held my ground. During a lunch break, Steve King explained to me that the wardens were understandably upset because my study made it look like they were not doing a good job. In time, their anger would subside and attention could be turned to prevention. Fortuitously, a head administrator joined us at our table for a candid discussion about solutions for prison sexual assault. She believed there was an immediate need to include sexual assault education in the staff orientation and training program. Steve told me later that the lunch meeting was very profitable and that the Nebraska DOC intended to pursue some of the ideas we discussed. I returned home from the four-hour meeting in a dazed state, feeling that I had finally earned my stripes as a sex researcher.

The Aftermath

It has now been over a year since the meeting with the Nebraska DOC. I find that my life has been inexorably changed by the prison sexual assault study, now a publication in *The Journal of Sex Research*. Since that May, I have received several phone calls and letters a week from students, researchers, legal scholars, inmates, defense lawyers, and news reporters from all over the country urgently seeking new information on prison sexual assault. Consequently, I have spent many hours packing up materials and trudging to the post office. I remind myself that it is a researcher's duty and privilege to share information. Psychology secretaries Lois and Pam have enjoyed taking calls from CNN and various television news and talk shows. Alas, these calls were requests for information, not a live researcher! It was exciting to give information to Debra DeLuca of *60 Minutes* for a segment on prison rape featuring Stephen Donaldson. My closest brush with celebrity was when Ann Landers published my prison sexual assault statistics in a column last spring. Despite the good-natured teasing from my colleagues, I was pleased that my information had become household reading. The study had also gained recognition from social scientists. Alan Beck, a director from the Bureau of Justice Statistics, recently included my sexual coercion survey items in pretesting for the first national survey on sexual assault of federal prisoners. This fall, I was honored to receive the 1996 Outstanding Achievement Award for the Nebraska prison study from the Critical Criminology Division of the American Society of Criminology.

During this time I have decided that I am a researcher, not a prison rape activist. Although Donny and I remain good friends, I declined his kind offer to serve on the board of the now-thriving Stop Prisoner Rape. I intend to continue research on prison sexual assault and hope that my results contribute to educational and prevention efforts. My chief goal is to conduct at least one more sexual assault survey in another state prison system. I have recently submitted an application to survey an East Coast prison, chosen because a chaplain there asked me to investigate the problem-prone system. The prison officials first refused my application outright. A week later, they reconsidered and said that they would be interested in the study *after* the elections and political battles end next fall. I feel optimistic about my chances there. Unfortunately, my "in" at the Illinois prisons did not materialize last year. Cal Skinner's prison sexual assault bill did not make it out of committee. However, just a few weeks ago, an Illinois DOC official called to ask for a copy of my survey. She said that I had been recommended by Mothers Against Prison Rape. Fate seems to be keeping me in contact with activists. Most of all, I would like to rejoin forces with Lila Rucker. We have been on hold now for nearly two years. The new warden is in place and there have been no more riots. Perhaps the time will come when we can complete our break in to the South Dakota prison system.

Suggested Readings

Anderson, P., & Struckman-Johnson, C. (1997). *Perspectives on female sexual aggression*. New York: Guilford.

Braswell, M. C., Montgomery, R. H., & Lombardo, L. (Eds.). (1994). *Prison violence in America* (2nd ed.). Cincinnati, OH: Henderson.

Cotton, D. J., & Groth, A. M. (1982). Inmate rape: Prevention and intervention. *Journal of Prison and Jail Health, 2*(1), 47–57.

Donaldson, S. (1993). *Prisoner rape education program: Overview for jail/prison administrators and staff*. Brandon, VT: Safer Society Press.

Dumond, R. W. (1992). The sexual assault of male inmates in incarcerated settings. *International Journal of the Sociology of Law, 20,* 135–157.

Dumond, R. W., King, M., & Brouhard, K. (1995, August). *Ignominious victims: Effective treatment of male sexual assault in prison*. Symposium presented at the 103rd annual convention of the American Psychological Association, New York.

Heilpern, D. (1994). Sexual assault of New South Wales prisoners. *Current Issues in Criminal Justice, 6,* 327–334.

Lipscomb, G. H., Muram, D., Speck, P. M., & Mercer, B. M. (1992). Male victims of sexual assault. *Journal of the American Medical Association, 267*(22), 3064–3066.

Mezey, G. C., & King, M. B. (Eds.). (1992). *Male victims of sexual assault*. New York: Oxford University Press.

Scacco, A. M., Jr. (Ed.). (1982). *Male rape: A casebook of sexual aggressions*. New York: AMS.

Struckman-Johnson, C. J., & Struckman-Johnson, D. L. (1994). Men pressured and forced into sexual experience. *Archives of Sexual Behavior, 23,* 93–114.

Struckman-Johnson, C. J., Struckman-Johnson, D. L., Rucker, L., Bumby, K., & Donaldson, S. (1996). Sexual coercion reported by men and women in prison. *The Journal of Sex Research, 33,* 67–76.

Wooden, W. S., & Parker, J. (1982). *Men behind bars: Sexual exploitation in prison*. New York: Plenum.

Chapter **14**

My Life in Prostitution

Jacqueline Boles

        Jacqueline Boles (Ph.D., University of Georgia) is a Professor of Sociology at Georgia State University. Dr. Boles is on the editorial boards of *The Journal of Sex Research* and *Deviant Behavior* and was, with Kirk Elifson, a corecipient of the Hugo C. Biegel Research Award from the Society for the Scientific Study of Sex. She has more than 30 publications in the areas of deviant occupations, HIV risk factors, and women's issues. Dr. Boles and her husband continue to play carnivals occasionally, and she is writing a book about show business.

My dad was a coal miner, and we moved on average three times a year. During all these moves, I met a diverse group of people: farmers, lumberjacks, coal miners, fishermen, itinerant farm laborers, and showgirls (my uncle who lived with us was a fan). As an only child, I spent most of my childhood talking to adults. I was most interested when the people I met talked about the work they did: how they felt about their work, and the meaning it had for them.

When I was a sophomore in high school we moved to McMinnville, Tennessee. After graduating, I entered Vanderbilt University. The summer of my first year, I met my future husband, who came to our house to tune the piano. He was working in a carnival and tuning pianos during the day. We started corresponding and married three years later.

After our marriage, we toured Tennessee and Kentucky playing theaters with a mind-reading and spook show. My husband, who was also a magician, adopted the stage name Rex Dane. On Friday nights we would do a mind-reading act, and then on Saturday night we put on a spook show that contained magic acts with a mystery/ghost format and always ended with a blackout when spooks (cloth strips dipped in florescent paint) floated through the darkened theaters.

After a number of near-disastrous experiences (e.g., the guillotine malfunctioning) we decided on a more settled life. We moved to Atlanta; my husband went to college, and I taught elementary school. Eventually I got my M.A. degree in sociology and taught part-time at Georgia State University while our four children were growing up.

In 1968 my husband and I decided that I should go back to college to get my Ph.D. in sociology; so I left him with our children during the week and spent a year in residence at the University of Georgia. Dr. Al Garbin had just joined the faculty, and his primary area of interest was work and occupations. With his help I decided to write my dissertation on the anatomy of an occupation.

Stripping for a Living

At the time, Atlanta was a mecca for strippers. In 1969 there were 11 strip clubs located in the downtown area, each employing 10 to 12 dancers. Most of the stars of stripping played here: Kalantan, Morganna the Wild One, Evelyn West, Gladyce Night and Her Two Pips, and Babette Bardot. On impulse, Dr. Garbin suggested that I do my dissertation on strippers, and I agreed. I had been around showgirls, and I had a friend, Michael Motes, who was the entertainment editor of *The Atlanta Journal-Constitution*.

My husband and I went with Michael to see Sally Rand, the great fan dancer. She wrote a letter of introduction for me, but my access to strip clubs was greatly facilitated by Michael, who took me to the clubs and introduced me to the performers. From these initial introductions, I snowballed my sample by asking dancers to introduce me to their friends. I became a fixture in the dressing rooms of the clubs, mending torn costumes, making pasties (discs decorated with sequins worn over the nipples), and otherwise being useful.

My research focused on stripping as work; I developed an interview protocol that examined their occupational choice, recruitment, and career paths. In the beginning I made several false starts. For example, I wanted to examine the value system of strippers; so I obtained a widely used scale, the "Study of Values." All the items were similar to this one: "If you were a university professor and had the necessary ability, would you prefer to teach: (a) poetry; (b) chemistry and physics?" It took me two interviews to realize that this scale was totally inappropriate for my respondents.

My first real interview was scheduled at a club that had matinees. I was very nervous because I was afraid that I might say or do something that the dancers would find offensive. I started my interview around two in the afternoon. It seemed to be going well, but after about half an hour, my dancer said, "I have to go; I'll be back in about 20 minutes." She excused herself twice during our three-hour session. I kept wondering what I had done to offend her. When two other dancers also excused themselves during our interviews, I finally got the nerve to ask one dancer what was going on. She said, "Don't you know? We're hooking." So began my involvement with prostitution.

During the three years that I worked on my dissertation, I spent hundreds of hours in strip clubs, after-hours clubs (clubs that opened after the others closed), illicit gambling casinos operating outside the city limits, and parties frequented by strippers, prostitutes, and other denizens of the night world.

Hooking for a Living

At that time most Atlanta prostitutes were controlled by pimps. A successful pimp would have a "stable" of five to ten prostitutes. Typically the pimp took all the money the prostitute made and paid her expenses. Pimps set their "girls" up in apartments managed by the "bottom bitch," usually an older prostitute who had been with the pimp for a long time.

During times I was interviewing strippers, I observed the strategies pimps used to control their women. For example, one night a pimp brought around seven or eight of his women to a strip club. One of these women was complaining about how badly he was treating her and threatened to leave him. Finally, he asked the manager to bring a phone to his table. He demanded that this woman give him her parents' phone number, which she finally did. He put through a long distance call to her parents and chatted with them without revealing his connection with their daughter. He finally hung up. He needed to say nothing more; the threat was understood.

After graduating in 1973 I was hired as an assistant professor at Georgia State University. In 1975, a police officer who was head of research for Atlanta's police department came to my office to ask me about prostitutes. He said the city had been overrun by street prostitutes, and he was supposed to find out why they were coming to Atlanta. He had developed a short questionnaire that he attempted to distribute to arrested prostitutes, but the women would not fill it out. When he showed it to me, I thought I knew what the trouble was; the women found it offensive. They didn't like the suggestion that they were atheists or drug addicts, nor did they view some of the acts they performed as "perverted."

A graduate student (Maxine Atkinson) and I volunteered to interview these women. Over the course of a year, we sat in the vice squad office and asked all the women arrested for prostitution if they would consent to be interviewed on condition of anonymity. Typical of the stories we heard was one by a 17-year-old girl who had been arrested her first night on the street. She was from a small Georgia town where she and her family worked in a chicken processing plant. One day she decided that there had to be more in life than processing chickens, so she bought a bus ticket to Atlanta. Waiting at the bus station was a pimp who was on the lookout for runaways. He befriended her and gave her a place to stay; a week later he "turned her out," that is, made her go into prostitution to pay him back for room and board. The vice cop who arrested her said that he would not book her if she would call her family to come to get her. She called her brother, a deacon in the Church of God.

Maxine and I began interviewing prostitutes in other locations, such as a "hooking bar" located in a seedy hotel, massage parlors, and floating brothels where housewives worked during the day. One of the massage parlors, the Roman Bath House, featured a large plate-glass window that fronted Peachtree Street. The prostitutes sat in ornate red plush furniture facing the window. One day we were sitting in the window area with some employees. A customer came in and demanded Maxine. When he was informed that she did not work there, he accused the bathhouse owner of false advertising.

Though Maxine and I never paid prostitutes for interviews, we did offer an exchange. While spending time on carnivals with my husband I learned how to read palms from Gypsy women who worked in the "mitt camps," that is, fortune-telling booths. While Maxine conducted the interviews, I "told fortunes," concentrating on changes in the "head line" that foretold new career directions.

As a result of our interviews and observations of prostitutes in all these work situations, we drew a number of conclusions.

The Ecology of Prostitution

Prostitution may be conceptualized as an ecological niche that flourishes in some specific geographic areas. Some members from a substantial number of occupational groups form this niche: prostitutes, pimps, madams, police officers, politicians, customers, procurers, public health and social welfare personnel, professional gamblers, and nightclub owners. Members from all these occupational categories are connected in a complex set of relationships governed by their involvement in prostitution. For example, there is a symbiotic relationship between the police and prostitutes. Prostitutes are excellent informants about criminal activities such as illegal gambling, organized crime, and various forms of vice. They will engage in free sex with police, and the police are often asked to recruit prostitutes for sex with politicians and judges. On the other hand, the police help the prostitutes "work the system," for example, get free medical care at the public hospital or find a good, cheap criminal lawyer for their boyfriends. Some of the vice cops care about the working girls and protect them from vengeful pimps and even give them money to leave town. Usually, efforts to eradicate or control prostitution fail because they are targeted toward the prostitute, who is just one component of this network of relationships.

Prostitution Is Work

Prostitutes work. They "put in" many hours a week, the number usually fixed by a pimp, madam, or escort service manager. Their work location is usually determined by others. For example, often pimps control the best locations for streetwalkers, so, a working girl's "stroll" will be a function of her pimp's power and her ranking within his hierarchy of favoritism.

Like other workers, a prostitute's tasks are prescribed largely by others. Most street prostitutes and "crack whores" (who prostitute out of crack houses in exchange for the drug) will engage in any sex act requested, with or without condoms. Escorts and call girls usually limit the kind of sex acts they will perform. While many refuse to engage in "water sports" (urination) or similar acts, some escorts specialize in these and sadomasochistic (s/m) acts. In the area of sexual services, s/m is a growth area; many customers and sex workers prefer these acts because they are deemed "safer" than "flatbacking" (vaginal intercourse), "butt fucking" (anal intercourse), or "blow jobs" (active oral sex). An ever-increasing number of sex workers specialize as dominatrices in master-slave relations.

Prostitution is alternately boring and dangerous. Maxine and I spent hours sitting in a hooking bar with prostitutes, waiting for "johns" to come in. Some prostitutes smoked, drank alcohol, and used illicit drugs to excess, largely as a response to the boredom of waiting for something to happen. However, prostitution is dangerous; we knew many working women who were beaten, robbed, and murdered by pimps, johns, and passersby. Also, some prostitutes committed murder. Most working girls carried weapons; they hid razors in their hair or carried small knives concealed on their persons. Sometimes they robbed and murdered their customers or killed their pimps. Juries are usually unsympathetic to prostitutes arrested for any type of crime.

The choice of an occupation is usually conceptualized in one of two ways: (1) a more or less rational process of choosing an occupation that fits a person's needs, or (2) an adventitious, largely nonrational approach founded on situational contingencies such as immediate need for money. The great majority of both strippers and prostitutes were pushed into their occupations through a combination of situational contingencies, almost always including immediate need for money. For example, one sex worker was married to a racing car driver who needed large sums of money to finance his cars. He persuaded her to work as a waitress in a strip club, and when her income did not meet his needs, he pushed her into prostitution.

Prostitute Career Patterns

There is a prestige hierarchy within prostitution, with call girls and escorts having the most prestige, making the most money, and being the least threatened by disease, violence, and arrest. At the bottom are the streetwalkers, who are the most vulnerable to all the physical and emotional threats a life on the street entails. Prostitution, like athletics and show business, is an "early ceiling" occupation; that is, incumbents reach their highest income level and occupational success at an early age; thereafter the process is one of downward mobility. A young attractive woman may begin her career as an escort, but if she stays in the business long enough, she will eventually end up on the streets.

Many, if not most, prostitutes have difficulty thinking in terms of career tracks. In our interviews we asked them, "What do you see yourself doing five years from now? Ten years from now?" We used a medical career analogy: "You go four years to college, then four years of medical school, then . . . and so on." Typical answers would include "being happy," "owning my own beauty shop," "being a lawyer," and "having a husband and children." When asked how they intended to become a lawyer or the owner of a business, they were unable to conceptualize the process. While I "read their palms," I tried to help them visualize the steps they would need to take in order to attain their career goals. For example, one sex worker had saved $20,000 toward her goal of owning a beauty shop, but did not know that she could take a course to become a beautician.

Viewing sex work as work like plumbing or accounting focuses the researcher on occupational processes like patterns of recruitment and career tracks rather than on the perceived "pathology" of the worker. Most efforts to control sex work, especially prostitution, are directed at changing, curing, or rehabilitating the prostitute. That approach, in my opinion, is misguided because it views the choice of sex work as inherently flawed, resulting from the psychopathology of the sex worker.

Sex workers, like many of the rest of us, do the work they do because it seems like the best option at the time; that, over time, it may be a bad choice is a mistake often made. When I started interviewing sex workers, I was not interested in the societal implications of that work. However, I came to realize the importance of understanding the place of prostitution and exotic dancing in human history as well as contemporary strategies to control them.

The Regulation of Prostitution

In 1977 Delores French, an outspoken local prostitute, organized a self-help group for prostitutes. Modeled on Margo St. James's COYOTE (Call Off Your Old Tired Ethics), we formed HIRE (Hooking Is Real Employment); I was the first treasurer.

In 1978 Delores and I were appointed to the Mayor's Task Force on Prostitution (MTFOP). Our mandate was to devise a strategy for controlling prostitution in Atlanta, particularly in the area known as midtown. Large numbers of suburbanites had moved into midtown seeking the amenities associated with the area, such as art galleries, theaters, and good restaurants. One of the amenities they had not counted on was the ubiquitous presence of prostitutes.

Because of my involvement on MTFOP, I began studying the history of prostitution and strategies used to control it. As an institution, prostitution is directly tied to the political economy and the gender-, age-, and class-stratification systems of the societies in which it is found. The children of the most powerless usually become the prostitutes or other sex workers.

The origin of prostitution may lie in the development of state religions in which young women and men were attached to temples and engaged in prostitution with supplicants. For example, in India, temple prostitutes (*devadasis*) danced at public ceremonies and also provided sexual services. The original Japanese shrine maidens developed the Kabuki, a dance-drama that came to be associated with prostitution but now is part of the classical theater tradition.

Prostitutes who were often slaves or serfs usually came from low-born castes and classes and were frequently sold into prostitution. In China, India, and Japan, prostitutes were often placed in the same castes as beggars, convicts, and lepers. Today, as people become more physically mobile and separated from their roots, prostitution flourishes. Poor young men and women travel to commercial and tourist centers in central Africa, South America, and Thailand to prostitute themselves. As in the past, boys and girls are sold into prostitution by their impoverished parents.

Across cultures, people have generally felt the need to control prostitution. By some, prostitution is judged to be immoral or sinful; for others, prostitution is a public nuisance. Some feminists abhor prostitution because they see it as an instrument of women's subjugation; others argue that prostitutes should have the right to practice their occupation without the interference of the state. These conflicting attitudes toward prostitution and its practitioners have led to a variety of approaches aimed at regulating it.

In many, if not most, contemporary societies, brothels, bars, or prostitutes are licensed by the state. Advocates of legalization argue that through licensing, prostitutes will be checked for sexually transmitted diseases, and both prostitute and customer will be physically protected. Often when prostitution is legalized, the sex worker is relegated to a bounded community like a bordello or a restricted geographic area. For example, in Nevada, where prostitution is legalized by county, prostitutes are isolated in licensed brothels in a few rural counties. In many of these counties, prostitutes are not even allowed to go into the nearest town on their days off. Even though prostitution is illegal in Las Vegas and Reno, prostitutes flourish there because there are so many tourists with money. The strategy of trying to keep prostitutes in a bounded community has not and will not work.

Some societies have tried to eliminate prostitution altogether. In Russia during the Communist regime, female prostitutes were sent to prison, and pictures of their customers were put up in their workplaces. Often citizen groups or individuals attempt to eliminate prostitution through public harassment. For example, in Atlanta a businessman put up a large sign warning prostitutes that they were under surveillance and being photographed. Evidently, the sign discouraged prostitutes from strolling on that corner, but it was taken down by the police.

Another approach is to decriminalize prostitution, that is, to make no laws affecting its practice. To control prostitution, most societies try a combination of criminal sanctions and benign neglect. They may penalize pimps, procurers, and madams while not penalizing the prostitute; most have laws prohibiting child prostitution, though in countries as diverse as India, Thailand, and parts of South America, child prostitution flourishes. In general, those countries that have the fewest prostitutes have the fewest young men and women living in poverty.

While on the MTFOP, Delores French and I, along with the other task force members, attempted to develop some strategies that would reduce the visibility of prostitution in areas like midtown. Though some of us favored decriminalization, that option was not seriously considered because prostitution is a state offense, and our task force had no mandate from the state.

David Whittier, a graduate student, and I collected data on prostitution arrests by examining all the cases made in the city of Atlanta for one year. We identified more than 300 cases, a majority of which were "loitering for the purpose of prostitution." Slightly more men (a substantial number of transvestite prostitutes practiced in certain areas of the city) than women were arrested.

We also noted that the vice officers used practices bordering on entrapment in making arrests. To make an arrest for prostitution, a police officer must hear the sex worker "make an offer." Vice cops encouraged the prostitutes to "tell me how much you charge." In one case a young man told the policeman, "I'll blow you for nothing." The officer said, "No, I want to pay. How much do you charge?" Finally the man gave the officer a price and then was arrested.

Delores ably represented the interests of female prostitutes, but neither David nor I was able to entice a member of the gay community to address the concerns of male hustlers (prostitutes) with the task force. David did persuade one transvestite prostitute to share his experiences with task force members. He spoke about the humiliations he endured from police and correctional officers, hospital personnel, and the general public.

The MTFOP made a number of recommendations geared to (1) controlling street prostitution, the type that most residents found objectionable; (2) providing counselling and other services for first-time arrestees; and (3) training the police and correctional officers to deal with transgender (transvestite and transsexual) prostitutes. None of our recommendations were enacted. In Atlanta as elsewhere prostitution is a political football. Politicians are determined to "do something about the problem" when the public is annoyed but are usually loath to develop any long-term policy that takes a commitment of resources and money. Usually after the public loses interest, it's prostitution as usual.

The War on AIDS and Male Prostitution

In 1984 my friend Bill Darrow (who has a chapter in this book) began telling me about a strange new disease he and his colleagues at the Centers for Disease Control and Prevention (CDC) were investigating. They determined that this illness, which was caused by the human immunodeficiency virus (HIV), was sexually transmitted. As the nature of this transmission became better understood, researchers began to question the role of prostitutes in its spread. Bill initiated a multisite study of HIV seroprevalence (rate of infection) among female prostitutes. At a meeting of his collaborators at the CDC, I learned about the exciting research they were conducting and the importance of their findings for understanding the role of female prostitutes in HIV transmission.

It was after this CDC conference that my colleague Kirk Elifson and I began work on a grant application to study HIV seroprevalence among male prostitutes. While working on our proposal, we began to confront some of the problematic issues related to doing research with hidden populations. Research focused on people who are engaged in illegal or stigmatized activities is notoriously difficult. These people are usually hostile to strangers who might be police informers, and, conversely, often view outsiders as people to be hustled or exploited.

One major research problem when studying hidden populations like prostitutes, illicit drug users, or burglars is that it is difficult to construct a probability sample. If I wanted to study attitudes toward abortion among Georgia State students, I could obtain a list of all students registered for one quarter and select a random sample (each unit in the population has an equal chance of being chosen) from that list. After completing my study, I could then say with assurance that a certain percent of the population of students are prolife or prochoice. The use of probability samples is what allows pollsters to make accurate predictions about people's voting preferences.

There is no comprehensive list of prostitutes from which a probability sample might be drawn. Street prostitutes are occupationally and geographically mobile. We decided to locate the centers of male street prostitution and then "hang out" in those areas while distributing condoms. We would engage the hustlers in conversations and ask those who seemed receptive for interviews. Using the classic "snowball" technique, we would ask our initial respondents to refer us to their friends.

In reviewing the literature on HIV transmission, we learned that for men, HIV seropositivity is associated with sexual behavior in which body fluids are exchanged and with intravenous (IV) drug use. Consequently, in developing our interview schedule, we focused on these two areas. Studying the sexual behavior of sex workers, male or female, is complicated indeed. We decided that it was important to distinguish between paid and nonpaid (recreational) sex. Because there may be as long as ten years before infection with the HIV virus manifests itself in symptoms, researchers are usually concerned about sexual or IV drug behavior over at least a ten-year period. However, we knew that our respondents would not be able to account for their sexual or drug-use behavior over such a long period.

We limited the time span over which we asked them to remember their sexual and drug use behaviors. First, we asked them how many paying and nonpaying male and female sex partners they had in the last month. Second, we asked them, "Out of the last ten times how often did you engage in the following sex acts with customers and recreational partners?" This question was followed by a list of sex acts. They reported condom use for each sex act.

We also asked them if they had ever used a number of illicit drugs. If they reported using one or more of these drugs, we asked if they had used the drug in the last month. We asked additional questions about drugs that they injected and about needle-sharing practices.

Besides questions on sexual behavior and drug use, we included a number of standard demographic questions including age, race, education, and residence. In addition, we inquired about our respondents' self-identified sexual orientation, hustling behaviors, friendship patterns, length of time hustling, and attitudes and knowledge about HIV and AIDS.

For example, our respondents identified their two best friends (no real names were ever used) and characterized the strength of each relationship on a scale from 1 to 10. With the exception of the transvestite sex workers, most of our respondents had only fleeting friendships. One hustler had known his best friend for only three weeks. Most of the questions in this section were for the purpose of establishing the extent to which our respondents were embedded in various social networks. For example, the transvestite respondents in one area associated almost exclusively with other transvestite prostitutes (drag queens) while heterosexual-identified hustlers were strongly involved with drug-using networks.

Our entire interview packet took about 35 to 40 minutes to complete and included the following: (1) an informed-consent form (which means that our respondents understood the risks and rewards related to their participation in the research); (2) a receipt with their patient identification number (PATNO); (3) a checklist about the procedures for the interview and blood draw; and (4) the interview form itself. The blood drawn from each respondent was sent to the CDC for testing for HIV, hepatitis B, and syphilis.

One of the major ethical dilemmas we wrestled with as we began establishing our research procedures was how to guarantee our respondents' anonymity while making their blood-test results available to them. Each respondent was identified only by his birth date and mother's first name. At the end of the interview, the respondent was given a receipt with his PATNO, and this same number was placed on the tube containing his blood sample and interview schedule. Each respondent was encouraged to go to the local public health department and obtain his test results and counseling. The respondent was not required to identify himself by name, only by PATNO.

We received a research grant from the CDC in 1987 and began by hiring two employees: an interviewer and a phlebotomist, who was responsible for drawing our respondents' blood. Our team went out on the streets, distributing condoms and introducing themselves. Some nights there would be 30 or more men on the street; other nights the streets might be deserted. Our team's standard procedure involved giving a potential respondent a five-minute introduction that included "and we pay $15 cash for the interview and blood draw." If the man agreed, the team and respondent sat on a low cement wall under a streetlight and started the interview. We were more often harassed by the police than by the hustlers as the police were naturally suspicious when they saw us on the street with needles and money. We had a letter from the police chief; yet, when an officer said "Move on," we moved on.

After we had been on the street for a year, the CDC asked us to interview female sex workers, too. We trained a female team and developed a new interview schedule for female respondents. Most of the questions were identical to those asked of males, but we added questions about birth-control methods used, pregnancies, and problems associated with menstruation.

Unlike male prostitutes, females worked all over the city. Some worked on Peachtree Street and in the midtown area; others hustled out of all-night restaurants along the expressways. In Atlanta, as in many other large cities, a number of prostitutes traded sex for crack cocaine. These women usually work in or near crack houses that are often located around low-income housing. We interviewed in a 1940s-style motel, consisting of a number of separate cabins located in an enclosed area behind the motel office. All the units were occupied by prostitutes and their pimps.

The following year we began interviewing drag queens who were located in two primary areas: midtown and a predominately black business area that we called Foggy Bottom. The transvestites, especially those working in Foggy Bottom, usually did not begin their activities till around 11 P.M. and did not conclude until dawn. They were so desperately poor that they worked winter and summer; many nights our interview team was out with them in below-freezing weather.

Over the course of the four years we interviewed sex workers, Kirk and I went out with the teams on occasion, managed the finances, kept the teams on target, negotiated with the police, consulted with our project directors from the CDC (Bill Darrow and Linda Doll), and otherwise kept the project afloat. Our major research assistant, Mike Sweat, not only conducted some of the interviews but also entered all the data from the interviews in our computer database and worked with us on analyzing the data.

I handled many of the day-to-day problems. I often delivered supplies to our teams. The trunk of my car was piled with boxes of condoms. One evening I had a flat tire, and a passing motorist stopped to help me. I opened the trunk to get the spare, and he saw the boxes of condoms. He stared at me for a few moments and then said, "Lady, are you selling them or giving them away?"

As my office phone number was on the receipt we gave our respondents, they often called me looking for help. I functioned as a general referral service for our respondents in need of various kinds of services. While most of the respondents who called me needed health, legal, or housing services, a few needed more. One respondent insisted that we buy him a pair of shoes; he described the size and style he wanted in detail and called me weekly to check on my progress. He was difficult to discourage. One day I got a call from the mother of one of our respondents. She had found his PATNO with my phone number on it, and she demanded to know what kind of "crazy research" he was involved in. I kept saying, "That information is confidential; ask your son." Finally, she said that she would call the president of the university to complain about my failure to cooperate. After that experience, we always told our respondents not to leave their PATNO around for others to see.

During our fifth research year, we began interviewing customers of male and female prostitutes. At first we tried to recruit customers from a gay bar adjacent to the major hustling area, but that proved unsuccessful. I went there with our interview team and read tarot cards in an effort to recruit respondents. A number of the customers tried to pay me for their readings but would not agree to an interview. Finally we placed an ad in a free newspaper that is widely read over the entire metropolitan area. If a person had been a customer of a male or female prostitute, he could call a number given in the ad. A recorded message told him more about the study and gave him my number. When he called me, I tried to make sure that he was a genuine john or customer. When we first placed our ad, we got a number of joke callers, including several men who had been set up by their friends. When I told one man that his friends had played a joke on him, he indignantly replied, "I work in a brokerage; nobody here would do anything like that." I heard laughter in the background, and the caller quickly hung up.

If I believed that the caller had been a customer of a sex worker, I set up an appointment for the interview. Our research team had a room in a midtown motel. We scheduled three interviews a night, 8 P.M. through 11 P.M. Our interviews were spaced so that our respondents would not run into each other on their way to and from the room. I brought supplies to the room, which was located in the rear of the motel. One night, I was knocking on our door when a friend of my husband emerged from the room next to mine with a woman who was not his wife. Just as he saw me, the door to our room opened, and our interviewer said, "Hi Jackie; its about time." The four of us stood there in the doorways staring at each other. After a few seconds of embarrassed silence, I said "We all must stop meeting like this" and entered the room. I decided I'd let my husband straighten it out later.

In many ways customers were more difficult to deal with than the hustlers. I was trying to set up an appointment with a customer and told him the hours we interviewed. He wanted an afternoon appointment, and I patiently explained that we did not interview in the afternoon, but he could come at 8 P.M. He refused, and I asked why. He told me that he was afraid to come downtown at night. I wanted to shout, "You're not afraid to have sex with a street hustler, but you're afraid to come downtown at night. Are you crazy?"

In contrast to the hustlers, many of our customer-respondents wanted over-the-phone counseling. Several told me that they were addicted to sex; one told me, "I am in the grip of sex mania." Many expressed guilt feelings over their use of prostitutes, especially the married men. One man who was planning to get married wanted the results of his test for HIV. He kept calling the health department, but his test results had not yet come from the CDC. So he started calling me. I told him I could not give him his test results over the phone, and he became abusive. He finally called the head of the CDC and demanded his test results. I finally got them from the lab and told him, "I can't give you your test results over the phone, but I would say that it's okay to consummate your marriage."

In sum, over a five-year period we interviewed and drew blood from more than 700 male and female sex workers and their customers. Now our task was to communicate our findings to public health professionals, other sex researchers, sociologists, other academics, and the general public. We first looked at risk factors associated with HIV among male prostitutes. Of the 235 nontransvestite male prostitutes interviewed, 29.4% were HIV positive. Those factors that we found most strongly associated with HIV seropositivity included having engaged in receptive anal intercourse with a nonpaying partner in the past month, having had hepatitis B and syphilis, and having been physically abused before the age of 16.

These findings reinforced other studies that have found a consistent positive relationship between receptive anal sex and HIV seropositivity in male to male sex.

Generally, HIV rates are higher for men who engage in nonpaid anal receptive sex because they are less apt to use condoms with recreational partners. The positive relationship between HIV seropositivity and syphilis and hepatitis B further suggests that those who are HIV positive have engaged in high-risk sex and/or intravenous drug use. Interestingly, however, intravenous drug use was not a major predictor of HIV serostatus in our sample, which suggests that HIV did not yet have a strong presence among IV drug users in the Atlanta area. Our data showed that childhood physical abuse was a significant predictor of HIV serostatus, although this has not been reported elsewhere to our knowledge. We wished that we had included a better measure of physical abuse. (We asked, "Were you physically abused before the age of 16?") Reading studies of the correlates of physical abuse led us to speculate that early abuse may lead to a lack of self-esteem, which translates into a lack of care and concern about one's health and safety. Without better data, however, we were unable to draw any conclusions about the correlates of abuse on HIV-related behaviors.

We were interested in the role that self-identified sexual orientation plays in explaining HIV serostatus. Sexual orientation is not, in and of itself, a predictor of HIV status; rather, it is specific sexual behaviors such as receptive anal sex that are the predictors. However, we found that in our sample of male hustlers, 50% of the homosexual, 36.5% of the bisexual, and 18.5% of the heterosexual hustlers were HIV positive.

From data collected in our interviews as well as ethnographic field notes written by our field teams, we found that the men in the three sexual orientation groups had different styles of dress and demeanor and were willing or unwilling to engage in different types of sexual activities. The heterosexual-identified men were strongly committed to a "straight" identity; most had or claimed to have girlfriends, and most importantly, refused to engage in anal receptive sex because "only queers do that." Conversely, the homosexual-identified men were most likely to engage in anal receptive sex with both paying and nonpaying partners. Many of these men reported that condoms interfered with their sexual pleasure. The bisexuals presented a sort of "jock" persona and were less apt to engage in receptive anal sex than the homosexuals but more likely than the heterosexuals. We concluded that sexual orientation is related to HIV serostatus in that one's sexual orientation is related to the kinds of sexual behaviors engaged in, condom usage, and general involvement in high-risk sexual behavior.

We interviewed 53 transvestite prostitutes in two primary geographic areas and found that 81.1% of the transvestites in Foggy Bottom, in contrast to 37.5% of those in midtown, were HIV positive. We identified the networks of associations in the two areas and found that the transvestites in Foggy Bottom were tightly interconnected into three major cliques or groupings. The members of these three cliques generally lived together in rooming houses near their stroll. They usually slept until noon, ate together in a soup kitchen, and met at a neighborhood bar before going out on the street. Although they did not use IV drugs, they did use crack. These sex workers were strongly committed to transvestism: they adopted female names, dressed in female clothing at all times, and adopted female mannerisms. They dreaded going to the public hospital because they were stared at, ridiculed, and humiliated when they left their community. These sex workers often engaged in receptive anal sex both to please their customers and to enhance their own feelings of femininity. Those in the midtown area were less committed to transvestism. They maintained male names and only dressed completely in drag (female clothing) when working. They had lower HIV seropositivity rates and were less apt to engage in receptive anal sex, particularly without using condoms.

We interviewed 172 female prostitutes, 11% of whom were HIV positive. The male, female, and transvestite prostitutes were similar on a number of demographic characteristics including age, education, and years hustling. However, the females differed from the others in several important dimensions. They were more apt to use crack cocaine, have been physically and/or sexually abused, and have more paying sexual partners than respondents in the other two groups. We found that they generally asked their paying partners, but not their nonpaying partners, to use condoms. The women were more apt to engage in receptive anal sex with partners than were male hustlers. Of the 19 females who were HIV positive, 11 had lived with or were living with male partners who were HIV positive.

We are still in the process of reporting our data. We have two articles in progress: one on risk factors for customers of male and female prostitutes and another comparing risk factors among male, female, and transvestite prostitutes. We have made a number of presentations to public health officials, outreach workers, medical practitioners, and others in the anticipation that our data will be useful to those on the front lines of combating the transmission of HIV.

Prostitutes' Rights: Is There a Future?

When I first started "hanging out" with female prostitutes back in 1968–1969, the prostitution scene was quite different from what it is today. Then, most street prostitutes were controlled by pimps; there were no escort services and no women who exchanged sex for crack. Most prostitutes did not use drugs other than alcohol and marijuana. They thought of themselves as "working girls" and had a professional attitude toward sex work. Today the ranks are filled with younger and older women who engage in sex work to obtain drugs. In many cases, these women's situations are truly desperate; they are driven by their need for drugs and their extreme poverty.

And so it is with the men. Transvestite prostitution is more common today than it was 25 years ago. Although there are male escorts who, like their female counterparts, are relatively safe from the hazards of the street, most male prostitutes work off the street and are vulnerable to arrest, harassment, violence, and disease.

In the United States and around the world, children are used in pornography and prostitution. There is a worldwide trade in female and male prostitution; children are bought and sold into a lifetime of sexual servitude.

What to do? Those who are concerned about the welfare of both sex workers and society ponder this question: Is decriminalization or legalization the answer? Some prostitutes, like Delores French and Priscilla Alexander (California Prostitutes Education Project), argue that women should have the right to control their own bodies. The International Committee for Prostitutes' Rights World Charter and World Whores' Congress have set forth a charter demanding: (1) the decriminalization of adult prostitution; (2) the regulation of third parties, such as madams and pimps, according to standard business codes; and (3) enforcement of all laws regarding violence, coercion, and related offenses. Most of the prostitute rights organizations in the United States, such as the Association of Seattle Prostitutes, Prostitutes of New York, Friends and Lovers of Prostitutes, support decriminalization.

Also, there have been a few organizations representing the interests of male and/or transvestite prostitutes. In 1993, The Gay Men's Health Crisis received a grant from the American Foundation for AIDS Research to fund an organization, Coalition Advocating Safer Hustling (CASH), to advocate for the rights and protections for male and transvestite hustlers and to identify successful HIV-prevention programs. Kirk made a presentation based on our research at the organizational meeting of this group in San Francisco in 1994. Those who attended included sex and outreach workers, as well as researchers like ourselves. Some of the outreach workers were, themselves, former prostitutes. Unfortunately, CASH has ceased to exist; however, there are still some independent sex worker organizations like Sex Workers Alliance of Toronto.

The only major organization of which I am aware that does *not* advocate either decriminalization or legalization is WHISPER (Women Hurt in Systems of Prostitution Engaged in Protest). WHISPER sees prostitution as inherently harmful to women because it dehumanizes them. WHISPER advocates do not believe that decriminalizing prostitution will improve the lot of any but the more sophisticated prostitutes who are educated and self-directed. They argue that women like Margo St. James (founder of COYOTE), Delores French (HIRE), and Priscilla Alexander (prostitute activist) are not typical; rather, most working women are uneducated and lack the life skills to take control of their own lives without assistance.

Over the years, I have wrestled with this issue. Most of the prostitutes—male, female, and transvestite—whom I have met were uneducated and untrained. They were often victims of childhood physical and sexual abuse; today they are often serious drug users. Many of these sex workers were or had been physically ill, often with sexually transmitted diseases. The women had boyfriends or husbands who were drug users, and their children were usually poorly cared for. Most of these sex workers were both victims and victimizers, hustlers and the hustled.

I argue that in a free society, those who wish to trade sex for money have a right to do so. However, I also believe that most of those who prostitute themselves in the United States and other countries do so out of desperation. As a researcher I maintained a value-neutral stance toward our respondents. Neither Kirk, nor I, nor any of our interview team members lectured our respondents about their occupation, drug use, or lifestyles. However, when asked, we referred them to those few agencies that offer help to street people. I continue to advocate for private and government services for sex workers, and I work for the abolition of child and youth prostitution in all countries where it exists.

Acknowledgments

Special thanks to Kirk Elifson, Don Boles, and the editors for their invaluable help on this manuscript. I also wish to acknowledge my colleagues who, over the years, have shared my research adventures: Kirk Elifson, Maxine Atkinson, Al Garbin, Claire Sterk, David Whittier, Mike Sweat, and Jeff Cornet. Finally, I wish to express my gratitude to all the sex workers who have taken the time to share their lives with me.

Suggested Readings

Boles, J., & Elifson, K. (1994). Sexual identity and the male prostitute. *The Journal of Sex Research, 31,* 39–46.

Boles, J., & Elifson, K. (1995). The social organization of transvestite prostitution and AIDS. *Social Science & Medicine, 39,* 85–93.

Cohen, B. (1980). *Deviant street networks: Prostitution in New York City.* Lexington, KY: Lexington Books.

Elifson, K., Boles, J., & Sweat, M. (1993). Risk factors associated with HIV infection among male prostitutes. *American Journal of Public Health, 83,* 79–83.

French, D. (1988). *Working: My life as a prostitute.* New York: E. P. Dutton.

Jenness, V. (1993). *Making it work: The prostitutes' rights movement in perspective.* New York: Aldine de Gruyter.

Wasserheit, J., Aral, S., Holmes, K., & Hitchcock, P. (Eds.). (1991). *Research issues in human behavior and sexually transmitted diseases in the AIDS era.* Washington, DC: American Society for Microbiology.

Chapter **15**

No More Dr. Nice-Gal: Finding a Public Voice as a Feminist Sexologist

Gina Ogden

Gina Ogden (Ph.D., Institute for Advanced Study of Human Sexuality) is a licensed marriage and family therapist and certified sex therapist in independent practice in Cambridge, Massachusetts. Author of three books on women's sexuality, her latest is *Women Who Love Sex* (PocketBooks, 1994), which has been published in eight foreign editions. She is producer of the 24-minute educational video *Women Who Love Sex: Creating New Images of Our Sexual Selves* (Out of Line Productions, 1994). She writes for national magazines including *Ms.*, *Glamour*, and *Parade* and conducts workshops and seminars on women, sex, and spirit. She is an active member of the Society for the Scientific Study of Sexuality; has served since 1991 as Editorial Advisor for *Contemporary Sexuality*, the monthly newsletter of the American Association of Sex Educators, Counselors, and Therapists; and is chair of the National Writers Union Boston Book Collaborative.

During a radio interview about my most recent book, I was introduced as an expert on "S-E-X." The host spelled it out, as if his listening public were small children he was shielding from a dirty word. Later, when I mentioned the word "orgasm," he cried out: "Oops! That's something I'm afraid we don't say on the air!"

"Oh. What *do* you call that on your program?"

"We call it a hot fudge sundae!"

"Well," I countered, "let's hope my book can help your listeners discover at least 57 ways to get to the ice cream parlor."

The book is *Women Who Love Sex*. It came out in paperback last year and has been published in eight foreign editions so far. It is the product of 20 years of interviews, thinking, angst, and personal growth. It explores women's capacity for whole-person sexual relationships from lust to intimacy—the complex interfaces of body, mind, heart, soul, memory, and imagination. These are facets of sexual response that have not been explored by sexual science, because science cannot count or measure them. Although I wrote two other books on women's sexuality while this one was still gestating, I have such a close personal history with *Women Who Love Sex* that it sometimes seems like a member of my family.

With its publication, I have spent countless hours on the talk-show circuit, which has challenged me in a way that nothing else could about the necessity to develop a strong voice on behalf of women's freedom to express all aspects of sexuality. I learned that if we cannot talk openly and intelligently about sexual relationships, all the scientific research in the world is not going to change attitudes.

Media treatment is symbolic of how our culture biases information, or just plain suppresses it. As we near the millennium, our culture is shaped by television, talk radio, and the popular press with its many millions of listeners, viewers, and readers. If you pay close attention to the kinds of messages about sexuality these media transmit, you will find that most are erotophobic, homophobic, and misogynistic. In particular, they trivialize women's power and perpetuate a double standard in which male locker-room attitudes prevail. Moreover, the media perpetuate a giant double message about sex. Every form of the media sells explicit X-rated (and often sexually violent) material to anyone who will buy. Yet, when we try to use those same media to speak out directly about what feels good, we are supposed to pretend sex does not exist—especially if we are women.

I found all of the above to be true on my book tour. It seems that the title *Women Who Love Sex* acted like a Rorschach for prevailing attitudes. Although many interviewers welcomed the concept of strong, sex-positive women in charge of their own lives, others were downright terrified or repelled: "Oh, you must mean sluts and bimbos," they told me. Or, "Are you talking about addicts—women who love sex *too much?*"

Traveling around the country with this book turned out to be a rigorous training program in assertiveness and in reframing situations that spelled disaster. It also gave me the opportunity to practice a kind of Zen humor. The radio host spelling out "S-E-X" was only the tip of the iceberg. I learned to empower and encourage women interviewers who felt they should give over control of the mike by calling in male doctors to ask me the questions. I learned to speak energetically and authoritatively when male interviewers pontificated and joked, filling space on the airwaves as I imagine they might fill it in the bedroom. I learned to stand my ground when callers said I should go back home to Massachusetts where they burn witches. I learned to confront when a technician interrupted a radio interview by cutting in the orgasm sounds from *When Harry Met Sally*. To the station's credit, the technician was fired and I was invited back on the air to discuss the dynamics—the insidious co-opting of women's sexual energy.

One of my personal defining moments occurred when I was actually thrown off a rock radio station in San Antonio, Texas. The host of the program knew what he was getting into. He introduced me as an author in town for the National Organization for Women conference to give a paper on "Sex as an Activist Issue." Then he introduced himself as an easterner who had moved to Texas because it was the last bastion of sexism. "All I have to do is snap my fingers and 40 women will bring me beers."

We began chatting about women's sexuality and the phones lit up with callers. Lively discussions followed, including what I thought was some good-natured bantering between me and the host. He made comments like, "You make it sound as if you think our sexual attitudes are dictated by some white males in corporate offices." I made answers like, "Well, since you mention it, *yes*"—and then asking the callers for their opinions.

Then I noticed that the host was becoming increasingly agitated and had slipped over into frenzy-faced, neck-bulging rage. He bellowed into his mike, "You can't come on *my* station with your secret feminist agenda!" I said, "It's not a secret."

Strangely, instead of fear, what I was experiencing at that moment of attack was total calm. I felt in control, because I understood the dynamic of what was happening, and he did not. As he continued roaring and posturing over the air, I leaned up close to my mike and described that dynamic: "You women out there listening, this is important for you to hear. This is what abuse sounds like. When you try to take control of your sexuality—when you say what you want, or ask a guy to wear a condom so you can be safe—you may get the same kind of reaction you're hearing right now. So listen well. The kind of anger you're hearing isn't my fault. And when this kind of anger is aimed at you it's not your fault either. Remember, our sexual energy is at the core of all of our energies, and there are some men who are just too scared to allow women to be connected with our power. If this kind of thing happens to you, talk with your friends about it, talk with people you trust."

The host was so self-involved in his rage that he let me get quite a lengthy message out before he pulled the plug on the microphone.

The upshot of these media experiences? I learned that when I keep my thinking clear and resolve to tell the truth, even the worst-case scenario can create energy to underscore my most important points. Being blitzed by the media has moved me well beyond a lifelong fear of public speaking. I have learned to report what I know, speak with passion, and talk in sound bites when necessary. In short, I have given up being a tractable, deferential WASP. As my partner so aptly puts it, "No more Dr. Nice-Gal."

Growing Up Without a Voice

I didn't grow up knowing how to speak openly about sexual issues. I was born in Boston at the tail end of the Great Depression. "Banned in Boston" was the buzzword of the times and the predominant sexual message was "nice girls don't." We not only *didn't,* we didn't talk about it either. In my household, there was a lot we didn't talk about, such as the family traditions of alcoholism, divorce, and suicide. But mostly, we didn't talk about sex. We didn't talk about the women my father had visit him in his artist's studio, and we didn't talk about the out-of-wedlock daughter borne by my grandmother in 1906 and hustled out of the family house in a black leather suitcase, never to be seen again.

I learned early that "nice girl" meant repressed, ashamed, confused, and absolutely secretive about sexual desire and pleasure. On the bookcase where I kept my treasures sat a tiny brass statuette of three monkeys, one blind, one deaf, and one dumb. Today, we might call these monkeys differently abled, but back then, they seemed to sum up our family values and the tenor of the times. The first monkey had its hands covering its eyes, the middle one had its hands covering its ears, the third had its hands muzzling its mouth. Engraved in diminutive letters on the statuette's base was: "See No Evil, Hear No Evil, Speak No Evil." By "Evil" I knew was meant any kind of sexual involvement. I knew all about "just say no" long before Nancy Reagan popularized the phrase. I was living it.

But despite my family and my brass monkeys, I grew up harboring enormous curiosity about the vital signs of human life, and that included—I can say it aloud today, and without spelling it out—*sex.* Even before the Kinsey group published its landmark studies, I was hungry for details about what leads people, especially women, to search for warmth and love and satisfaction in the interesting and mysterious ways they do. I wanted to understand the kinds of obstacles they had to overcome. But even more passionately, I wanted to know about the pleasures they experienced. It is that curiosity that eventually led me into the field of sexology.

My original training was in family therapy, a discipline I had discovered in my mid-30s as my second marriage was falling apart. I became a client, hoping I could find a key to free me and my two children from the legacy of constraint and denial that had crippled every one of my ancestors. The opportunity to open up and talk about the dynamics brought dramatic results. In due course I graduated from client to therapist and began professional training in the early 1970s.

I noticed that many couples and families who came to the clinic where I trained were asking searching questions about their sexuality. ("Why aren't we getting pregnant, Doc?" "Can you tell me if my kid is gay?") But none of the therapists training me was able to answer questions like these in a way that was helpful. Note that this was when the United States was at the height of the women's health movement and the so-called sexual revolution. Even so, most clinicians (especially those in the Boston area) did not talk about sexual issues any more than repressed, ashamed nice girls did.

Back then, the stores were not yet filled with all the books we rely on for information and guidance today. There was *The Joy of Sex,* now a classic. *Our Bodies Our Selves,* now also a classic, was then only a grassroots booklet. There was a wildly popular volume of misinformation and stereotypes titled *Everything You Always Wanted to Know About Sex but Were Afraid to Ask.* For the professional, there were Masters and Johnson's *Human Sexual Inadequacy* and Helen Singer Kaplan's just-published *New Sex Therapy.* But I could find little that was directly helpful for clients struggling with issues of sexual identity and fear of pleasure. When I turned to the family therapy literature and looked under "S," sex wasn't even listed.

I felt a mission coming on. I decided to seek specialized training in sex therapy and by 1978 was enrolled in a doctoral program at the Institute for Advanced Study of Human Sexuality in San Francisco. Part of the institute's appeal for me was that the focus was practical and solution based without a great many academic hoops to jump through. Most importantly for me as a single parent, there was no residency requirement, other than two or three weeks each trimester. I could continue to live at home, bring up my children, and support myself with my private practice of individual, couple, and group therapy, along with occasional workshop leading and professional training programs.

Recognizing the Male Authority Voices in "Human" Sexuality

It was as a doctoral student over the next four years that I became acutely aware of the male bias in both sex research and therapy. I learned that the study of "human" sexuality essentially left out 51 percent of the population, namely women. It is true that women might be included as necessary for male pleasure, or as partners to be pleasured by men, or even as beings who deserved pleasure in their own right. But—and this is a big *but* for me—women had no substantial voice in defining what pleasure is or in setting the research parameters for the definition.

I listened to lectures on sexual politics and religion, medicine, and law—by experts, female and male. I reviewed the literature on sexual attitudes and behaviors through history and across cultures. And I began to feel as if I were experiencing déjà-vu. I seemed to be looking at the complex, flowing, ever-changing subject of sex through a kaleidoscope, one that focused only on male genital needs and constructs. No matter which way I twisted and turned all this material or faced it toward the light, the little pieces inside always seemed to reconstruct into the shape of a penis.

There was one incident in particular that jolted me into acknowledging the gender gap in the study of sex. An expert in animal behavior showed us laboratory films of how he had intentionally created sexual dysfunction in a macaque monkey troupe by isolating out the dominant males, thereby disturbing the social order. No longer motivated to hump and cuddle at will, the formerly manic monkeys now skulked in corners, downcast and ungroomed, knuckles dragging on the cement. How like home, I thought. How like the therapy room. Dysfunctional dynamics cause sexual dysfunction.

Then the animal expert went on to show us techniques for curing the dysfunction in the male macaques. Only the *males*? Suddenly, I flashed on the image of the three moralizing brass monkeys on my childhood bookcase—don't see, don't hear, don't speak. But I was an adult now, and a doctoral student, too, with the support to drop my defensive layers. I could see and hear that learning about sex was good, not evil. Moreover, I knew I finally had something worth speaking up about.

I raised my hand and asked, "What about the female monkeys? What did you do in the lab for them?"

"Nothing," he replied. "We don't know whether the females experienced sexual dysfunction or not. We don't know whether or not female macaques even come to orgasm. Our research protocol doesn't include females."

I gathered the courage to challenge the animal expert: "I think it's time our research protocols started including females."

Looking back, I realize this was the very first instance of finding my public voice as a feminist sexologist.

I began to listen closely to how those male voices bias our notions of sexual normality. It seemed to me then, and sometimes seems to me now, as if they owned the language, by creating the terms that shape how we think about sexual relationships. For instance, a word like *foreplay* marginalizes the exquisite all-over body pleasure and emotional joy women were telling me was so important to their sexuality. It suggests that these are merely preambles to something much more important—the real thing. The real thing is penis-vagina intercourse, which researchers from Kinsey on have documented is immensely satisfying to most penises but less than satisfying to most vaginas. A particularly insidious phrase routinely used by traditional sex research is "*achieving* orgasm." This puts a can-do, competitive spin on the idea of pleasure and letting go, as if orgasm is some kind of Olympic event like the pole vault or the shot put. The performance aspect of sex means that women have to be extraordinary to qualify for a gold medal. Their male partners have performance issues as well, but at least they get to define the events.

In addition, I began to examine the linear, quantitative, analytical methods of scientific research. Although these methods have elicited a great deal of valuable information about sexual behavior in recent decades, they have not elicited the whole story of human sexuality. No amount of scientific rigor can elicit the spherical, lyrical way women often say they experience sexual feelings and relationships. Nor can it convey the nuances of sexual meanings that women consistently report are crucial to their experiences of sexual ecstasy.

As I listened to the chorus of mostly male voices who trained me, I came to a radical conclusion back in the late 1970s, a conclusion that still holds true today. Mainstream sex research and therapy discount much that is essential to women's sexual experience. Moreover, I began to notice a kind of old-boy/old-girl agreement among sex researchers that encouraged a double standard based on male constructs—even when the researchers were women. The animal expert's admission about the macaque monkeys underscored that in sex research as in the rest of our culture women were still the second sex. Even now, the scientific study of sex is largely characterized by the following methods that marginalize the experience of many women:

- *Quantitative inquiry.* In traditional sex research, the prevailing attitude is: If you cannot measure it, it is not really sex. This limits sexual experience—and the reporting of sexual experience—to events that can be counted, such as number of partners, duration of erection, or velocity of vaginal spasms per incidence of orgasm. Yet many women I have interviewed describe their physical experience in terms of emotions and meanings that cannot be counted or measured.
- *Goal-oriented standards of achievement and satisfaction.* Sex has come to be synonymous with the act of penis-vagina intercourse (as in "having sex") and sexual satisfaction has come to be synonymous with the spasms of physiological orgasm. Researchers from Kinsey to Masters and Johnson and beyond have based their premises on the successful performance of intercourse as the measure of sexual activity and on the achievement of orgasm as the measure of sexual health. Yet these goals create anxiety and dysfunction for many women (and men) and do not take into account the oceanic, tidal way many women say they experience their sexuality.
- *Gender-loaded sexual norms.* Notions of sexual function and dysfunction are based on the intercourse standards and orgasm standards described above. The result is that more men than women measure up as normal. What women report wanting most from their sexual relationships is a sense of connectedness and intimacy along with physical pleasure. No wonder disorders of sexual desire are the major complaint of women who enter sex therapy.
- *Heterosexual norms.* The main focus of sex research and therapy is on penis-vagina intercourse, which requires a biological man and a biological woman. Although there is a vastly growing body of gay and lesbian sexological literature, this literature often uses the same methods of quantification, goals, and norms to lend it validity and reliability. The result is that gay and lesbian sexual health is often measured by standards developed for heterosexual men and women by male researchers.

Listening to Women's Voices and Discovering Whole-Person Sexuality

When I think of defining moments in developing a voice as a feminist sexologist, I remember a rainy April weekend in 1987 when I attended two sexuality conferences. On Saturday was the annual meeting of the Society for the Scientific Study of Sex in Philadelphia. The keynoter opined that a feminist critique had no legitimate place in the scientific study of sex. That night I drove to New York to attend a rude and radical feminist conference called "Sexual Liberals and the Attack on Feminism." The very title blasted the misogyny epitomized by the keynote speaker of the day before.

I don't know at which conference I felt more uncomfortable. After squirming through the Saturday pronouncements of the "liberal" scientist, I had looked forward to the feminist group as an antidote, an escape, or at least the sense that I was among kindred spirits. What I found on that Sunday, however, was not positive direction, but hard-boiled negativity. One speaker categorically maintained that all intercourse is rape. She was followed by another who spoke of sexual pleasure as the body's way of betraying a woman. Another characterized women as victims in *all* sexual encounters. Therefore (she maintained) consent is meaningless as a sexual term. Heterosexuality is a trap, men are the enemy, and sexual pleasure is an enemy, too. At this conference it seemed as if a new standard was being set for satisfaction: sex negativity. There were plenty of problems discussed but no solutions. Tables in the hall were spread with a smorgasbord of pamphlets from organizations *against*—from Women Against Pornography to Women Against Sex.

I learned that even women dedicated to making the world a safe and empowering place for other women do not necessarily have the final answer, at least where sexuality is concerned. The women at this conference were superbly aware of important and virtually neglected issues of sexual context, such as race, class, age, and ability. But in an effort to rid sex of its centuries of sexism, subordination, slavery, addiction, rape, battering, and incest, these women were creating a categorical hierarchy of their own. Further, they had appointed themselves pleasure police. In the course of battling patriarchy as the oppressor, it seemed they had turned with venom on sex as the oppressor. I could see that something essential was being thrown out with the bathwater—many somethings: humor, play, comfort, softness, and the transformative possibilities inherent in ecstatic sexual relationships.

The hard-line, negative approach to sexuality also leaves out the experience of many women. It is characterized by:

- *Politically correct sexual norms.* To challenge the norms that discount or coerce women, feminism has provided an opposing discourse to help women create a separate sexual identification. But rigid adherence to this discourse, without acknowledging the complexity and redemptive power of sexual relationships, may be trading one conceptual straitjacket for another. Moreover, although a strong political identity helps to create a sisterhood of the sexually oppressed, it is divisive in the long run because it excludes women who feel good about their sexuality and who are vocal about it.
- *Focus on violent and destructive aspects of sex.* To raise awareness about the epidemic proportions of sexual abuse and coercion that plague women, sexual experience is shaped by social issues like the abortion debate or the pornography debate and defined from the point of view of oppressed women. A problem here is that labels are created that may reinforce victim identity beyond its usefulness and prevent forward movement. Also, ironically, when war becomes the only acceptable response to the war against women, there is a systemic collusion with the oppressor that may result in oppressed women inadvertently becoming sexual oppressors (or suppressors) themselves.

These two conferences in April represent polar opposites of the spectrum and do not begin to represent the attitudes of *all* sex scientists or *all* feminists. There are sex scientists who do take women's issues to heart, whose research and therapy have helped liberate countless women from the dark ages of Victorian repression. And throughout history, there have been sex-positive feminists, creating a heritage that is evident today in a healthy explosion of books, performance artists, sex boutiques, and the like. But experiencing the negative poles on that April weekend helped me clarify the direction my own research would take.

I saw a need for a dramatically new approach to researching women. To bridge the gaps between mainline sexology, which marginalized women's experience, and hard-line negativity, which focused on the defensive, I envisioned research that would add an integral element to the discourse on "human" sexuality: a full spectrum of women's positive experiences. I envisioned questions that would allow women to describe what they meant by pleasure, orgasm, and ecstasy rather than having these interpreted for them by "experts" with agendas of control, whether these experts were female or male. Working independently and in conjunction with like-minded scholars, I have spent much of the last decade interviewing women to find the answers to these questions and to broaden the parameters of women's sexual health.

Interviews included as diverse a population as I could muster: heterosexual, bisexual, and lesbian women from the United States, Canada, England, Ireland, Italy, and India; women who are African American, Native American, and Latina; women who are working class, suburban, and professional; women who grew up in brutal families, others who were raised by virtual angels. For some, it was the first time they had ever been asked to talk about their sexual experiences. Many relished the opportunity to break the silence. Many were altruistic. They wanted their voices to be heard in the hopes that they would be an inspiration to others.

My research questions and procedures have evolved organically over the years, much as my garden has, according to what takes root and flourishes. In a beginning effort to address positive issues for women that were not being fully discussed in the literature, I interviewed 50 easily orgasmic women for a 1981 dissertation study. I met with each woman face-to-face for one to two hours, asking structured questions about her perception of touch during a peak sexual experience with a man and/or a woman and during masturbation with herself. I asked each woman to detail "essential ingredients" of these remembered experiences of sexual ecstasy, including setting, sensual flooding, and emotional factors such as romance, love, commitment, and intimacy. In these interviews, I asked a number of questions about the women's experience of orgasm, two of which have led to even more questions about the nature of sexual satisfaction: "Have you ever come to orgasm on extragenital stimulation alone with no genital stimulation?" and "Have you ever come to orgasm spontaneously, on imagination alone, with no physical stimulation at all?" ("Oh," said one woman, "You mean *thinking* off.") I outline answers to these questions in pages that follow; the entire dissertation questionnaire can be found in the appendix of *Women Who Love Sex.*

The question on spontaneous orgasm led directly to a 1992 laboratory study on the physiological correlates of imagery orgasm, involving 20 women, all of whom had the ability to "think off" to imagination, fantasy, or other means of nonphysical stimulation. This was an opportunity to further explore the mind-body connections of spontaneous orgasm, witnessing and measuring the women's sexual responses in the lab (something Masters and Johnson had been unable to do), and asking "What were you thinking or feeling or imagining as you came to orgasm?"

Colleagues, students, and clients have proved to be a rich, ongoing source of interview material from the early 1970s to the present. Listening to women reflect on their sexual experiences has continually honed my research questions and has moved me, finally, to research in earnest the ultimate mind-body subject: sex and spirituality. In 1995, I distributed a nine-page pilot questionnaire to 151 health care professionals and college students preparatory to creating a 65-question survey on sexuality and spirituality, now accepted by a national women's magazine. Questions I ask here are intended for a broad, nonacademic audience and explore such concepts as: What does sex mean in women's lives? Where does sexual response begin and end? What is the role of memory? A question that concretizes the relationship between sexual and spiritual experience is: Did you ever cry out "Oh God!" at the moment of orgasm?

Finally, I cannot talk about interview populations without mentioning material I have obtained from many hours spent on call-in talk radio while on various book tours from 1990–1996. As talk radio serves as a kind of national confessional, I found myself privy to the most intimate of anecdotal material from women all over the country. (One of my favorite calls was from a woman in her seventies who confided, for the first time ever, that her interview with Alfred Kinsey in the 1940s had removed all sexual shame and guilt from her life. She gave her name to the station, and I subsequently asked her to tell her story on a panel on "The Golden Years of Women Who Love Sex" that I was organizing for my alma mater, the Institute for Advanced Study of Human Sexuality.) Anonymous radio conversations may not qualify as a valid and reliable research sample, but many of the women's comments and questions moved my thinking.

These are the women with whom I formulated the ideas for *Women Who Love Sex* and for my ongoing research since the book was published. From conversations with them, I have found (and continue to find) that whatever their orientation or cultural differences, there are similarities in how women talk about their positive sexual experiences. Call it energy, call it soul, call it mind-body connection, women who have talked with me seem to share a positive sexual core. They also share another commonality. They almost universally agree that there is not adequate language to describe that core with accuracy, detail, and feeling. Try as they might to make their own voices heard, many reported feeling as if they were starting with a double handicap—cultural interdiction along with their own internalized monkeys that told them to deny their sexual truths.

What have I learned from interviews with these women who love sex?

- *Sex is a whole-person proposition.* Every woman who talked with me about her peak sexual experiences reported that her physical feelings were inseparable from her emotional feelings, her life situation, her quest for meaning, and/or her sense of connectedness in her relationships—heart to heart, soul to soul, even mind to mind.

- *Sexual response begins long before the bedroom.* These women reported that their sexual responses were directly affected by a whole host of issues that preceded their sexual encounters. These issues include cultural customs, economics, self-esteem, children in the next room, relationship with their partners, and fear of pregnancy or HIV/AIDS. Moreover, their sexual response was affected by early memories and recent memories of both pleasure and abuse.
- *Sexual response can last long after a sexual encounter.* More than half the women in my dissertation study and many more anecdotally reported that sex was often a source of energy that radiated beyond this or that randy encounter. Satisfaction could lead to personal integration and rewarding relationships of all kinds, from "something I can take on the bus the next morning to make my whole day go wonderful" to a paradigm shift in physical or spiritual outlook. One woman reported that a peak sexual experience marked the permanent ending of a six-month-long depression.
- *"Sexual activity" means more than intercourse.* All of the women I interviewed reported pleasure responses from outercourse as well as from intercourse or direct genital stimulation—that is: stimulation all over their bodies, including fingers and toes, hips, lips, neck, and earlobes, as well as clitoris, vagina, and G spot. Seventy percent of the women in my dissertation study reported more pleasure from extragenital stimulation than from genital stimulation. Perhaps even more remarkable, 52 percent of the women in my dissertation interviews affirmed that they were able to experience orgasm from extragenital stimulation alone, with no touching of the vulva, a finding corroborated by my 1996 pilot survey. There is nothing in the sexological literature with which to compare these figures; extragenital orgasm is virtually unresearched in sexual science.
- *Sexual imagination is vital to sexual response.* Even though sexual science generally acknowledges that the most important organ of sexual pleasure is the brain, little research exists on the sexual imaginations of women. Sixty-four percent of the women in my dissertation study and 81 percent of the women in my pilot survey reported ability to experience orgasm "spontaneously," without any physical touch at all. For these women, sexual imagination was a source of safety, pleasure, healing, empowerment, and locus of control, framed by themselves and not by stereotypical media or pornographic images.
- *Sexuality is connected to spirituality.* This finding is still a work in progress and awaits more data from my soon-to-be-published survey. Many of the women I interviewed reported experiencing sexuality as a path to spiritual experience—that is, their search for positive energy and meaning, their need for love, romance, nurturing, touching, and emotional bonding, and their capacity for fully conscious and connected partnerships. For these women, deep sexual satisfaction was more than physical release; it was also a sense of oneness with the deity, by whatever name they called it—God, Goddess, Great Spirit, Higher Power, or Universal Energy.

Finding My Own Voice—and Message

The most important element in finding my own voice as a feminist sexologist has been discovering the passion to speak out about what is most important to me. This I found not from reading books or sitting at the feet of experts but from my many, many conversations with women.

The more I listen to women, the more I become aware of the cultural factors that shape our sexual attitudes and behaviors. I have found that many of the women I have talked with have had to *learn* to love sex—by transcending pain and misinformation and by having the courage to let their partners know how they feel.

As I continue to listen closely to interviewees and clients, colleagues and friends, I find myself looking at sex through a new kaleidoscope, a colorful women's kaleidoscope, with no two patterns coming up exactly alike. Yet there is an overall pattern to these women's stories, which holds a crucial message for women and for the partners who love them: Sexual pleasure is good. It is not evil, as the three brass monkeys of my childhood would have had me believe.

For these women, sexual pleasure is life enlarging, particularly as women become more adept at exploring the vast arena that pleasure is. To celebrate the erotic, to feel motivated by satisfaction rather than by guilt and suffering, is a radical reframe for many women. It means women do not have to give up sex to be safe. It means they can orchestrate the positive instead of mustering all their energy to block sexual pain: danger, abuse, manipulation, inequality. It means shifting from control—the ability to say no—to power—the ability to say yes.

After all the years of the women's movement and the women's health movement, women have finally earned the right to say no to sexual abuse and violence. (Although saying no does not always stop abuse and violence, it is a giant step for womankind.) However, there is still no widescale encouragement in this culture for women to say yes to pleasure. (Women who love sex are still often labeled sluts, bimbos, and out-of-control addicts.) Until women have the right to say yes to pleasure, we remain at risk of being defined by somebody else.

The question I am addressing today is: How can women of all ages and sexual and spiritual orientations rethink erotic experience in a world in which women are not supposed to define sexual pleasure?

There is no one right answer to this question. The answer is as complex as the history of sexual pleasure itself. It is embedded in the life experience of women who are ready to move beyond guilt and victimization, dismantle good-girl/bad-girl myths, listen to the intelligence of their bodies, and affirm sexual energy in safety and celebration. The answer is embedded in the language, too. For this reason, I am constantly challenging both women and men to change the names they call women who love sex. Think about it. If we change those names from "slut" and "addict" to "energized," "self-aware," "courageous," and "powerful," we can change the entire culture.

To keep my voice strong as a feminist sexologist takes daily attention, just like any other spiritual practice. Sexual denials and negativities die hard and are so ingrained in the language that they surface everywhere. Only yesterday, when I consulted my computer's thesaurus for synonyms for the word "orgasm," there was nothing there—"word not found." At least it didn't say "hot fudge sundae." For the word "erotic," my thesaurus spewed back adjectives that felt like throwbacks to my proper Bostonian upbringing: "indecent," "improper," "racy," "unbecoming." It was as if my childhood monkeys had invaded cyberspace to chide "speak no evil."

Yet, as I write this chapter, I sense a subtle turning of the tide away from shame-based sexuality that divides women from themselves and from their partners, female and male. I see women of all ages and orientations creating new sexual rituals, from using vibrators to experimenting with gender roles to creating more empathic partnerships with men and women. I see increasing interest in ecstatic traditions, such as tantra, that use breathing, imagery, and movement to connect mind and body. I see academic challenging of sexist and heterosexist paradigms. I witness a groundswell of interest in the cultural transformation that would bring sex back to its sacred roots—and equal participation by both women and men.

On the personal front, the direction my work is taking is stimulating, varied, and demanding of an increasingly public voice. A major national magazine has just asked me to do a cover story on recovery from sexual abuse. I am negotiating with another magazine for a piece on the healing potential of sexual pleasure—the interface between medicine and politics. For yet another, I am creating a survey on women, sexuality, and spirituality. When the results of this survey are in, they will form the basis for my next book. This coming month, I am scheduled to teach a sex-and-spirit workshop at a New Age healing center; to keynote a sexological conference on pleasure, power and culture; and to present a talk on "Sex Therapy for the Millennium" at a Harvard Medical School symposium. I just got off the phone with a reporter from the *Los Angeles Times,* who called to interview me about the cultural meanings of foot fetishes for the 1990s.

Today, life is interesting and good. So far, no radio shows want me to burn at the stake or insist that I use a substitute for the word "orgasm." Going public as a feminist sexologist definitely has its rewards. Most days, it is more satisfying than pigging out on a hot fudge sundae. And a whole lot healthier.

Acknowledgements

Portions of this chapter appeared in *Women Who Love Sex,* Chapter 1, "Portrait of a Feminist Sex Researcher" (PocketBooks, 1994), and in *Ms.,* "Media Interruptus: Sexual Politics on the Book Tour Circuit" (November/December 1995).

Suggested Readings

Boston Women's Health Book Collective. (1992). *The new our bodies our selves.* New York: Touchstone.

Eisler, R. (1995). *Sacred pleasure.* New York: HarperCollins.

Heyward, C. (1989). *Touching our strength: The erotic as power and the love of god.* New York: HarperCollins.

Jordan, J. V. (1987). Clarity in connection: Empathic knowing, desire and sexuality. *Work in Progress No. 29.* Wellesley, MA: Stone Center for Developmental Services and Studies.

Ogden, G. (1988). Women and sexual ecstasy: How can therapists help? *Women and Therapy, 7,* 43–56.

Ogden, G. (1990). *Sexual recovery.* Deerfield Beach, FL: Health Communications.

Ogden, G. (1994). *Women who love sex.* New York: PocketBooks.

Ogden, G. (1995). Media interruptus: Sexual politics on the book tour circuit. *Ms.,* November/December.

Whipple, B., & Ogden, G. (1989). *Safe encounters.* New York: McGraw-Hill.

Whipple, B., Ogden, G., & Komisaruk, B. (1992). Physiological correlates of imagery-induced orgasm in women. *Archives of Sexual Behavior, 21,* 121–133.